Private Sector
Strategies for
Social Sector Success

Private Sector Strategies for Social Sector Success

The Guide to Strategy and Planning for Public and Nonprofit Organizations

Kevin P. Kearns

JOSSEY-BASS
A Wiley Company
San Francisco

The case study that appears on pp. 33–37 concerning William "Bill" Strickland and the Manchester Craftsmen's Guild is reprinted herein with kind permission of William Strickland.

The case study that appears on pp. 168–171 concerning John Murray and Duquesne University is reprinted herein with kind permission of John Murray.

The case study that appears on pp. 218–224 concerning the Banksville Human Services Center is from Leslie, D. "To Grow or Not to Grow," in K. Koziol (ed.), *Nonprofit Management Case Collection*. Institute for Nonprofit Organization Management, College of Professional Studies, University of San Francisco, 1992. It is reprinted herein with kind permission of Donald R. Leslie and Ken Koziol.

TCF Manufactured in the United States of America on Lyons Falls Turin Book. This paper is acid-free and 100 percent totally chlorine-free.

Library of Congress Cataloging-in-Publication Data

Kearns, Kevin P.
    Private sector strategies for social sector success: the guide to strategy and planning for public and nonprofit organizations/Kevin P. Kearns.—1st ed.
        p.   cm.—(Jossey-Bass nonprofit & public management series)
    Includes bibliographical references and index.
        ISBN 0-7879-4189-1 (alk. paper)
        1. Nonprofit organizations—Management.   2. Public administration.   3. Strategic planning.   I. Title.   II. Jossey-Bass nonprofit and public management series
    HD62.6.K4   2000
    658'.048—dc21   00-020566

FIRST EDITION
HB Printing   10 9 8 7 6 5 4 3 2 1

The Jossey-Bass Nonprofit & Public Management Series

To Bernard and Dolores Kearns, with love

Contents

Part Three: Strategy in Practice

Tables, Figures, and Exhibits

Figures

Exhibits

Preface

Today, perhaps more than ever before, public and nonprofit organizations are using strategic management methods to help them survive in a volatile and competitive environment. Nonprofit organizations of all types have launched entrepreneurial commercial ventures and are aggressively using fees for service to augment charitable donations and government grants (Skloot, 1988; Weisbrod, 1998). Municipal governments have used sophisticated marketing campaigns to attract tourists and businesses, and they too have turned to entrepreneurial enterprises to supplement stagnant or shrinking tax revenues (Osborne and Gaebler, 1992). Government agencies at all levels, federal, state, and local, have divested parts of their service portfolios to the private sector, focusing their finite resources on their core mission rather than trying to be all things to all people. Nonprofit hospitals and other health care organizations are using strategies of horizontal and vertical integration in order to gain greater control and stability in their turbulent industry.

If you work in a government or nonprofit organization, you may be using a vocabulary today that was once heard only in the executive suites of private corporations. Perhaps you are looking for *market niches* that capitalize on your organization's *comparative advantages*. Maybe you are worried about *competitive threats* in the *marketplace* and how to provide your *customers* with *value-added* products and services. You may be using management techniques like *portfolio analysis* or *break-even analysis* and tracking financial indicators like *profit margins* and *liquidity ratios*. Perhaps your organization is designing a sophisticated *marketing* and *promotional* campaign or contemplating creative ways to measure and report its *return on investment* to key constituencies.

Until recently these business concepts were not part of the management lexicon in public and nonprofit organizations. Today they are standard practice in some municipalities, some federal and state government agencies, and many nonprofit organizations.

Yet government and nonprofit organizations are *not* businesses and cannot be managed as such. Unlike your counterparts in the business world, you cannot think of clients and taxpayers merely as *customers* or *consumers* of goods and services. Unfettered commercialism in public and nonprofit organizations can disenfranchise marginal members of our communities who rely on government and charitable organizations to meet their needs (Hasenfeld, 1996). Not all of your clients are *customers* who are exercising free choice in the *purchase* and *consumption* of public services. Some of them simply have no choice or are incapable of exercising or unwilling to exercise whatever choices they do have. They depend on you to keep their best interests at the forefront of all that you do. In addition, the competitive paradigm that is one of the drivers of the business world is not totally applicable in the public sector. Instead, you look for opportunities to collaborate with other organizations (even with your competitors) in finding lasting solutions to public problems. A purely competitive mind-set in public sector organizations can waste precious public resources and blind these institutions to their true missions. Finally, you cannot worry only about financial indicators and ratios because these measures represent only part of your organization's total performance. Critical decisions regarding people in need cannot be made on the basis of your organization's balance sheet or cash flow statements (Rosenman, 1998).

What the public sector needs therefore is an approach to strategic management that borrows concepts from the business sector when those concepts are relevant and helpful but that is tempered by an understanding of the distinctive missions, contexts, and constituencies of public and nonprofit organizations.

Purpose and Audience

Private Sector Strategies for Social Sector Success is a practical guide for busy decision makers in the public and nonprofit sectors who need to chart a course for their organizations. It is targeted primarily to professionals in government and nonprofit organizations of all types. The objective is to help you improve the ways you accomplish the following tasks:

Understand the environment in which your organization exists. Strategic management demands that you identify and interpret the important trends that affect your organization and your portfolio of programs and services. Businesses use environmental scanning (also known as industry analysis) to help them identify and interpret important trends. With the caveats and the modifications to concepts and terminology that I discuss, government and nonprofit organizations too can use some of the principles of industry analysis.

Understand your organization's distinctive competencies and your comparative advantages. Any organization will fail when it strays too far from its core competencies into programs or markets in which it has little experience. Most of the techniques presented in this book require a candid assessment of your organization's strengths and comparative advantages. Your organization's portfolio of programs and services should embody its strengths. To cling to weak programs and services, especially when other organizations can better serve the same needs, is a waste of scarce community resources.

Identify and select organizational strategies that advance the mission and goals of your organization and are consistent with your strategic environment. At the broadest level of organizational strategy, all organizations have essentially three choices—*growth, retrenchment,* and *stability*—and each choice also has several subcategories (Wheelen and Hunger, 1992). Business firms use this paradigm to plot their overall vision and direction (see also Andrews, 1980; Chaffee, 1985). With some caveats, this paradigm has value for public and nonprofit organizations as well, and therefore I discuss these three strategies extensively.

Explore opportunities for collaboration with other organizations. Public and nonprofit organizations have been urged to explore collaborative relationships to reduce redundancy and enhance effectiveness. Collaboration can be a method for pursuing many types of business strategies under the general categories of growth, retrenchment, or stability while making the best use of finite public resources.

Encourage a culture of strategic thinking and strategic action throughout the organization. There are many executives who are brilliant strategists but totally incompetent planners. Some of the most celebrated executives and even prominent management scholars actually seem to have contempt for strategic planning. This book is designed to stimulate strategic *thinking* rather than to promote a particular approach to strategic planning.

Here are some of the important issues this book can help you address in your organization:

- Why is growth such a seductive strategy?
- How can you evaluate growth strategies objectively?
- When does retrenchment make sense as an organizational strategy?
- If you decide to cut back, how can you do so without endangering the core mission and purpose of the organization?
- How do you turn around a troubled organization?
- Under what conditions should you seriously consider liquidation?
- Should your organization try to compete against other public and nonprofit organizations? If so, what are your comparative advantages?

- When does it make sense to collaborate with other organizations rather than compete against them?
- What factors should you consider when you try to implement your strategy?
- What role does politics play in the formulation and implementation of organizational strategy?

Not only executives, policymakers, and top-level managers in government agencies and nonprofit organizations will benefit from the ideas and applications discussed here. This book is also appropriate for students in schools of public management and social work. It will be useful as a primary or supplemental text in courses on strategic management or strategic planning at the graduate level and in some instances the advanced undergraduate level. And it will be particularly useful in academic programs designed to meet the specific needs of midcareer students who have some professional experience.

Some Assumptions

The approach I take in this book assumes that the environment of public and nonprofit management is often collaborative but also sometimes intensely *competitive*. It is a good bet that your organization is competing directly or indirectly with similar organizations for finite resources. Municipal and state governments compete for tax-paying residents and businesses. Universities compete for students. Hospitals compete for patients and for doctors. Opera companies compete for singers and patrons. Social service agencies compete for government contracts and grants. To the extent that your organization "wins" a certain amount of resources in this game, another organization probably "loses." Perhaps this is not the type of cutthroat, winner-take-all competition that we see so often in the business world. But the supply of resources cannot accommodate all needs, and therefore some organizations are more successful than others in garnering resources, attracting clients, serving community needs, and gaining legitimacy in the political environment.

Consequently, this book assumes that some of the concepts and methods of strategic management developed for use in the private sector can be adapted for use in the public sector. This is a controversial assumption because over the past few years there has been backlash, primarily among scholars, against the business-oriented philosophy espoused by David Osborne and Ted Gaebler in their best-selling book, *Reinventing Government* (1992). Critics of the reinvention movement remind us, quite appropriately, that government agencies and nonprofit organizations are *not* businesses and should not be operated as such. Moreover, we see examples every day that prove private businesses are hardly paragons of effective management. We do not need to look very far in the business world for shocking examples of mismanagement, strategic blunders, and ethical lapses that rival even the most famous management gaffs in the public and nonprofit sectors.

Still, even though they are not a panacea, some of the concepts and tools developed for use in the private sector have transferable value for government and nonprofit organizations.

Approach

I borrow from the business management literature in the presentation of techniques like market environmental scanning, portfolio analysis, and strategy design, and the reader will notice frequent references to the work of business scholars like Michael Porter, Henry Mintzberg, David Hambrick, James Thompson, Thomas Wheelen, David Hunger, and many others.

Only in the last fifteen years have we seen attempts, primarily in scholarly journals, to apply the concept of competitive strategy to public and nonprofit organizations (MacMillan, 1983; Young, 1988; Osborne and Gaebler, 1992; Kearns, 1992a; Stone and Crittenden, 1994; Roller, 1996). This book tries to synthesize and expand these various approaches, illustrating their application to the strategic choices facing public and nonprofit organizations.

It should be said at the outset that some readers may find the business terminology I use occasionally to be controversial or even inappropriate in its application to public and nonprofit organizations. Can we really conceptualize social programs and services as *portfolios?* Do strategies like *divestment* and *liquidation* make any sense in government, where agencies rarely go out of business? This book is evidence that I believe these concepts do have value in public service organizations. But I also recognize that these concepts must be qualified, carefully illustrated, and often modified to be meaningful and helpful for public sector managers.

Overview of the Contents

Chapter One of *Private Sector Strategies for Social Sector Success* lays a foundation for the remaining chapters by describing some of the forces affecting the ways government and nonprofit executives do their jobs. In what respects is your organization behaving more like a business? What lessons can you learn from business about effective management in public and nonprofit organizations? Conversely, what are the limits on what you can learn from business? What types of skills will be needed by public and nonprofit executives as we enter the twenty-first century?

Chapter Two provides a brief overview of three approaches to strategy formulation. Sometimes strategy is derived rationally, through analytical techniques designed to assess the fit between an organization and its strategic environment. At other times strategy seems simply to evolve, through political bargaining and power plays, through informal experimentation, or through the gestaltlike insights of a visionary leader. Moreover, strategies do not always require dramatic shifts in direction intended to optimize performance. Sometimes strategies are nothing more than efforts to survive, even temporarily, to fight another day. They can even be incremental efforts to meet suboptimal objectives. I believe that strategy development can be usefully informed by the techniques presented here, but strict adherence to these strategic management methodologies should not supplant your own insights, imagination, and creativity.

Chapter Three presents concepts and techniques for conducting an environmental scan. The environmental scan provides crucial information on important environmental trends affecting your organization and others like it. What business are you in? In what markets do you compete? What are the distinctive features of these markets? Are these markets growing, shrinking, or remaining stable? Do you have competitors? A systematic review of these and other questions can help you identify opportunities and challenges in your strategic environment.

Chapter Four presents the concept of product and service portfolios and explores how portfolio management can help your programs and services work together to achieve the organization's goals. Portfolio analysis used in conjunction with environmental scanning is a powerful tool for deciding whether you want to grow, retrench, or simply stabilize your organization.

Chapter Five presents the various types of growth strategies and explains the pros and cons of each. Growth strategies are always appealing because they signify vitality and success. But they have pitfalls as well that need to be avoided.

Chapter Six looks at retrenchment as an organizational strategy. Retrenchment is never easy because most of us have been conditioned to think of retrenchment as a sign of failure or even impending demise. But when used wisely, retrenchment strategies can help your organization live to fight another day.

Chapter Seven explores strategies designed to stabilize your organization in a turbulent environment when neither growth nor retrenchment is appropriate. Much of Chapter Seven focuses on how to turn around a troubled organization.

Chapter Eight discusses collaborative strategies, which are appropriate when you want to partner with another organization to

achieve common objectives. Collaboration is a valued ideal, especially for public and nonprofit organizations, but it is not easy to
develop and sustain meaningful collaborative programs with other
organizations. There are important issues to consider as you select
and implement opportunities for collaboration.

Chapter Nine addresses important issues of strategy implementation. As you think about implementation, you will likely need to
consider whether your organizational structure will facilitate or hin-
der your strategic objectives. You will also need to consider the impact of your strategy on staffing, information, and control systems.
Lastly, you must consider how you will evaluate and, if necessary,
modify your strategy.

Finally, the Conclusion examines the politics of strategy development and implementation. Political considerations are presented
throughout the book; however, this section highlights some specific
concerns and political management strategies.

Throughout I offer illustrations and examples from public and
nonprofit organizations that are applying the concepts discussed.
Also, I conclude each chapter with a series of questions that you
might ponder on your own or discuss with your colleagues as one way
of getting started on applying some of the ideas in your organization.

March 2000   Kevin P. Kearns
Pittsburgh, Pennsylvania

The Author

Kevin P. Kearns is associate professor and director of the Master of Public Administration program at the Graduate School of Public and International Affairs (GSPIA), University of Pittsburgh. During his fifteen-year career in universities, he has held positions as an administrator, teacher, and researcher. He has served as associate dean of GSPIA, assistant to the president of the University of Pittsburgh, and director of executive education at the H. J. Heinz III School of Public Policy and Management at Carnegie Mellon University.

Kearns is the author of *Managing for Accountability: Preserving the Public Trust in Public and Nonprofit Organizations* (1996) and coauthor of *Analytical Planning* (with Thomas Saaty, 1985). He has published articles in such leading journals as *Public Administration Review*, *Nonprofit Management and Leadership*, *Public Budgeting and Finance*, and *Public Productivity and Management Review*. He serves on the editorial boards of the *Nonprofit and Voluntary Sector Quarterly*, *Journal of Public Affairs Education*, and *Public Productivity and Management Review*. He has won awards at both the University of Pittsburgh and Carnegie Mellon University for the quality of his teaching. Most recently, he received the GSPIA 1998–99 Annual Teaching Award. He has also delivered more than one hundred seminars for high-level executives in business, government, and nonprofit organizations.

Kearns has served as a trustee and adviser for many nonprofit organizations in Pittsburgh and nationally. He currently serves on the board and chairs the planning committee of the American Red Cross of Southwestern Pennsylvania. In the private for-profit sector, he is a member of the board of directors and chairman of the strategic planning committee of PHICO Group, Inc., a national provider of risk transfer and risk management services.

Kearns received his bachelor's degree from the University of Dayton and his master's and Ph.D. degrees from the University of Pittsburgh. He lives in Pittsburgh with his wife, Lorna, and their children, Maura and Ned.

Acknowledgments

Twelve years ago I developed and taught for the first time a master's level course on strategic management of public and nonprofit organizations at the Graduate School of Public and International Affairs, University of Pittsburgh. Since then, nearly four hundred students journeyed (and sometimes suffered) with me as we developed and refined the course. I want to thank those students, unfortunately too numerous to mention individually, for their enormous contribution to this effort. Many of them have come to the class with extensive practical experience as leaders of public and nonprofit organizations. They have challenged me to make the material relevant to their needs, and they have gladly taught me about their world. Others, though less experienced professionally, have come armed with sophisticated technical skills and an eagerness to explore the methodologies of strategy development and evaluation. All of them have provided me with inspiration, enrichment, and boundless joy.

Also, I have had the pleasure of working with senior executives around the country and abroad on issues of strategic management. Some of these encounters have been in executive development seminars. Others have been in consulting relationships. Still others have arisen from my work on nonprofit and corporate boards. I am indebted to the many colleagues I have met through these real-world experiences for their contribution to my thinking.

Intellectually, I am indebted to several prominent scholars in the field of strategic management. Not surprisingly, they span the intellectual spectrum in terms of their approach to the field. Michael Porter, writing primarily for business executives, has prompted me to think about applications of business strategy to public and nonprofit organizations. The thoroughness and logic of his analytical models has earned him the sparkling reputation he so richly deserves. On the other end of the spectrum, the work of Henry Mintzberg has inspired me to think critically and reflectively about the limitation of the analytical models that are the planner's toolkit. Mintzberg, who also writes primarily for a business audience, is skeptical of the value of analytical methods like Porter's and his observations on the field are at once insightful, irreverent, and marvelously entertaining. Perhaps in the middle between these two poles, John Bryson has contributed extensively to the literature on strategic management in public and nonprofit organizations. I used his textbook in that first strategic management course twelve years ago, and I use the revised edition of it today. Bryson blends his extraordinary mastery of the literature and methods with hands-on practical advice for doing strategic planning in government and nonprofit settings.

Closer to home, I want to express thanks to my colleagues at the Graduate School of Public and International Affairs (GSPIA), especially William Dunn, Iris Young, Martin Staniland, Leon Haley, David Miller, Paul Hammond, Susan White, and Carolyn Ban. The marvelous feature of a school like GSPIA is the amount of intellectual diversity, and sometimes the collision of viewpoints, contained under one roof. Several of these colleagues are not management scholars per se but rather do their work in fields like international diplomacy, ethical reasoning, and institutional advancement. Their observations on my work, even when they are skeptical, have been among the most valuable to my own development.

I am enormously indebted to several people at Jossey-Bass who nursed this project along. Alan Shrader served for sixteen years as senior editor of the Jossey-Bass Nonprofit and Public Management Series before moving on to other challenges. Alan worked with me on my first book published by Jossey-Bass, in 1996, and provided invaluable assistance with this one as well before he left. His knowledge of the field and his editorial eye are extraordinary. Just as important, Alan is a sensitive critic and a supportive motivator. Alan's successor, Dorothy Hearst, has taken up where he left off. Her assistance with the final stages of this project was supportive and most appreciated. Johanna Vondeling, editorial assistant, was simply superb. She interpreted and synthesized the observations of the anonymous reviewers of the draft manuscript and added insights of her own that proved to be most useful in editing the final version of the manuscript. And speaking of anonymous reviewers, I am deeply grateful to these three unknown colleagues for their comments and suggestions on the draft manuscript. Reviewers receive little in terms of tangible rewards, yet in order to contribute to their field, they spend days poring over manuscripts and providing thoughtful and constructive commentary. I also want to thank Elspeth MacHattie for her careful and thoughtful copyediting. Her suggestions greatly clarified and strengthened the manuscript.

Finally, I want to thank my wife, Lorna, and our two terrific children, Maura and Ned, for their love, companionship, and unwavering support through this and many other demanding endeavors. My gratitude for my family grows stronger every day.

Naturally, despite the contributions of everyone mentioned here, I alone remain responsible for errors or omissions in this book.

K.P.K.

Private Sector
Strategies for
Social Sector Success

PART ONE

Preparing for Strategic Planning

1

Embracing New Challenges and Opportunities

Strategic Management in Government and Nonprofit Organizations

At this dawn of a new century, government and nonprofit organizations look vastly different than they did one hundred years ago, or even ten years ago. They have become more market driven in their delivery of public goods and services. They no longer enjoy monopolies; rather they must often compete for public support and scarce resources. From a managerial perspective the boundaries between sectors—public, private, and nonprofit—have blurred almost to the point of irrelevance (Lipsky and Smith, 1993). Nonprofit organizations are using profit-making enterprises to diversify their revenues, and for-profit firms are operating welfare programs, schools, prisons, and other services that once were the exclusive domain of government (Ryan, 1999; Firstenberg, 1996).

Millersburg Public Library

Carla Anderson had worked through the weekend preparing her annual report for the city council.* As director of Millersburg Public Library, Anderson has oversight over the central library in downtown

* This is a hypothetical case constructed by the author and based on his experience as a trainer and consultant to corporate and public libraries. For another example of a case dealing with the evolving mission of public libraries, see Moore, 1995, pp. 13–16.

Millersburg plus three branch libraries located in outlying neighborhoods. The central library was founded in 1910 with a bequest from Edwin Miller, under the stipulation that subsequent operating costs would be borne by the community. Since then the central library and the three branches have relied almost exclusively on annual tax appropriations from the Millersburg City Council. User fees, overdue fines, and other revenue sources account for less than 10 percent of the library's budget.

Anderson's annual report and its accompanying five-year trend analysis portray a troubling picture for the library. Patronage, as measured by book circulation, is down more than 20 percent over the five-year period. Yet Anderson knows that this measure of output, required by the city council, is a deceptive measure of the library's overall value to the community. Even though patrons are borrowing fewer books, all four library facilities are nearly full of people and bustling with activity at all hours of the day. Some people use the library's computers to access Web-based research materials. Others use the library as a quiet place to read out-of-town newspapers or do genealogy research. Also, Anderson had made the library more accessible to cultural groups and book clubs and for other community gatherings. Anderson knows that the city council, especially Councilman Jones, will use her declining output measures as justification for reducing her budget. But her operating expenses are higher than ever, and all four of the facilities are in need of new equipment and other capital investments. She needs a way to convey to the city council that the library is busier than ever producing positive outcomes for the residents of Millersburg.

Anderson reflected on a few other issues as she put the finishing touches on her proposal.

Mandate and Mission

The original deed of gift from Edwin Miller specified the purpose of the Millersburg Library: "to collect, maintain, and circulate books and other printed materials and to provide free and open access for the education and general enlightenment of the citizens of Millersburg." Shortly thereafter the very same language was incorporated into the authorizing legislation, which was passed into law by the city council and which committed public funds for the operation of the library in perpetuity. Thus the legal mandate for the library is unequivocal and permanent.

The problem for Anderson is that this mandate captures only part (and a shrinking part!) of the programs and services the library actually delivers to Millersburg and the surrounding communities. People who want to borrow books make up a smaller and smaller portion of the library's users.

So, with respect to its fundamental purpose, the Millersburg library has become something much different than its founders envisioned. It is now a sort of information broker, a taxicab on the information highway. Thus the original mandate for Millersburg Public Library, though an essential part of Anderson's accountability environment, is no longer sufficient as a management or political tool. Anderson realizes that the Millersburg Public Library needs a mission statement that captures its broader purposes and value to the community.

Competitive Environment

For generations the Millersburg Public Library was the only library within one hundred miles. It enjoyed a virtual monopoly as a collector and distributor of books and other printed materials. Now, of course, the situation is much different. To begin with, many people in Millersburg have computers at home, work, or school through which they gain instant access to the Internet, including the holdings of other libraries around the world. Resources available through the Internet provide a significant amount of competition for traditional public libraries. Fortunately, Anderson has kept pace with changing technology by providing services to help patrons use the Internet more productively and with greater sophistication.

But there is also competition from other libraries that appeared as Millersburg and its surrounding communities grew. The local community college has made a significant investment in its library facilities and has made these facilities more accessible to the general public. Large bookstores also provide competition with their vast collections, friendly and relaxed atmosphere, and special programs for children and adults.

Anderson knows that the business of information brokering has become more and more competitive. She worries that her library is in danger of becoming obsolete and noncompetitive in the new marketplace of ideas.

Diversification of Revenue

Financially, the Millersburg Public Library simply can no longer survive on its annual tax appropriation from the city council. Anderson has been trimming costs and delaying investments for years. Anderson must find new sources of revenue.

She is thinking about a variety of options for earning that revenue. For example, she would like to establish a cooperative arrangement with the Millersburg Public Schools that could result in a long-term contract for certain educational services for children. She wants to expand her evening programming with a public lecture series funded by foundation grants and subscription fees. Most significant, she wants the city council to support a proposal pending before the state legislature that would force suburban residents to bear a portion of the financial burden for large institutions like the Millersburg Public Library. Currently the suburbs enjoy the use of the library, but they bear none of the financial responsibility for upkeep and operations.

Anderson knows that the stakes are high. With her declining output measures, she will not be able to convince the city council to increase her budget. She must find the revenues herself to sustain the library.

Outputs and Outcomes

Finally, Carla Anderson is troubled by the perception among certain members of the council that the Millersburg Public Library is a luxury that can no longer be afforded. One council member was overheard referring to the library as "a relic, nothing more than a museum for books that sit there rotting on the shelves." Anderson knows that the library's real contribution to the quality of life in Millersburg cannot be measured in facts and figures on patronage, book circulation, or fees and fines collected. She sees the positive outcomes every day in the faces of children and adults who gather at the library for various purposes. But how can she measure these outcomes and convey them to the members of the city council in a way that convinces them of the library's value to the community?

A New Paradigm of Public Service

Carla Anderson works in an environment that is much different from that of her predecessors. Let's examine some of the practical implications of these changes, focusing especially on the skills needed by public and nonprofit executives today and in the foreseeable future.

The Goals of Public and Nonprofit Organizations: From Mandates to Missions

Generations ago professional public executives were trained to believe that their only job was to faithfully and efficiently implement mandates and programs handed down to them by elected officials. Over time this strictly construed ministerial perspective gave way to a more proactive managerial paradigm in which professional public executives are recognized as key players in the political process, individuals who work closely with elected officials in crafting policy as well as implementing it. Still, however, the notion of the legal *mandate*, with all its constraints on administrative discretion, has reigned supreme as the core job description for most public administrators.

Today most experts acknowledge that professional public executives' legal obligation to fulfill the official mandate must be complemented by a professional and leadership responsibility to craft and vigorously pursue a vision and mission for the organization. Carla Anderson is beginning to develop a broader vision for the Millersburg Public Library, well beyond its original and increasingly outdated mandate. As she does so she must ask at least two fundamental questions: What *must* the library do to be in compliance with its mandate? and, What *can* the library do and what *should* it do to serve a legitimate need in the community within a reasonable interpretation of its legal mandate?

Frances Hesselbein (1996), who brought the Girl Scouts of America back from the brink of extinction, has said many times that the secret of her success was "managing from the mission." Peter Drucker (1990), the preeminent management scholar, observes that the organization's mission and the extent to which that mission is embodied in daily decision making is a key to success. Harvard political scientist Mark Moore (1995) says that today's public managers are more than mere custodians of funds and overseers of mandated functions and activities. Rather, he says, they have been "entrusted with a bundle of public assets" (p. 16) and their job is to decide how to best employ those assets in the creation of "public value." And finally, case study research on the common characteristics of high-performing organizations consistently reveals that the clarity of the organization's mission is a contributor to outstanding performance (Peters and Waterman, 1982; Knauft, Berger, and Gray, 1991; Steckel and Lehman, 1997; Brinckerhoff, 1994). Managing from the mission requires such leadership skills and perspectives as these:

- The pragmatism to understand that your mandate must be fulfilled first, before you envision other roles for your organization

- The imagination, courage, and vision to see beyond your organization's legal and jurisdictional mandates

- A sophisticated understanding of the marketplace in which your organization exists, including the "industry" in which you operate

- The ability to identify and interpret unmet needs in that marketplace

- The ability to think of ways for your organization to prevent problems before they occur, not just solve them after they occur

- An entrepreneurial yet pragmatic view of your organization's core competencies and its ability to meet those unmet needs, including (most important) the ability to ascertain whether a given activity or initiative is within the domain of its mission

- An accurate understanding of your organization's strengths, weaknesses, and comparative advantages

- An understanding of the prospective programs and activities that are clearly *outside* the scope of your organization's mission and the conviction and concentration to keep your organization from straying from its core mission

The Mission as an Empowering Force. Carla Anderson might find it helpful to begin thinking seriously about an expanded vision for the Millersburg Public Library and then to articulate this vision in a new mission statement. Apparently the mission and the mandate of the library have been virtually indistinguishable for many years. The members of the city council seem to focus exclusively on the mandate, even when they disparagingly refer to the library as "a museum for books." A new mission statement would be a key component of Anderson's strategy to build and sustain support for the library from the city council and other key constituencies. Their support for her vision would likely be enhanced if they were involved in crafting the new mission statement. At a minimum, a new mission statement would clarify and make more explicit the distinction between the mandate and the mission of the Millersburg Public Library. Such a distinction would clarify for Anderson what the library *must* do to satisfy its legal mandate and what it *might* do to meet emerging community needs. The process of developing a new mission statement would also help Anderson better understand the values and priorities of the city council members.

A good mission statement should articulate (1) the organization's purpose and long-term goals, (2) the needs that the organization fills in the marketplace, (3) the organization's core values and operating philosophies, and (4) the organization's aspirations for the future (Kearns, 1998b). Many executives seem to prefer extremely short mission statements (one or two sentences) that succinctly articulate the organization's core purpose or its reason for existing. They prefer not to include operating values and aspirations in the mission statement, choosing instead to state these in a separate values statement or vision statement. Short mission statements do indeed have the advantage of being easily conveyed, and it is true that they can give you a great deal of flexibility, which can be valuable in a politically charged environment. But their brevity also brings with it ambiguity. A short mission statement can be so vague or all-encompassing that it does not provide much guidance to you in making choices among competing uses of your scarce resources. In other words, a bare-bones mission statement, even though sometimes the foundation for a good marketing slogan, is often not very helpful in guiding day-to-day decisions or larger policy choices. Moreover, short mission statements can confuse the mandate with the mission.

An expanded mission statement for the Millersburg Public Library could give legitimacy to programs and services that the library has been providing for a long time while also placing some important constraints on its activities. Exhibit 1.1 illustrates an expanded mission statement that Carla Anderson might submit to the city council.

The new mission statement would be an empowering document for Anderson and her staff because it provides the library

EXHIBIT 1.1 Mission Statement of the Millersburg Public Library.

The duty of the Millersburg Public Library is to fulfill its mandate as outlined in the deed of gift from Edwin Miller in 1850: "To collect, maintain, and circulate books and other printed materials and to provide free and open access for the education and general enlightenment of the citizens of Millersburg." Consistent with the intent of the mandate, the broader mission of the Millersburg Public Library is to promote lifelong learning among the residents of Millersburg and surrounding communities. The library serves a unique need, not only as a repository for knowledge but also as a catalyst for inquiry and a facilitator of intellectual exchange among citizens of all ages.

Values and Operating Principles

To advance its mission, the Millersburg Public Library will adhere to the following values and operating principles:

- To provide a haven for intellectual inquiry of all types
- To embrace its role as a place where citizens of all ages gather to learn and exchange ideas
- To help citizens make maximum use of advanced technology as a tool of inquiry and learning
- To develop and deliver programs designed to stimulate intellectual curiosity
- To seek out collaborative ventures with public and private organizations whenever such ventures will enhance the library's ability to achieve its mission with maximum efficiency and effectiveness
- To engage only in activities that advance the library's mission and fulfill its mandate to the citizens of Millersburg and surrounding communities

with certain guiding *values* and *philosophies* but does not dictate or preclude particular actions. If the city council endorses this new mission statement, it will commit itself to certain guiding principles that serve the purpose of *opening*, not closing, opportunities for the library to serve legitimate needs in the community.

The Mission as a Constraining Force. Does an entrepreneurial manager try to stretch the mission as far as possible to accommodate all potential interpretations? Should managers chase opportunities, forcing them to fit within the mission? Absolutely not! Carla Anderson would likely face very strong opposition from the city council if her expanded vision for the library substantially weakened its ability to fulfill its legal and historical mandate.

The mission-driven executive needs to master the art of saying no when it is apparent that a proposed program or activity is beyond the scope of the mission and especially when it jeopardizes the mandate. The late Richard Cyert, renowned management scholar and former president of Carnegie Mellon University, continually emphasized this point to the faculty, trustees, and staff. Cyert is widely credited with transforming Carnegie Mellon from a good regional university to a first-class international institution. For Cyert, on the one hand, managing from the mission sometimes meant passing up opportunities when they would distract attention from the core mission and objectives. Early in his tenure some powerful stakeholders urged Cyert to open a medical school at the university. Cyert resisted, noting that such an investment would not be consistent with the university's operating philosophy, which was attached to its mission statement and which said unequivocally that Carnegie Mellon would engage only in those activities in which it could develop a leadership position based upon its *comparative advantage*. He was skeptical that Carnegie Mellon could develop a strong foothold in medical practice and research.

On the other hand, Cyert was a master at leveraging the resources of his institution, combining them in ways to *create* comparative advantages where none existed before. For example, in the 1970s he brought together cognitive psychologists and computer scientists to create one of the earliest and most impressive research programs in artificial intelligence. In fact, throughout his tenure at Carnegie Mellon, Cyert worked hard to break down the walls, real and imagined, that sometimes prevent university departments from collaborating on promising opportunities. In sum, Cyert was an expert at looking beyond narrow jurisdictional boundaries that sometimes constrain organizational missions and at the same time an expert in knowing when to say "no" to proposals that would have stretched the institution beyond its inherent comparative advantage.

Thus, managing from the mission requires vision, an astute sense of the marketplace, a mature understanding of your organization's place in the market, a commitment to the concept of comparative advantage, and the courage to act on your convictions. But all these qualities must be tempered by political pragmatism and an understanding that you will be judged by your mandate as well as your mission.

The Marketplace of Public and Nonprofit Services: From Monopoly to Competition

Many government executives and some nonprofit leaders believe they have a monopoly in the provision of goods and services. In some cases their perceptions are justified. At one time the Millersburg Public Library enjoyed a monopoly, but a newly competitive environment has forced it to reexamine its mission and role in the community.

Public and nonprofit executives today should look twice at their markets and question whether their monopolistic assumptions still hold (Menefee, 1997; Boyne, 1993). For example, in public education, charter schools and voucher systems have injected a higher level of competition, and private companies now compete for contracts to manage schools and school systems. Likewise, public housing authorities must compete against private landlords and nonprofit agencies for people (customers) who use vouchers and certificates to shop in the housing marketplace (DiIulio and Kettl, 1995; DeParle, 1996). New federal regulations and block grants are forcing public housing authorities to abandon their monopolistic "take it or leave it" attitude and behave more like entrepreneurial real estate managers in a free market (Quercia and Galster, 1997).

In the nonprofit sector there is a long tradition of competition, primarily because the *entry barriers* (see Chapter Three) to the marketplace are minimal. Nearly anyone can start a nonprofit corporation simply by filing the necessary registration forms with the appropriate state agency and the Internal Revenue Service. So the nonprofit marketplace is already crowded and becoming more so with every passing year. Moreover, nonprofit organizations are experiencing more intense and aggressive competition from the private sector. Many private firms, for example, are tripping over each other to win lucrative government contracts to administer welfare reform and managed care programs. Private firms bring expertise in data management, cost control, and policy enforcement to the task. These are activities in which the private sector generally has a comparative skill advantage over nonprofit organizations.

Skills for Responsible Competition.   Survival in a competitive environment requires such skills and perspectives as these:

- The ability to recognize when competitive behavior will contribute public value and when it will be destructive and have a negative effect
- The ability to recognize when competitive behavior will advance the mission of your organization and when it will merely waste scarce resources
- The ability to read and interpret market signals from competitors and consumers
- The ability to tailor your organization's programs and services to meet specific needs

- An understanding of consumer behavior, including consumers' sensitivity to price and quality and to promotional and marketing strategies
- An understanding of product life cycles and their effect on organizational strategy
- The ability to identify niche markets and opportunities for market penetration

To support these skills, management needs authorization from the governing body (the elected or volunteer board) to engage in competitive behavior.

Carla Anderson realizes that the Millersburg Public Library faces formidable competition from others in the knowledge industry. In fact, in this age of information overload, Carla Anderson works in one of the most competitive industries in the world. Moreover, much of the competition she faces is *passive* or *diffused* competition, coming not from comparable organizations but from technologies that compete with the library for the attention of its potential patrons. For example, the Internet is not an organization that is consciously trying to put Millersburg Public Library out of business, but it is an increasingly prevalent and powerful supplier of information that is available for people who might otherwise use the library to find that information. Anderson knows that it is pointless to compete against the Internet. Rather she must find a way to embrace this new supplier, using information technology to enhance the library's value to the community.

Tread with Caution. Some organizations in the public and nonprofit sectors have (implicitly if not explicitly) adopted *no competition* policies. They believe that competition is economically at odds with the provision of public goods or philosophically at odds with the notion of charitable activity. Even when they do not have such policies, organizations may fear the public perception that they are wasting public funds on needless competition and duplication of effort.

For example, the board of directors of a nonprofit organization spent many hours debating the prospect of entering the biomedical distribution industry, competing directly against an existing non-profit organization that enjoyed a monopoly in that line of programs and services. In the end the board members realized they had *no choice* but to compete because the managed care environment forced local hospitals to look for competitive pricing and quality from all their suppliers. Still, this decision to enter a competitive market was significant enough to require board authorization. Here are a few of the issues board members discussed:

- Is this line of programs and services consistent with our mission?

- Do we want to be perceived as engaging in head-to-head competition with another nonprofit organization?

- What will be the perceptions of the general public, the major donors, the United Way, and other important stakeholders? Will the competitor counterattack?

- Have we exhausted all opportunities for collaboration with the competitor?

- Overall, what are the threats, opportunities, and future prospects associated with this line of programs and services? What can we gain, and what might we lose? Will this venture contribute to other services in our portfolio, or will it distract our attention from our core mission?

The theory of free market economics tells us that consumers generally benefit from competition because it keeps prices affordable and quality high. But is the public always well served by competition? No. Competition in the public and nonprofit sectors can easily distract mangers' attention from the core mission and long-term goals. The competitive spirit can, for example, lead a nonprofit organization to make decisions based on its bottom line or market share rather than on the best interests of its clients or the community as a whole. For example, the competition between neighboring communities for economic development projects can blind decision makers to the reality that the communities' fates are interwoven.

Responsible competition requires mature judgment, a supporting set of corporate values and philosophies, a long-term view, and a commitment to the mission.

Revenue Streams in Public and Nonprofit Organizations: From Concentration to Diversification

Today taxes are only one of many revenue sources that government jurisdictions use to finance their activities. Service fees have a long and well-documented history, but we are also seeing the use of novel ideas like franchising, public-private partnerships, equity investments, and demand management (Osborne and Gaebler, 1992). Government executives are now looking beyond simply balancing their budgets to ways they can generate profits in some services to subsidize losses in others.

Similarly, in the nonprofit sector, the historical reliance on philanthropic contributions as the dominant source of revenues has given way to diversified revenue streams that include fees for service, unrelated business income, profit-making subsidiaries, contracts, and grants. Today, fees for service are the fastest growing source of nonprofit revenues. The result is not only the diversification of revenue streams but also the diversification of the programs and services in an organization's portfolio. As the diversification process becomes more sophisticated, the portfolios become more and more complex. Even museums are looking for ways to add a few more dollars to their earned revenues by, for example, opening their hallowed halls to birthday parties, sleep-overs for scout troops, wedding receptions, and the like.

Apparently Carla Anderson has concluded that the Millersburg Public Library cannot survive on its annual allocation from the city council. Even if the council accepts her new and expanded mission, they are unlikely to completely fill the growing gap between her revenues and expenditures. Therefore she must find additional revenues from grants and contracts with other organizations and higher earned revenues from the library's growing portfolio of programs and services.

Portfolio Management. In the business world, firms often produce more than one product in order to appeal to diverse customers and markets. Consequently, they must engage in *portfolio management*, designing and implementing an appropriate competitive strategy for each of several product lines. In multiproduct firms the dimensions and characteristics of the product portfolio are constantly being adjusted to maximize the company's overarching goals and objectives.

Public and nonprofit organizations sometimes manage diverse portfolios just as multiproduct firms do. For example, municipal governments have such programs and services as public safety, parks and recreation, land use planning, economic development, public works, transportation support, and many others. Similarly, many social service agencies offer a continuum of care from crisis intervention to long-term support and counseling. Until recently, however, the notion of portfolio management was nonexistent in public and nonprofit philosophies.

When parts of its portfolio provide an organization with earned revenue over and above expenses, then it is generating a profit *on that part of its portfolio*. Those revenues might be used to subsidize other programs and services in the portfolio that earn nothing or that spend more than they earn. Multiproduct for-profit firms use a set of techniques (see Chapter Four) to understand flows of money and other resources among the various parts of their portfolios. Naturally, in public and nonprofit organizations there are limitations on the use of such portfolio management techniques. For example, an organization cannot move restricted funds from one part of its portfolio to another.

Responsible Portfolio Management. If allowed to run unchecked, commercialization of the nonprofit sector will fundamentally alter the relationship between public service organizations and their clients, who would be viewed as consumers at best and buyers at worst (Hasenfeld, 1996; Young, 1988). The risks are especially great for the most vulnerable populations, who could easily be overlooked or even victimized in a fully commercialized human service marketplace. Entrepreneurial management in government organizations also poses a special set of considerations. The bankruptcy of Orange County, California, illustrates many of the potential dangers of public sector entrepreneurship (Kearns, 1995). In that affluent community the county treasurer succeeded for years in supplementing restricted tax revenues by investing public funds in highly lucrative (but very volatile) derivative markets. The strategy worked beautifully until a shift in market conditions brought the investment fund to its knees, causing the largest municipal bankruptcy in history. Some critics of the reinvention movement have argued that a certain degree of inefficiency and rigidity is a small price to pay for the time-honored system of representative bureaucracy. Government, they argue, should not be run like a business (Moe, 1994; Goodsell, 1994).

Responsible portfolio management requires such special skills and perspectives as these:

- The ability to recognize not only the synergies among your organization's programs and services but also the programs' and services' distinctive identities as semi-autonomous units

- The establishment of an unambiguous set of priorities regarding the parts of your organization's portfolio that are central to its core mission and the parts that are ancillary

- Attentiveness to the fact that a portfolio of multiple programs and services can generate multiple cultures within your organization and that these cultures may not always complement each other

- Implementation of budgeting and accounting systems that allow you to track the finances, performance, and outcomes of the various programs independently

- The ability to develop separate business plans for each major program and service while simultaneously linking these plans to your organization's overall direction and philosophy

As Carla Anderson expands her portfolio and diversifies her revenues, she must keep a close eye on her mandate and her core mission, which is to provide free and open access to the library to all citizens of Millersburg. Each new program she adds, especially those that generate earned income, will have an impact on the total organization. She must be vigilant in not allowing the profitable parts of the portfolio and the innovative programs that attract favorable consumer response to drive out unprofitable or routine programs that represent the core of the library's mission.

For many executives who work in public and nonprofit organizations, revenue diversification is not a choice, it is a necessity. The challenge is to maintain the organization's core values as a public service institution while simultaneously using business skills to strategically manage a portfolio of programs and services.

Performance of Public and Nonprofit Organizations: From Outputs to Outcomes

In the public and nonprofit sectors, *outputs* have historically been the primary measure of organizational performance. Especially during the decades when government was growing, the order of the day was to produce more and more programs and services. Even in the current era of government cutbacks and downsizing, many public executives remain obsessed with maintaining or even increasing expected levels of output. "Do more with less" is a familiar battle cry in both the public and nonprofit sectors.

Certainly, Carla Anderson is concerned with outputs because she knows that the city council has been keeping a watchful (and critical) eye on the library's declining circulation figures. Fewer books are going *out* the door, but more people are coming *in* the door. Anderson cannot ignore or trivialize her declining output trends, for they tell an important story about the viability of the library's programs and services. But she must find a way to focus the attention of the council and other important stakeholders on *outcomes* as well as outputs.

Outcome measures are concerned not with how many people are served by an organization but with the differences those activities make for clients, beneficiaries, and society at large. Citizens want evidence from public and nonprofit agencies not only of high productivity and high efficiency but also of the ways the community is somehow better off as a direct result of the agencies' efforts. They want to know not just how many more police were hired with last year's budget increase but whether the streets are really safer as a result of the investment.

In the nonprofit sector, funding agencies like the United Way, private foundations, and even individual philanthropists are demanding that organizations demonstrate that they are making a difference in the lives of the people they serve. The following skills and attitudes are just a few of the ones you need as a public or nonprofit manager to survive in this new environment:

- An ability to conceptualize and explain exactly how the programs and services your organization offers contribute to filling unmet community needs

- A willingness to put your theories to the test by subjecting your programs and services to close scrutiny, identifying as precisely as possible the extent to which they succeed in filling those community needs

- An adherence to the principle that there are no sacred cows in your organization, that each program or service in your organization's portfolio must be able to prove its worth and its contribution to the organization's mission

Carla Anderson has a challenging task in demonstrating to the city council that the Millersburg Public Library is providing positive outcomes to the community. On the one hand it is obvious that the library is a popular gathering place for people of all ages. On the other hand city council members are skeptical that those people are engaged in meaningful or productive activities that are facilitated by the library. Although Anderson is convinced that people are benefiting from the services offered by the library, she needs to cultivate an objective view and back up her intuition with data and evidence. Is the library really providing positive outcomes to the community that could not accrue through any other source? What are the outcomes, for example, of the library's Internet classes? Can she demonstrate, first, that residents have been empowered to become more informed consumers of information? If so, she then needs hard evidence that the library is substantially responsible for these positive outcomes. Could these fledgling Internet users have acquired the same skills elsewhere? Third, she must convince city council members that public investments are needed to sustain these positive outcomes. Why should tax dollars be used to support Internet usage? Why should the city council subsidize an after-school program for latchkey kids?

The advent of advanced and relatively affordable information technology will only intensify the pressure on public and nonprofit organizations to maintain and disseminate more and more information about clients, services, and outcomes. If properly used, this technology will permit agencies to maintain far more sophisticated databases on client outcomes, correlating those outcomes with different interventions, programs, and treatment modalities and benchmarking their performance against that of other agencies through sophisticated information networks. Information technology will also facilitate multiple measures of performance, including the use of far more sophisticated financial indicators such as ratio analysis and financial modeling.

The Jobs of Public and Nonprofit Managers

To summarize the prior discussion, the jobs of public and nonprofit executives will likely change significantly to the extent that executives are under pressure to accomplish these tasks:

- Provide executive leadership in the pursuit of a vision that encourages the members of the organization to think beyond the confines of their legal mandate.

- Help the organization adapt to a competitive marketplace where it no longer enjoys a monopoly over certain products and services.

- Exercise responsible entrepreneurship in the search for opportunities to earn more revenue and to continually control costs.

- Keep key stakeholders focused on organizational outcomes, not just outputs.

The new paradigm I have been describing is having profound impacts on the roles and functions of public and nonprofit executives and the skills they need to lead their organizations into the next century. Appointed government executives once were viewed as relatively passive *implementers* of directives and policies handed down from elected officials. They were expected to bring professionalism and politically neutral competence to public bureaucracies and to use their managerial expertise to improve the efficiency and effectiveness of public services. But their focus was on means, not ends, and they were careful not to show too much initiative lest they be accused of bypassing the official policymaking machinery of a representative democracy. Their accountability to the general public was exercised indirectly through accountability to superiors in the bureaucracy and, ultimately, to elected representatives.

Today government executives are encouraged to think of accountability in broader terms and to continually prove their contribution to the public good and justify the resources they consume. They recognize that the price of failure in today's competitive marketplace is the loss of their resources to another organization, often a private for-profit firm that is waiting on the sidelines and anxious to play the game.

Similarly, the image of the "typical" nonprofit executive is undergoing a metamorphosis. Not long ago, executives in a nonprofit organization were widely viewed as poorly paid idealists, social reformers, artists, or educators who knew little and cared even less about the messy details of organizational management. Today, of course, the image of the nonprofit executive is vastly different. For one thing, most people nowadays have at least some understanding of the complexity of the nonprofit sector itself and its powerful impact on the social and economic life of the nation. The sector has grown and has become more visible than at any time in the past. Many of the organizations that the sector comprises are themselves a reflection of this complexity. They offer an array of services to a diverse clientele. They manage multiple streams of revenue including government grants and contracts, philanthropic contributions, fees for services, and unrelated business income. Even more so than their government counterparts, executives in the nonprofit sector must sing for their supper, competing for a slice of the resource pie. Accordingly, they must engage in virtually every task that a typical business executive does:

- Identifying unmet needs in the marketplace
- Designing programs or services to meet those needs
- Pricing those programs and services to ensure financial viability
- Marketing those programs and services directly to consumers and indirectly to the philanthropists and government officials who subsidize them

- Managing program and service portfolios
- Continuously evaluating program and service impacts on society

Today, nonprofit executives are among the most entrepreneurial managers to be found anywhere, including the private for-profit sector.

What Public and Nonprofit Organizations Should (and Should Not) Learn from Business

In this chapter I have focused on how government and nonprofit organizations are behaving more like businesses. As you brace yourself for the world of public and nonprofit management in the twenty-first century, what can you realistically learn from your counterparts in the business world? Certainly there are some business philosophies that will serve you well in this new environment. Conversely there are many distinctive characteristics of public and nonprofit organizations that should be preserved. A public service organization should never fully embrace the business mentality, lest it lose sight of its core mission and values.

What Business Can Teach You

Here are some lessons that many business leaders have learned to their advantage and that should also serve public and nonprofit leaders well in a competitive marketplace:

Know your business better than anyone else does. Executives in any organization have no excuse for not knowing the trends affecting programs and services delivered by that organization and the markets it serves. Businesses must continually monitor the competitive forces affecting organizations in their industries and markets. So, if you are in the "industry" of adult day care, then you should strive to know that field better than anyone, including the ways it is likely to change in the future. If you are in the "business" of crime prevention, then you should strive for the highest level of knowledge in that field.

Have a realistic image of your organization and its environment. Business executives cannot afford to look at the world through rose-colored glasses. For example, if they need to seek venture capital to develop a new product, they know that lending agencies will demand a brutally honest appraisal of the prospects for success. Similarly, you should cultivate an objective view of your organization in relation to comparable organizations, acknowledging their comparative advantages as well as your own (Letts and others, 1997).

Protect your organization's comparative advantages, recognizing that it is highly unlikely it will ever be all things to all people. Successful businesses build on their comparative advantages. Similarly, don't allow your organization to stray too far from its core strengths. Sometimes managing from your mission means knowing when to say no to a new initiative or venture. Executives cannot afford to become complacent about current comparative advantages, perhaps allowing them to wither and die. Another organization is waiting to snatch your comparative advantage at the first sign of ambivalence.

Use portfolio management. Businesses do not usually succeed with a one-size-fits-all philosophy. Develop a separate strategy for each of your programs and services, recognizing their distinctive markets and performance benchmarks as well as their synergistic contributions to the overall corporate mission.

Recognize that the continued existence of your organization is a privilege to be earned, not a right to be protected. The business world has taught us that even the largest and most powerful organizations are not invincible. Even in government, survival demands continuous success in meeting public needs and creating something of value.

Try to see your organization through the eyes of consumers and other important stakeholders, not just from your own professional perspective. Too often the advocacy role played by public and nonprofit organizations can cross over that thin line between advocacy on behalf of others and a paternalistic attitude that blinds us to the beliefs and preferences of those we profess to serve.

Set tangible performance targets for your organization, and hold your employees and yourself accountable for their attainment. Public and nonprofit executives sometimes protest, "You can't measure our contribution to society." This mentality gets passed downward to employees who say, "You can't hold me accountable for goals that have not been made explicit." Ultimately, then, no one is accountable for anything.

Create perceptions of your organization, and continually reinforce them. Marketing and promotion are ways of facilitating exchanges between your organization and the people it serves. Marketing has become an essential skill for public and nonprofit managers.

Understand that competition is a fact of life. At some level you organization *is* competing with other organizations whether you want it to or not.

The following chapters explore ways for you and your staff to develop and refine these essential skills and perspectives.

What Business Cannot Teach You

Although much can be learned from our colleagues in the business world, it is wise to take their philosophy with a grain of salt. Public and nonprofit organizations are *not* businesses, and your leadership role is *different* from the role of the corporate CEO in some very important ways. Graham Allison, former dean of Harvard University's John F. Kennedy School of Government, suggests that public managers operate under tighter constraints than their private sector counterparts in three important areas: (1) defining the mission, objectives, and strategy of their organizations; (2) designing and managing internal operations; and (3) interacting with external constituencies, especially legislators and the media (Allison, [1980] 1991; see also Ring and Perry, 1985). Paul Nutt and Robert Backoff

(1993) itemized twenty differences between public, nonprofit, and for-profit organizations, categorizing these differences as environmental factors, transactional processes, and organizational characteristics. They argue, for example, that the flexibility of public and nonprofit organizations to respond to market shifts is severely constrained by a complex web of interorganizational contracts, legal mandates, negotiated franchises, limited control over diverse stakeholders, and political pressures from all sides.

These and other operational constraints will always distinguish public and nonprofit organizations from their counterparts in the business world. Beyond operational issues, there are these important philosophical differences to keep in mind:

The mission must follow the mandate. Even though they ultimately answer to shareholders and directors, business executives can define, refine, and redefine the mission and corporate strategy of their organizations with relative ease. Their mandate, which they receive from shareholders through the board of directors, and their mission are essentially indistinguishable. Public and nonprofit executives, however, must strike a more reflective and sometimes delicate balance between mandate and mission. Libraries cannot throw out their books and become community recreation centers. Police departments cannot simply transform themselves into social service agencies.

To think of citizens only as customers is to degrade their central role in a representative democracy. In the business world the consumers of sellers' products are nearly always the paying customers. There is a straightforward *quid pro quo* relationship between buyer and seller. In contrast, the relationship between citizens and public servants is much more complex than simply that of buyer and seller. For one thing, many of us "purchase" (through our tax dollars or charitable contributions) public services that we know (or hope) we will never actually consume. We are, in effect, partners in the production of public goods and services in a way that private consumers are not. Consequently, we as citizens have a more symbiotic relationship with government and nonprofit organizations than we do with, say, the neighborhood supermarket or auto dealership. We are not just consumers, we are coproducers and ultimately we give sanction to the actions of government (Moe, 1994).

Public servants' roles are much larger and more complex than those of business executives. For the most part, business executives are rewarded for simply delivering a valued product at a fair price. They are held responsible and accountable to their shareholders for delivering a quality product and producing a profit for the company. However, public and nonprofit executives are stewards of the public trust and enforcers of societal values. Thus they have the power to coerce as well as the obligation to provide (Moore, 1995). Stewards must be more deliberative and inclusive in their decision making than entrepreneurs, who need to act quickly to take advantage of market shifts. Unlike the business entrepreneur, stewards must master the fine art of political management: respecting political institutions and processes, building winning coalitions, and bargaining and compromising (Bolman and Deal, 1996).

An organization's portfolio will always have loss leaders. Business executives, knowing that their primary objective is to make a profit and increase shareholder value, can abandon losing products and services very quickly. In government and nonprofit organizations, an executive's primary objective is to serve people, regardless of financial performance. Making a profit on certain services may help an executive accomplish that goal, but profit making is incidental to the primary mission of filling social needs that are not filled by the private market. Thus your approach to portfolio management will, by definition, be much different from that of the typical business executive. Your approach to portfolio design will be focused primarily on mission fulfillment.

Managing external constituencies is essential to organizational success. Managers in the private sector are masters of their own destiny. True, they must answer to boards of directors, shareholders, regulators, and other groups. But as long as they meet corporate goals and manage the affairs of the firm in a responsible way, they will likely be left alone to chart the course and carry it through. Your strategic initiatives, however, can be pursued only after you have done a great deal of work to secure political support from myriad constituencies including legislators and their staffs, donors, contractors, special interest groups, media representatives, professional associations, accrediting agencies, regulators, employee unions, lobbyists, and on and on. This deliberative process takes time, energy, and a set of skills that set you apart from business executives.

There is no doubt that the public and nonprofit sectors in the United States have become more entrepreneurial and businesslike. And it is clear that public and nonprofit executives can learn much from their colleagues in the business world about market analysis, competitive strategy, comparative advantages, marketing, and customer service. But it is not accurate to suggest that public and nonprofit executives can fully embrace the business frame of mind toward management. Their role in society is qualitatively different and in many ways more demanding and complex than that of their business counterparts.

Conclusion

The environment described in this chapter demands a shift in the mind-set with which we regard the missions and strategies of public and nonprofit organizations. The traditional values and operating philosophies of public and nonprofit management will not suffice in the twenty-first century.

The remainder of this book presents tools and concepts to help you and your organization adapt to this new environment. For some organizations it is an environment rich with opportunities for growth. For others the future holds a different scenario, perhaps retrenchment or simply holding their own in a hostile environment. In any case, there are proven tools and techniques to help you make necessary decisions intelligently and with foresight.

Getting Started

1. Thinking back to the case study used in this chapter, consider how Carla Anderson might use the new mission statement to convey to the city council and the public the emerging role of the Millersburg Public Library in the community. What is the true mission of the library—to collect and distribute books or to stimulate lifelong learning and enlightenment? Is it appropriate for Anderson to encourage use of the library as a kind of surrogate town hall, a place for people to gather for meetings and other events? Are there any limits on what Anderson should encourage or allow? What are example of activities or programs that would be outside the scope of the new mission? What political risks would Anderson take by promoting a public dialogue on her mission statement?

2. In what respects is your organization operating more like a for-profit business than it did, say, five years ago? What have been the results, both good and bad, of this businesslike approach to management?

3. What parts of your organization should be managed more like a business? In what respects should your organization never behave like a business?

2

Understanding Three Models of Strategy Formulation

Studies of strategy formulation have uncovered many different models used by organizations to chart their futures. One of the most thought provoking and entertaining overviews of these models is presented by Mintzberg, Ahlstrand, and Lampel (1998), who identified ten schools of thought on strategy formulation. John Bryson (1988, 1995) also developed a useful typology for comparing various approaches to strategy formulation. For our purposes, the many models of strategy formulation can be summed up in three broad categories.

The first approach to strategy formulation, the *analytical approach,* is favored in most textbooks on strategic planning. It recommends that you use logic and in-depth analysis to improve the strategic fit between your organization and its environment. The second approach to strategy formulation, the *visioning approach,* starts with the leader's vision for the organization and then works backward to determine what resources or core competencies must be leveraged to achieve that vision. The third approach to strategy formulation is the *incremental approach.* When using this model, you avoid both the analytical approach and the visioning approach. Rather, you develop your strategy step by step, attacking problems and opportunities as they arise and allowing the overall strategy to evolve from the cumulative tactical adjustments made throughout various parts of the organization. This approach to strategy development often is described as the dominant approach in government organizations, because of the prevalence of bargaining, compromising, and political maneuvering in these institutions (Lindblom, 1959).

These three approaches to strategy formulation are not mutually exclusive, but obviously there are some important differences among them. Before examining the features of these three approaches, consider the following case.

Bill Strickland and the Manchester Craftsmen's Guild

As a young African American growing up in Pittsburgh in the 1950s and 1960s, William "Bill" Strickland could easily have been defeated by prejudice, poverty, violence, or simply the malaise of inner-city neighborhoods. Instead, with the help of a mentor, he discovered and developed his skill as a potter and sculptor, finding an artistic outlet for his energies, his passions, and his dreams.

After earning a degree from the University of Pittsburgh, Strickland returned to his neighborhood in 1968 to establish the Manchester Craftsmen's Guild, a nonprofit organization dedicated to introducing inner-city youngsters to their own talents in artistic expression. Early on Strickland ran the organization out of his home. "I used to just go out and bring neighborhood kids in off the street, give them a hunk of clay, and say make something of it," Strickland recalls (personal communication). Despite these humble beginnings, Strickland's vision was clear and unequivocal—to create an artistic community where at-risk youths could discover a constructive outlet for their energy and passions. The goal was never measured in terms of their artistic achievements, though some of Strickland's young craftsmen have achieved artistic success. Instead, Strickland simply wanted to make a positive impact on the lives of kids, some of whom had little hope.

Soon the Manchester Craftsmen's Guild began to attract the attention and assistance of community leaders, who were impressed by Strickland's vision, energy, and entrepreneurial skills. But his benefactors are the type of people who are not satisfied with words and visions alone. They demand actions and results. Naturally, therefore, they were impressed that over 60 percent of the youths who participated in Strickland's program finished high school and went on to participate in some form of postsecondary education.

Opportunities for growth and expansion of the Manchester Craftsmen's Guild began to appear. In some cases the opportunities might seem at first to have materialized out of thin air, but on closer examination it is clear that Strickland purposefully created the opportunities with a carefully crafted and masterfully executed strategy. Strickland assessed each opportunity from the perspective of his organization's primary mission and with an eye toward his organization's core competencies and comparative advantages. For example, Strickland agreed to take over responsibility for the Bidwell Training Center, a troubled job training program for adults. His organization had already acquired quite a bit of expertise in building the artistic skills of inner-city youths. He concluded correctly that these same competencies could be applied to the management of job training programs for adults. From one perspective this was a carefully constructed strategy of concentric diversification (see Chapter Five), but it was also a leap of faith and an entrepreneurial gamble. However, Strickland recognized that the Bidwell Training Center would add visibility and political clout to his organization.

After operating the joint organization out of a dilapidated warehouse for nearly ten years, Strickland launched a two-year capital campaign to construct a new 62,000-square-foot home for the two organizations. He secured the services of a top architect to design the new building, but he also played a central role in the design phase. The new center is a sparkling edifice with large common areas, a stunning exhibition hall, fountains, skylights, an acoustically perfect performing arts auditorium, and state-of-the-art training facilities for the Bidwell Training Center. Says Strickland:

I insisted that we put a fountain in the lobby. I like fountains. They symbolize vitality and hope. The building is bright and full of hope. We have filled the lobby and hallways with the products of the kids' work—beautiful ceramic art, clay pottery, paintings, and photographs. I want our kids to be surrounded by beautiful things, to be inspired by these things, and to feel that they are worthy of this beauty. If you show kids this kind of respect, they will respond in kind. We don't have a sophisticated security system, and we are located in the middle of one of the poorest neighborhoods in Pittsburgh. We have never once lost a piece of artwork from this building.

From there it seems that Strickland was again presented with one opportunity after another. A famous jazz artist who performed in the music hall as part of the Living Masters jazz series, offered to donate the recording rights to the Manchester Craftmen's Guild. Strickland immediately seized the opportunity to design a state-of-the-art recording studio to support a new training program in music production. Subsequently many other top performers have also donated recording rights to the guild. Some come to the center to record their own productions simply because the studio and the young people who staff it are among the finest in the nation.

The Bidwell Training Center thrived as well, the beneficiary of Strickland's strategic management and entrepreneurial skills. Strickland seems to be a master at leveraging his organization's core competencies, and those of other organizations, to address emerging needs in his community. For example, he entered into a partnership with the Bayer Corporation to train technicians skilled in the production of high-tech synthetic materials. He recognized earlier than most that federally funded job training programs should train people for cutting-edge technologies, not dead-end, minimum wage jobs. He added a culinary arts training program when he saw that Pittsburgh's economy was becoming increasingly service oriented. He formed strategic partnerships with business organizations, schools, community groups, and political leaders.

When Strickland talks about these alliances, it is easy to get the impression that none of them evolved from a master plan. "I just called people and asked them to come out to our building to look around and see what we are trying to do here. They always say, 'I like what you are doing here. How can I help?'" (personal communication). But upon deeper analysis it is evident that each of the partnerships filled a very specific strategic need, and moreover, each one positioned Strickland's organization for future growth. They were not short-term marriages of convenience but long-term strategic alliances.

Soon Strickland's gleaming new building was a physical embodiment of his vision—a beehive of activity and a beacon of hope in a depressed neighborhood. Children of all ages flock to the Manchester Craftsmen's Guild for training and apprenticeships in ceramic art, photography, music recording, film production, literature, and painting. Distinguished artists and musicians from around the world gladly come to Pittsburgh to give lectures, exhibitions, and concerts. The children regularly stage professional quality exhibits of their work, which have become community events, attended by people from all over the region and lavishly catered by students in Bidwell's culinary arts training program.

The building, in fact, became one of Strickland's key marketing and fundraising tools. "I bring corporate leaders and foundation executives here for a tour," he says and then adds with a wry smile, "Something usually comes of it." Sometimes, Strickland just lets the product speak for itself: "I invite our corporate visitors to stay for lunch, prepared by the students in our culinary arts program. A few years ago some of them were so impressed by the quality of the food and professionalism of the service, they began to ask if the students would cater social events—birthdays, holiday gatherings, office parties, anniversaries, and so on. Soon the students were in such high demand that we decided to set up a separate for-profit corporation, Bidwell Food Services, Incorporated. We'll use the profits to subsidize our other programs" (personal communication).

Bill Strickland's vision is as intangible as a dream, but that dream is now embodied in real bricks and mortar and is being carried out through a dizzying array of programs and activities. But even before the gleaming new building, Strickland had more than just a vision. He had all of the qualities of an outstanding strategist—a clear sense of purpose and mission, an astute understanding of what resources would be needed to sustain his mission, a keen eye for opportunities in the external environment, and an extraordinary sense of how it all fits together in a master strategy for growth.

Strickland not only anticipates new needs in his community, he secures support for his vision and he delivers a quality product, giving his benefactors an excellent return on their investment. The story of the Manchester Craftsmen's Guild and the Bidwell Training Center is more than just a story of one man's vision. It tells of vision plus strategy plus competent management.

The Analytical Approach

The analytical approach to strategy formulation tries to improve the alignment or fit between an organization's internal strengths and weaknesses and the external opportunities and threats that are presented by the environment (Schmid, 1992). Thus, when you use this model, you are constantly looking for ways to match your organization's strengths with observed opportunities in the external environment, thereby maximizing your *comparative advantages* (Kearns, 1992a).

The analytical approach is data driven and uses specific templates and methodologies to help executives compile and interpret those data. For example, environmental scanning (see Chapter Three) following a systematic template can help you detect and even anticipate opportunities and challenges in the external environment. Portfolio analysis (see Chapter Four) helps you understand and achieve a good relationship between the programs and services delivered by your organization and the opportunities in the external environment. Other analytical methods help you evaluate specific strategic options (see Part Two).

Strengths and Weaknesses of the Analytical Approach

The analytical approach to strategy formulation has many favorable attributes. First, the analytical approach is data driven. Therefore, it creates an appetite for facts rather than anecdotes or "hunches" in the strategy formulation process. But it also accommodates discussion of judgments and assumptions in the interpretation of data. Thus, when properly designed, the analytical approach can provide a good blend of scientific rigor and experiential judgment.

Second, the conceptual schemas and visual representations used in the analytical approach seem to be intuitively appealing to most people, simplifying a very complex set of interacting forces. For example, certain schemas for visually presenting the results of your environmental scan can help you make the conceptual linkage between your organization's distinctive competencies and emerging opportunities in the external environment (Kearns, 1992a).

Another advantage of the analytical approach to strategy formulation is that it can be institutionalized in the management practices and information processing activities of your organization. In other words the analytical approach, unlike the visioning and incremental approaches to strategy development, can be *taught* to and *learned* by members of your organization. It is hard to teach someone to be a visionary, but you can teach him or her to be a strategic analyst. Thus the analytical approach to strategy formulation contributes directly to organizational learning.

Finally, the analytical approach may be more egalitarian than the visioning and incremental approaches, because it gives many people in the organization, analysts as well as leaders, the opportunity to have a direct impact on the formulation and design of the strategy. In contrast the visioning approach is usually reserved for CEOs and top managers and the incremental approach is dominated by political stakeholders and power brokers.

But the analytical approach to strategy formulation has some shortcomings as well that should be acknowledged and addressed. First, the emphasis on gathering and interpreting data and using analytical rigor can easily mask the inherent subjectivity of these methods and the ease with which they can be manipulated to "verify" predetermined conclusions, giving the false impression of objectivity. Also, the emphasis on data and research can lead to a process dominated by analysts and professional planners rather than by the executives and managers who will ultimately have to implement the strategies.

Second, the analytical approach can become an overly conservative method of strategy formulation because it forces the strategist to think within parameters defined by the intersection of organizational strengths and external opportunities. As we will see in later chapters, these parameters specify relatively narrow boundaries (for example, market niches and comparative advantages) in which strategies can form and flourish. It does not encourage speculation about unforeseen events, nor does it encourage thinking that challenges established patterns of interaction among other organizations in the environment.

Strickland as Analyst

From one perspective it appears that Bill Strickland does not use any of these methodologies as he charts the strategy for the Manchester Craftsmen's Guild. In fact he might say that there is no overall strategy at all, just a series of initiatives that respond to needs and opportunities. But from another perspective it is evident that he relies on the fundamental logic of the analytical approach, even if he does not necessarily pursue that logic through formal processes of strategic planning and management. In other words, although it looks at first like Strickland manages by intuition and is driven only by his entrepreneurial vision, the way he *thinks* about his organization in relation to its environment is very much a reflection of the analytical approach. Here are some examples:

All his initiatives begin with a clear sense of his organization's mission and purpose. Strickland does not pursue growth strategies to build an empire or to satisfy some entrepreneurial urge but rather to create more opportunities for inner-city kids to experience the rewards of artistic expression.

He watches changes in his environment like a hawk and has mastered the fine art of matching his organization's competencies and comparative advantages with opportunities in the environment. In fact Strickland seems to *anticipate* these opportunities long before other people see them. He has developed an eye for subtle changes in the environment that might create opportunities for his organization.

He sees his organization's total portfolio of programs and services as a system of interacting parts. Each program or service plays a specific role in advancing the mission of the organization.

He produces results. Strickland knows that words and enthusiasm go only so far in building community support and in building strategic alliances with corporations, government agencies, and other nonprofits. These organizations want to align themselves with someone who can deliver the goods, not just make a good sales pitch. The analytical approach supports results-driven strategy.

Admittedly, the Manchester Craftsmen's Guild would probably not be a good case study for illustrating formal deliberative processes of strategic *planning.* There is not a lot of organizational energy devoted to initiating and sustaining formal planning processes or to using specific methodologies to guide strategy formulation. The plans and the strategies are largely Bill Strickland's, and the process he uses to develop them seems to be intuitive as well as rational. In other words, Strickland seems to think and behave like many other seasoned executives who have so thoroughly mastered the analytical logic of strategic management that they employ it instinctively (Isenberg, 1984).

The Visioning Approach

Visioning, the second approach to strategy development, begins with a goal or performance target, usually formulated by the organization's leader. Then, the organization works backward from that target to determine what strategies, tactics, actions, and resources are needed to achieve it.

The visioning approach to strategy development has grown out of the observation that many very successful organizations do not confine their strategies to the boxes or cells of a portfolio matrix as advocated by the analytical approach. Instead, the people in visionary organizations, especially the leaders, think outside these boxes by envisioning stretch performance targets. This is not to say that they never use analysis or that they are not influenced by data. But data and formal analysis do not form the bedrock of the vision.

The visioning approach to strategy development is built on the foundation of entrepreneurship characterized by an obsession with opportunities instead of threats, a belief that growth is the ultimate goal, and the concentration of power in the hands of the chief executive (Mintzberg, 1973, cited in Mintzberg, Ahlstrand, and Lampel, 1998). Because the visioning approach to strategy development begins with an envisioned goal or target and then works backward by mobilizing and leveraging the necessary resources to achieve the goal, in effect, the visionary leader is saying: "Here are our aspirations for the future. What do we have to do to get there?" Consequently, the visioning approach to strategy development sometimes walks a thin line between reality and fantasy. The ambitious vision of the leader is sometimes in stark contrast with the modest performance of the organization. Hamel and Prahalad (1989) state that "companies that have risen to global leadership over the past 20 years invariably began with ambitions that were out of all proportion to their resources and capabilities" (p. 64).

The strategy in the visionary organization is to be in a position to capitalize on a variety of opportunities, most of which are unforeseen, rather than to commit the organization to a carefully prescribed set of actions or a formal plan. Because visionary organizations are not locked into specific strategic or tactical plans, they enjoy a higher level of flexibility than do organizations driven by the analytical approach. They understand that in a dynamic environment not every threat or opportunity can be foreseen. Some of the most promising opportunities will appear out of the blue.

Visioning organizations don't imitate the strategies of others; they set their direction and pace on their own. Commentator and sailing enthusiast Walter Cronkite once observed that famed yachtsman Dennis Conner seems to ignore his competitors on the racecourse: "Conner sails as though he were alone on the water. And as often as not, he might as well be" (Cronkite, 1988). So too the visionary organization tends to ignore the strategies and tactics of competing organizations, except to the extent that those tactics and strategies create entrepreneurial opportunities. The visioning approach is not particularly concerned about the goals and strategies of other organizations. The visionary organization is completely consumed, even obsessed, with its own vision and how to advance it.

The visioning approach to strategy development requires leaders who are extremely skilled at communication, persuasion, motivation, and promotion. The leader must constantly sell the vision to important stakeholders inside and outside the organization, finding creative ways to express the vision and to make it as compelling and relevant as possible to each stakeholder. But symbolism must be backed up by actions in order to generate trust in the leader's vision.

Strengths and Weaknesses of the Visioning Approach

The visioning approach can be inspirational and highly motivating. The visioning approach is driven by ambition, aspiration, and a challenging goal. The visioning approach tries to capture the imagination and energy of followers, appealing to their values and aspirations not just those of the leader.

Also, the visioning approach is opportunistic and action oriented. Visionary organizations are willing to seize opportunities as they arise, taking calculated risks. Yet the visionary organization is also pragmatic enough to realize that the environment is too complex to be accurately predicted and not every contingency can be formally planned for, no matter how sophisticated the forecasting and planning tools (Sheehan, 1999).

For all its strengths, the visioning approach has some very serious shortcomings as well. The most obvious one is that the strategy of the visionary organization is driven almost exclusively by the vision of the leader. What if the leader's vision is simply wrong? What if the vision advances the leader's hidden personal agenda above the organization's mission? What if the leader is malicious or even deranged? What if the leader finds a better job or keels over from a heart attack? Any of these contingencies could leave the organization in a dire condition.

Also, the visioning approach can be blind to emerging threats in the environment. The attitude is almost always "full steam ahead." Rarely, if ever, will a leader's vision be based on retrenchment, even when retreat is the appropriate strategy. The visionary leader therefore may be inclined to ignore or squelch arguments for any strategy that is not growth oriented, even when the evidence supports a more modest vision. Moreover, a few successes can make the visionary leader overly confident, even arrogant. The captain of the *Titanic* tried to race through the icebergs because he was blind to the ship's vulnerabilities.

Finally, the visioning approach cannot be taught or institutionalized. The visioning approach requires leadership traits and skills that are difficult to teach. There are no prescribed steps to follow in the visioning approach and no specific tools that can be learned, mastered, and passed along from one generation to the next.

Strickland as Visionary

It is not difficult to see how the visioning approach to strategy development applies to Bill Strickland and the Manchester Craftsmen's Guild. Strickland is the consummate social entrepreneur and, indeed, has won a national award for entrepreneurship from a major foundation. He shows all of the entrepreneurial traits described above. First, he is a leader who is focused, perhaps obsessed, with opportunities rather than threats. Listen to him describe how he has added one program after another to his portfolio, and you will hear him say again and again, "We saw the opportunity and we never looked back." Second, although he says that the secret to his success is "hiring good people and giving them the opportunity to succeed," it is clear that Strickland himself is the driving force of the organization. It is *his* vision and *his* entrepreneurship that has been the foundation for the organization's strategy. Third, Strickland's strategy is focused almost exclusively on growth. It is as if the words *retrenchment, cutback,* and *retreat* are not even part of his vocabulary. He is constantly looking for new growth opportunities, even to the point of exporting his vision to other cities. He is currently working with leaders in San Francisco to build an arts community there. Fourth, Strickland does not operate according to conventional wisdom and rarely if ever does he imitate the strategies of other organizations. He points to some of his strategic alliances as evidence. "Why would a high-tech German chemicals company [Bayer] want to partner with an inner-city job training program in Pittsburgh? On the surface it makes no sense. But if you put the right pieces together it makes perfect sense" (personal communication). Finally, Strickland has succeeded in achieving his vision without much of a formal planning process. Although all the logic of strategic planning is evident in the initiatives he has undertaken, few if any formal planning processes and methodologies are in place at the Manchester Craftsmen's Guild.

The Incremental Approach

The incremental approach, the third approach to strategy development, is, according to some observers, not a strategic approach at all. The incremental approach says that organizational strategies evolve slowly and gradually, through a continual process of political bargaining and negotiating. Thus the incremental approach stands in sharp contrast with both the analytical approach and the visioning approach. The incremental approach suggests that the strategic environment of any organization is too complex to be accurately modeled and analyzed and that the bold visions of entrepreneurial leaders ignore the inevitable fact that multiple stakeholders will have their own visions of the organization that will have to be negotiated and resolved. In the incremental approach the use of bargaining, coalition building, and power diminishes the need for analysis and vision. Instead, strategy evolves slowly and in marginal increments that result from fragile and often temporary agreements between political factions, coalitions, and other stakeholders inside and outside the organization. The incremental approach to strategy development reflects the work of Herbert Simon (1947), Charles Lindblom (1959), and James Quinn (1978) and the more contemporary works of theorists on organizational learning such as Peter Senge (1990) and Henry Mintzberg (1994).

A twist to the incremental approach to strategy development was added by James Quinn (1978, 1980a, 1980b, 1982), who developed the theory of *logical incrementalism*, which suggests that decision making in private firms, although incremental, is not as *disjointed* as decision making in government agencies. In Quinn's model the chief executive uses an incremental approach to nudge and prod the various parts of the organization toward a consciously conceived and loosely coordinated strategic agenda.

Strengths and Weaknesses of the Incremental Approach

The incremental approach to strategy formulation recognizes the roles played by power, conflicting values, and politics in any strategic issue. Consequently, the incremental approach can encourage leaders to focus on partnerships and strategic alliances. With its focus on stakeholders and shrewd attention to the role of power, the incremental approach can help leaders understand that there are times when their organization cannot go alone into the strategic jungle.

Another benefit of the incremental approach is its flexibility. Like an organization following the visioning approach, the organization that follows the incremental approach does not commit itself to a particular strategy or set of tactics. It remains flexible enough to address new circumstances as they present themselves.

Finally, the incremental approach is pragmatic. It recognizes that successful implementation of a partial solution to an issue is better than a failed effort to implement a comprehensive, optimal solution.

But for all its attractive features, the incremental approach has some very serious shortcomings that cannot be overlooked. It can be justly criticized for its lack of clarity and for several negative consequences when blindly followed. First, the incremental approach can produce a rudderless ship. That is, the central difficulty with the incremental approach is that it can lead to a situation in which the organization has no identifiable strategy at all. Its direction is merely the summation of individual and uncoordinated tactical adjustments made by various organizational actors. The apparent lack of strategy can contribute to confusion and even cynicism among internal and external stakeholders, who have a legitimate right to know where the organization is heading and why. Also, the open use of political maneuvering can lead stakeholders to become cynical, concluding that the only value or ideal that the organization stands for is power and influence.

The incremental approach can also compound errors. The disastrous experience of the United States in Vietnam is often used to illustrate this tendency. The organization that never takes a bold move or makes a major new commitment may have difficulty seeing that its small nibbles at an issue are leading it gradually and imperceptibly toward disaster. This is sometimes referred to as the boiled frog syndrome. Supposedly, though I know no one who has actually witnessed this, if you put a frog in a pot of water and turn up the heat gradually, the frog will not notice the incremental temperature change and will stay in the water till it dies. However, if the heat is turned up quickly, the frog will leap out of the water when it detects the sudden change in temperature.

Finally, the incremental approach often deals with symptoms, not causes, and with processes, not solutions. The incremental organization tends to make marginal adjustments in its procedures as circumstances warrant. But these marginal adjustments rarely challenge the assumptions underlying the organization's strategy or its processes. In addition, the incremental organization rarely takes the initiative (and the risk) of implementing proactive strategies to prevent problems before they occur. Instead, it tends to focus on solving problems after they occur.

Strickland as Incrementalist

Admittedly, it is a bit of a stretch to think of Bill Strickland as an incremental strategist because his vision and strategy for the Manchester Craftsmen's Guild are so bold and creative. Yet Strickland also displays the political savvy and pragmatism that are the hallmarks of the incremental approach. For example, he understands better than anyone that the Manchester Craftsmen's Guild and the Bidwell Training Center could easily recede into obscurity without the assistance of powerful corporate and political leaders in Pittsburgh. Strickland has also sought and nurtured alliances with neighborhood groups, creating some extraordinary coalitions of corporate leaders and grassroots activists in the process. He has bargained and brokered agreements among diverse stakeholders from all over the country, and he is no stranger to the art of compromise.

Also, despite his dramatic vision and "never look back" approach to growth, there is an air of pragmatism about Bill Strickland and an understanding that incremental investments today can lay the necessary foundation for more substantial moves later. For example, he launched the for-profit Bidwell Food Services, Incorporated only after the concept had demonstrated its value with numerous clients who were retained informally.

Finally, Strickland understands that strategy cannot be developed without one eye on implementation. He knows that success will breed success, and consequently, he often starts new training programs with relatively modest objectives and resources. He knows that if he succeeds on a modest scale, he can make a stronger case to corporate partners and government agencies for more substantial support in the future. The difference, of course, between Strickland and a more single-minded incrementalist is that he always has his other eye on the long-term (and usually bold) vision for the program.

Conclusion

This chapter has described three very broad approaches to strategy development and has highlighted the strengths and weaknesses of each. As demonstrated by the case of Bill Strickland and the Manchester Craftsmen's Guild, we should not draw the lines too sharply between these three paths to organizational strategy. Strickland, admittedly an extraordinary leader, is at once an analyst, visionary, and even incrementalist. He defies easy categorization into one of these boxes, and I suspect that you too would find it difficult to assert that your organization follows one of these schools of thought to the exclusion of the others.

The point is that there are many possible paths to the development of an organization's strategy, and public and nonprofit managers can travel some of them simultaneously (Maranville, 1999). This book, by necessity, has a focus that leans toward analytical tools and concepts. But these tools can never be applied in a vacuum. They are merely aids that can, when properly used, suggest plausible courses of action or illuminate areas where more information is necessary before you commit resources to a strategic direction.

Drawing on all three approaches and the experience of Bill Strickland, the following are proposed as general guidelines for executives when developing a strategy:

- Know your organization and the "industry" in which it operates, but admit that the dynamics of the environment will require multiple data gathering strategies.

- Assume your leadership responsibility by developing and articulating the vision, values, and key operating principles of the organization.
- Remain open to change in the environment, acknowledging that strategies are a means to an end, not an end in themselves.
- Build in opportunities to adjust the strategy.
- Create opportunities for the organization to continually learn.

I address these and other skills in the following chapters.

Getting Started

1. Which approach to strategy formulation best describes your organization's approach?
2. How has your organization benefited from this approach?
3. To what extent is your organization vulnerable to the weaknesses of this approach?

3

Using Environmental Scanning to Track Trends and Prospects

Environmental scanning is a generic term referring to a systematic and disciplined effort to learn about external factors that have a powerful impact on the programs and services offered by an organization. Your environmental scanning will be concerned with economic factors that affect your organization and others like it, the intensity of competition (if any) among those organizations, the external forces that drive change among organizations like yours, and the prospects for your organization's portfolio of programs and services.

Businesses often use the term *industry analysis* to refer to this type of assessment. Insurance executives, for example, continually monitor trends in the insurance and risk management industry to try to position their organizations to take advantage of emerging opportunities or to avoid threats that loom on the horizon. Similarly, the owner of a restaurant, whether a national chain or a corner diner, monitors developments in the food service industry that are likely to affect his or her business. Multiproduct firms rely on industry analysis to inform their thinking about diversifying into other lines of business and also to stay on top of developments that affect their current portfolios of products and services.

Public and nonprofit organizations also operate within *industries*, defined as *groups of comparable organizations offering similar, related, or substitutable services to the public*. If we use this definition, it

USING ENVIRONMENTAL SCANNING 51

does not stretch our imaginations to think of the health care industry, the higher education industry, or even the juvenile justice industry, and so on.

Nonetheless the concept of industry analysis is foreign to public and nonprofit executives who do not think of themselves as working within industries, and perhaps even controversial. Therefore I usually use the generic term environmental scanning, as a more palatable label for this technique. The objectives and methods are comparable to those in industry analysis but have been adapted for application to public and nonprofit contexts.

Shadyside Rehabilitation Clinic

Bill Markov, executive director of the Shadyside Rehabilitation Clinic (SRC), sulked back to his office and quietly shut the door. He had just endured a difficult and embarrassing lunch with Alice Green, the new chair of the SRC board of directors. At the end of the lunch, Green rejected, at least temporarily, a key component of Markov's strategic vision for the agency. Worse yet, Green lectured him on the need to make strategic decisions less on the basis of intuition and anecdotal data and more on the basis of informed analysis of strategic factors in the external environment.

SRC is a nonprofit drug and alcohol rehabilitation clinic, located in a large Midwestern city. The managed care environment has severely diminished the demand for SRC's flagship program, a twenty-eight-day residential rehabilitation program for substance abusers. Markov believes that SRC must engage in an aggressive strategy of *concentric diversification* (see Chapter Five) by selling its expertise in drug and alcohol counseling to corporations in the region that want to help employees who may have problems with drugs or alcohol. He believes that this approach will increase the number of admissions to the twenty-eight-day residential program, because SRC will have greater control over referrals, and provide an alternative stream of revenue to offset declines in the inpatient treatment market.

Markov also suspects there is a rich and untapped market in the administration of employee assistance programs (EAPs). His friends in that field have told him there is plenty of room for more EAP providers. He has conducted a feasibility analysis, including a rough estimate of expected costs and revenues, an assessment of SRC's capabilities, and a description of how a strategy involving an EAP has been successfully implemented by other rehabilitation centers like SRC around country. His analysis was more rigorous than any prior market research that had been done at SRC.

Still, Markov was not prepared for the probing, in-depth questions Alice Green posed to him over lunch. She wanted specific information about the size of the EAP market in the region and its anticipated growth rate. She asked about the number of organizations that provided EAP services in the marketplace, the types of products and services delivered by the competitors, and the intensity of the competition among these organizations. She asked Markov to assess the factors that distinguished the dominant competitors from the rest. Finally, Green wanted to know all about the external forces affecting the future prospects for EAP programs in the local market and nationally.

As Green paid the bill for the lunch, her closing comments were especially stinging: "Bill, you and your staff must do your homework much more thoroughly on this proposal before I am willing to take it to the board of trustees for their consideration. I agree with you that we need to think seriously about diversification into related products and services. But give me something I can sell to the trustees, not just a lot of speculation!"

Defining the Boundaries of a Strategic Environment

With her questions regarding SRC's foray into EAP programs and services, Alice Green in effect asked Bill Markov to conduct an industry analysis, or environmental scan. An environmental scan is a systematic effort to gather information on the strategic environment in which an organization exists. The purpose is to assess opportunities and challenges facing the organization and others like it and to determine as best one can the overall prospects for the current or contemplated portfolio of programs and services. In the SRC case, Green demanded that Markov learn more about the strategic environment affecting EAP programs and services in order to better assess the overall prospects for SRC should the trustees decide to invest in that line of business.

The first question to ask when conducting an environmental scan is, What should be the focus of my analysis? or in other words, What types of organizations make up my strategic environment? Your strategic environment consists of organizations that offer portfolios of programs and services that are either *related* to your organization's portfolio, *similar* to your organization's portfolio, or *substitutable* for your organization's portfolio. This question keeps your focus on organizations like yours, in the same way that business executives focus their attention on companies in their industry. This is a far more focused and productive approach than the all-encompassing method recommended in many strategic planning texts, a method that asks you to catalogue every political, social, technological, and economic trend that might conceivably affect your organization. The approach recommended here keeps your attention on your programs and services and on the organizations that provide comparable programs and services. The following sections discuss each organizational type, that is, the dimensions of your strategic environment.

Organizations That Offer Related Programs and Services

Related programs and services are those that interact in meaningful ways with the delivery of your organization's programs and services. Thus, for example, if your organization is in the business of addictions counseling, it probably interacts regularly with such organizations as hospitals, social service agencies, vocational rehabilitation programs, and even religious organizations. Any significant change in the strategic environment that affects one of these organizations is likely to have at least some impact on your organization. Therefore your environmental scan will usually include at least some organizations that offer programs or services that are related to those in your organization's portfolio.

Shrewd judgment and also simple common sense should be used when deciding which organizations to include in your analysis and which ones to exclude. You should definitely include organizations that have a direct and meaningful impact on the *supply* of resources your organization needs to produce its programs and services, the *production processes* it uses, and the *distribution* of its programs and services. For example, if you were an executive in the auto industry you would monitor trends in the steel, plastics, glass, and fuel industries because they produce critical raw materials for your manufacturing process. You would also monitor trends affecting the rail and trucking industries because these trends might affect your distribution costs. Similarly, if you are in the addictions counseling business, you will include in your environmental scan organizations that facilitate or restrict the supply of clients, such as managed care organizations, as well as organizations that affect the distribution of your programs and services to people in need, including perhaps the criminal justice system and employers. If you are a chief of police, you will follow developments in such related organizations as schools and social service agencies, which might affect citizens' attitudes toward crime and their motivation to engage in certain types of criminal activity. And you will monitor developments in organizations that are important components in your distribution network, such as the courts and the prison system, because this is where the crimes you detect and solve are processed, adjudicated, and brought to closure.

Organizations That Offer Similar Programs and Services

Similar programs and services are comparable, if not identical, to those offered by your organization, but they are provided by other organizations to markets or jurisdictions that your organization does not serve. Even though your organization generally does not compete with organizations that offer these types of programs and services, they constitute an important part of its strategic environment because the trends affecting them are likely to affect it as well. For example, the police departments in Pittsburgh and Los Angeles offer a wide range of similar, perhaps even identical, programs and services to different jurisdictions. Both departments are part of the crime fighting industry, and consequently, both are affected by many of the same strategic forces, such as international drug trafficking, federal funding for crime prevention programs, social and cultural mores and trends, and emerging technology for fighting crime. They offer similar programs, but they do not compete with each other.

Bill Markov's environmental scan then should definitely include other drug and alcohol treatment centers, even those that serve markets different from SRC's. Again, judgment and common sense will dictate what types of similar organizations to include in your scan. Typically the most relevant organizations are those that serve markets and clients that are similar to your organization's own in some important respects, like overall size of the market, demographics, and so on.

Organizations That Offer Substitutable Programs and Services

Substitutable programs and services are those that consumers might choose instead of yours to meet a specific need. They serve essentially the same purpose as your programs and services, and each could be substituted for the other. The organizations that offer substitutable programs and services are your organization's *competitors*, even if they are not actively engaged in competitive strategies. For example, when moving to a new town, a family with school-age children may literally shop for the best school district in which they can afford a home, or they may compare and choose between

private schools and public schools. For some people, home school-
ing has become a viable alternative to both the public and private
school systems. In this example, similar programs and services are
also substitutable ones. Some people shop for the community
where they want to buy a home, perhaps considering only those
that have the most professional and best-equipped police forces,
the most experienced administrative staffs, or the best parks and
recreation programs. Again, when they make their choice, they are
substituting one product for another.

You may also find instances in which substitutable programs and
services are not identical or even similar to those offered by your
organization. For example, a wealthy philanthropist who has a deep
interest in promoting child welfare programs might consider giving
a sizable charitable donation to one of two vastly different agencies,
one that supports family planning and another that tries to combat
school violence. Those in these agencies probably do not see their
agencies as occupying the same strategic environment, but from the
point of view of this particular philanthropist these dissimilar organizations meet the same broad philanthropic objective of promoting child welfare. Now, if you were an executive in an agency
combating school violence and you had evidence that many other
potential donors shared the views of this philanthropist, then you
might need to expand your definition of your organization's strategic environment to include a broad array of child welfare organizations, even though they offer programs and services that do not
appear to be substitutable for yours.

As a further example, consider the many organizations engaged
in health advocacy, research, and direct services for people suffering
from certain diseases. The strategic environments of the National
Kidney Foundation, the American Heart Association, the March
of Dimes and the American Cancer Society have much in common
even though these organizations have different missions and offer
different portfolios of programs and services. Likewise, recall how
Carla Anderson and the Millersburg Public Library (see Chapter

One) face competition from a variety of substitutable products and services, like the Internet, that are not necessarily similar to the library's core programs and services.

Private Sector Industries as the Basis for Environmental Scans

Our colleagues in the business world have an advantage over us in that their strategic environments (their industries) have been well defined by investors, analysts, and regulators. For example, Wall Street analysts carefully monitor trends in industry groups—fast foods, telecommunications, financial services, pharmaceuticals, and so on. Industry analysts often use narrowly defined categories (stainless steel and specialty steel in the steel industry, for example) to monitor industry trends more precisely. Sometimes, conversely, they group industries together under very broad categories (such as *smokestack industries*, *green industries*, and *commodity industries*) when they want to accentuate shared characteristics, opportunities, or threats. These industry groups delineate the parameters of the strategic environments of different types of businesses.

Unfortunately there are no universally accepted groupings of public and nonprofit organizations that are appropriate for defining the boundaries of environmental scans. Your best bet, then, usually will be to follow the advice at the beginning of this section: focus on organizations that provide programs and services related to, similar to, or substitutable for those in your organization's portfolio.

More Tips for Defining a Strategic Environment

Here are some additional tips to follow when defining the boundaries of your organization's strategic environment:

Start with general categories and then try to be more specific. Remember the definition of a strategic environment provided at the beginning of this section: a group of organizations producing programs and services that are *related* to, *similar* to, or *substitutable* for the goods and services produced by your organization.

Be cautious about assuming that your organization is unique. You may encounter the dilemma that there are virtually no other organizations that produce a related, similar, or even remotely substitutable program or service. Your organization may have a perfect monopoly, at least within a certain geographical market. In this case, it is de facto the entire industry. Look again, however, to be certain there are no organizations that provide related, similar, or substitutable programs or services. For many years the U.S. Postal Service believed it had a virtual monopoly on mail delivery. When it finally realized that it faced intense competition from private providers like Federal Express, United Parcel Service, and others (and now from e-mail), it needed to act quickly to survive.

Recognize that markets and strategic environments are not necessarily the same, though they generally overlap. A *market* is composed of specific consumers, perhaps confined within discrete geographical boundaries, and a specific set of organizations that compete head to head to meet the same community needs. A *strategic environment* is defined by lines of programs and services that are similar, related, or substitutable, and it transcends the specific markets in which these programs and services are delivered and consumed. In other words, the trends and forces that affect your organization and its portfolio of programs and services may extend beyond the boundaries of the market it currently serves. If, for example, your organization provides programs and services that are extremely labor intensive and require special professional skills, then it needs to monitor the supply of skilled professionals not only in its market but perhaps nationally and even internationally as well.

Remember that you can select a very broad or very narrow focus for your environmental scan, depending on what makes sense for the decision or task at hand.

Conducting an Environmental Scan

There are four essential questions to address as you conduct your environmental scan (Porter, 1980, 1985; Thompson and Strickland, 1992).

- What are the key economic characteristics of our strategic environment?
- How intense is the competition (if any) in our strategic environment?
- What forces drive change in our strategic environment?
- Overall, what are the prospects for our portfolio of programs and services?

Here are the steps to follow when answering these questions in public and nonprofit contexts.

Step 1: Identify the Key Economic Characteristics of Your Strategic Environment

In the business sector, industry analysts monitor certain economic factors to identify opportunities and challenges for firms in each industry. Because the prime purpose of a business is to generate a profit, these economic characteristics are vitally important to executives, whether they are contemplating a move into a new industry or trying to remain competitive in their current industry. Some of the economic indicators used by industry analysts are also potentially useful to public and nonprofit executives who want to better understand their strategic environment. This discussion will focus on four especially important economic characteristics for your organization:

- The size and growth rate of your organization's line of programs and services

- The life cycle of your organization's line of programs and services
- The significant barriers organizations must deal with to enter or exit your organization's strategic environment
- The overall economic health of your organization's line of programs and services

Let's examine each of these economic characteristics in turn, using the Shadyside Rehabilitation Clinic case study as an example.

Size and Growth Rate of Programs and Services. Bill Markov is trying to increase SRC's earned revenues by expanding its portfolio to include EAP programs and services. Therefore Alice Green's first set of questions to Markov focused on the size and projected growth rate of the EAP business:

- How many corporations in this region have EAP programs for their employees? How does this compare with national trends? How big is the market? Are more organizations adopting EAP programs, or has the growth stagnated? How many employees participate in EAP programs in this market?

- How much money do these corporations spend on EAP programs each year? Is this up or down compared to what they spent three years ago?

- What are the national trends with respect to all of these questions? Do the trends in our regional market reflect the national trends in EAP programs and services?

Essentially, Green is asking, How big is the financial pie that SRC would be sharing with other EAP administrators, and is this pie growing or shrinking? Instinctively, most of us are probably more inclined to invest in programs and services that are large and growing rather than those that are small and shrinking. But on closer analysis the choice is not quite that simple. There are risks and benefits in each type of market, as indicated in Table 3.1.

The overriding question in this phase of the environmental scan is, What is the total volume of resources devoted to the production of programs and services in your strategic environment and is this volume likely to grow or shrink in the future?

Life Cycle of Programs and Services. Many programs and services provided in the public sector have a natural life cycle. They are born, they mature, and sometimes they eventually decline and die. This is especially true of social programs that are designed to solve a specific problem or to promote a specific type of behavior. In the arena of job training, for example, the Comprehensive Employment Training Act (CETA) gave way to the Job Training Partnership Act (JTPA), which has now given way to the Workforce Investment Act (WIA). On the one hand this is nothing more than an incremental evolution of a social program, with high levels of stability from one incarnation to the next. On the other hand there are fundamental philosophical differences among these job training programs, reflecting different social and political objectives. Certain management technologies also seem to have natural life cycles. For example, over the past thirty years there have been several waves of new government budgeting and financial management models that have emerged, gained momentum, peaked, and then passed away.

The notion of a natural life cycle for programs and services has even more relevance in the nonprofit sector than in the public sector (Hasenfeld and Schmid, 1989). Historically the nonprofit sector has been more problem focused and therefore more experimental than government. Consequently, many types of nonprofit programs and services display the familiar curve of the product life cycle illustrated in Figure 3.1.

Not all programs and services display the same life cycle curve. For example, programs and services based extensively on a particular advanced technology may have steeper curves on both the upward

TABLE 3.1 Assessing Size and Growth Characteristics: Risks and Benefits.

Size of the Market for Your Programs and Services	Growth Rate of the Market for Your Programs and Services	Risks	Benefits
Large	Growing	This market for your programs and services might attract large and powerful new competitors (including private sector competitors) that try to capture market share by either acquiring established organizations or using their overwhelming production capacity to compete aggressively against smaller organizations. Large competitors may have the capacity to drive out smaller, weaker organizations.	This market for your programs and services offers significant opportunities if your organization is large and has comparative advantages such as production capacity, marketing expertise, and distribution channels. If your organization is small, there may be opportunities to penetrate niches, meeting needs not being met by larger organizations.
Large	Stable	This market for your programs and services is difficult to penetrate. The stability of their environments	This market for your programs and services is not as volatile as others, thereby minimizing risks

	Shrinking	Growing
Large	often allows large, established organizations to build up impressive comparative advantages.	if your organization is already an established provider.
	Long-term prospects are suspect in this market for your programs and services. It may be difficult to penetrate this shrinking market if established organizations compete aggressively with each other to cling to their market share. Smaller organizations are especially vulnerable if they cannot find a stable niche market.	If your organization is well established, it might use its programs and services that have this market as *cash cows* to subsidize other programs and services. With skillful analysis, small organizations may be able to find relatively stable market niches as larger organizations abandon these markets.
Medium	This market for your programs and services can be very volatile as it begins to attract the attention of large organizations that want to penetrate the market before it explodes.	This market for your programs and services can offer attractive opportunities for established organizations. There may also be opportunities for aggressive entrepreneurial organizations.

TABLE 3.1 Assessing Size and Growth Characteristics: Risks and Benefits, *continued.*

Size of the Market for Your Programs and Services	Growth Rate of the Market for Your Programs and Services	Risks	Benefits
Medium	Stable	This market for your programs and services is difficult to penetrate because large and medium-sized organizations generally have established comparative advantages.	This market for your programs and services is relatively safe for established organizations.
Medium	Shrinking	Growth slowdowns in the market for your programs and services lead to increased rivalry among established organizations and a shakeout of weaker competitors.	This market for your programs and services may offer limited opportunities for you to capture niche markets that are abandoned by larger competitors.
Small	Growing	In this market for your programs and services, competition may be intense among a small group of entrepreneurial organizations.	In this market for your programs and services, there are potentially significant opportunities to establish leadership position early by getting in on the ground floor.

Small	Stable	This market for your programs and services offers limited prospects for long-term growth.	In this market for your programs and services, niche markets may be attractive.
Small	Shrinking	This market for your programs and services offers no prospects for long-term growth. It is characterized by intense competition among small providers.	This market for your programs and services offers few opportunities from a financial perspective. However, there is an opportunity to build a community reputation for providing essential (even if perhaps unpopular) services to people in need.

Source: Compiled and adapted from Porter, 1980, pp. 191-274.

FIGURE 3.1 The Life Cycle of Programs and Services.

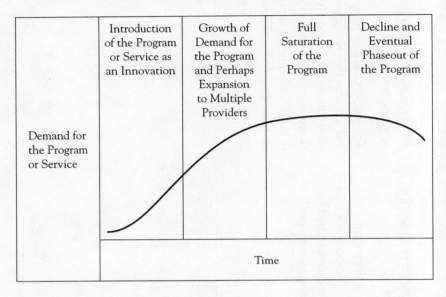

and downward slopes. Naturally, programs for which there is an artificial demand (created perhaps by a government subsidy) will have flatter and longer life cycle curves.

In our case example, Alice Green asked Bill Markov several pointed questions related to the life cycle of EAP programs and services:

- My impression is that EAP programs first appeared in the late 1970s and grew in sophistication and popularity throughout the 1980s. Is this a line of programs and services that has now matured, or is it still quite dynamic in terms of new competitors, new modes of intervention, new treatment methodologies for clients, and so on?

- Let's assume that EAP programs and services are on the mature end of the life cycle. What special challenges would SRC encounter trying to enter a mature line of programs and services?

- Several existing SRC programs and services are already in the mature or declining phase. Shouldn't SRC think about balancing them by adding something that has a brighter future?

All of us would like to have the foresight to anticipate the development of emerging programs and services and to get in on the ground floor as providers. Unfortunately we do not have a crystal ball to forecast the birth of new programs and services. With careful analysis, however, we can reach our destination even when we miss the early train. Table 3.2 highlights some organizational capabilities that contribute to success at each phase of the industry life cycle.

Bill Markov should pay very close attention to the questions posed by Alice Green. If indeed the EAP field is mature, as Green speculates, then SRC's success will be determined less by the distinctiveness of the particular EAP product that SRC introduces to the market than by SRC's investment in marketing and production efficiencies. In other words the trailblazing entrepreneurs in the EAP strategic environment have already done most of the research and development on how to design and implement an effective EAP program, and they have carved out their niche in the marketplace. It will be difficult for SRC, or any other organization, to gain a foothold in a mature line of programs and services.

Significant Barriers to Entry and Exit. You might find it helpful to think of each strategic environment as a large room where organizations offering related, similar, or substitutable services are jostling for seats at various tables (markets). Some of these rooms (environments) are easy to get into, requiring no special procedures for access. Others, however, require substantial investment in technology and expertise to unlock the door. Still other rooms require special credentials in order to enter, and gatekeepers (regulators, accrediting agencies) are posted at the doors to make sure that no one crashes the party. In other words, some lines of programs and services have high entry barriers and others do not. Thus an *entry barrier* is any phenomenon that restricts entry to a line of programs or services or penetration of a specific market. The health care environment typically has high entry barriers because of the cost of

TABLE 3.2 Life Cycles of Programs and Services:
Factors Contributing to Organizational Success.

Life Cycle Stage	Success Factors
New programs and services. These programs and services are developed and initially dominated by entrepreneurial organizations that are on the cutting edge of technology, community needs, or consumer preferences. Examples: distance learning, virtual universities.	• New product development and testing • Technical competence • Heavy and sustained investment in R&D • Intensive efforts to capture and retain market share • Promotion of product awareness among customers • Rapid and responsive decision making • Administrative systems that support growth
Growing programs and services. Programs and services begin to show signs of market segmentation and product differentiation. Organizations try to develop specialized products lines, and dominant organizations pursue horizontal growth strategies to increase their geographical coverage and market. Smaller organizations seek out niche markets. Competition is sometimes extremely intense during this phase. *Examples:* nursing homes, adult day care, hospices, community policing, charter schools.	• Increasing strength in market niche • Development of consumer loyalty as well as new markets • Product specialization and quality • Product improvement and successor product development • Cost control • Price or quality advantages • Heavy investment in production, marketing, and distribution systems • Vertical integration • Innovation in marketing and distribution

TABLE 3.2 Life Cycles of Programs and Services:
Factors Contributing to Organizational Success, *continued*.

Life Cycle Stage	Success Factors
Mature programs and services. Programs and services show more advanced signs of market segmentation. Typically, a relatively small number of organizations have achieved a dominant market share. Smaller organizations may compete with each other for niche markets but rarely pose a real threat to the largest established organizations. *Examples:* general health care, drug and alcohol counseling, symphony orchestras	• Production economies • Cost control • Vertical integration • Diversification • R&D expenditures to prepare for a new cycle
Declining programs and services. Consumer demand and community needs begin to flatten out due to many factors. Dominant organizations begin the process of abandoning these lines of programs and services in search of more fertile ground. *Example:* traditional welfare.	• Cost-cutting • Withdrawal of R&D from original product line • Retrenchment and divestment strategies • Administrative system geared toward retrenchment • Diversification

Source: Adapted from Hofer, 1975.

acquiring the necessary equipment, personnel, and infrastructure to deliver high-quality health services. Amazingly, in some states, including my home state of Pennsylvania, the entry barriers to forming a municipal government are relatively modest. The laws and regulations governing municipal incorporation are remarkably lax, which explains, in part, the proliferation of local government jurisdictions in Pennsylvania.

Some lines of programs and services also have high *exit barriers*. That is, once inside the room and seated at one of the tables, it is difficult to leave. Often sunk costs make it difficult to abandon a particular portfolio of programs and services. Or perhaps an organization is under intense political pressure to continue serving a particular need even though it can no longer justify the investment in objective terms. A few years ago, for example, my university tried to close one of its academic departments and experienced such a backlash from alumni, politicians, and other important constituencies that it was forced to retract its decision. Entry and exit barriers are a key consideration for business executives when they contemplate an investment in a particular line of programs and services or when they assess how secure the company's position is in its existing portfolio.

Here are some prominent entry barriers that apply to public and nonprofit organizations as well as private firms (Porter, 1980, pp. 9–15; Wheelen and Hunger, 1992, p. 100; Oster, 1995, pp. 32–36).

Brand identification and customer loyalty. It is extremely difficult to penetrate programs and services in which customers have lined up with favorite *brands*. This is especially true in the nonprofit sector, where trust and credibility are major criteria for organizational success. Thus reputation can be a major entry barrier in the nonprofit sector. Brand loyalty has relevance even in the public sector. Legislators and their staffs have pet programs and services that they protect at all costs. Often they have close professional relations with the administrators of these programs, on whom they rely for advice. In such circumstances it is nearly impossible for a newcomer to the area to

gain trust and credibility among an important group of consumers—
elected officials.

Selective access to scarce resources. Access to funds controlled by
foundations and other philanthropic organizations is often facilitated by interlocking networks of influence that can be difficult for
newcomers to understand and penetrate. Sometimes access is deeply ingrained in tradition and virtually exclusionary, as is the case
with the United Way and its access to workplace appeals. Limited
access to scarce resources can be a significant entry barrier in the
nonprofit sector. In the public sector, government jurisdictions and
their agencies obviously enjoy exclusive access to many resources;
their programs and services thus present formidable entry barriers
to potential competitors.

Credentials and government regulation. Many types of programs
and services require organizations to earn specific credentials, like
accreditation, licensure, certification, or to meet other standards to
ensure minimum levels of quality and professional competence.
Establishing and running schools, nursing homes, day-care centers,
vocational training programs, and many other important functions
are activities performed largely by public and nonprofit organizations, and they often have significant entry barriers deriving from
credentialing requirements and government regulations. The presence or absence of this type of entry barrier is likely to have an especially strong impact on competition.

Capital requirements. Some programs and services require large
investments in facilities and equipment, whereas others require very
little. Just as important, some require investments in equipment or
facilities that cannot easily be converted to other purposes should
the venture fail, thereby creating a substantial exit barrier. Churches,
hospitals, and certain performance venues are not only enormously
expensive to build and maintain but cannot easily be converted to
other purposes. Thus capital requirements may be both an entry barrier and an exit barrier.

Economies of scale. Some programs and services discourage new
entrants because they demand large-scale production in order to be

competitive. Large schools, hospitals, performing arts organizations, museums, and other organizations enjoy economies of scale over their smaller competitors. Large cities and towns support many amenities that small communities cannot afford. Economies of scale increase the size of the investment needed and the risk to new entrants, thereby posing a significant entry barrier.

At SRC, Alice Green asked Bill Markov several questions regarding entry and exit barriers in EAP programs and services:

- SRC has no name recognition in the EAP business per se, but it does enjoy an excellent reputation in the treatment of substance abusers. How important is customer loyalty in the EAP business? Can SRC establish a reputation as a cost-effective administrator of EAP programs, or will it always be viewed as a relatively expensive residential treatment facility?

- Some EAP administrators enjoy instant access to corporate clients through their connections to the corporation's insurance or employee benefits programs. SRC has some access to those networks already. How much of an advantage will this be to developing a book of business as an EAP administrator?

- Is there any type of credential that superior EAP administrators boast of when seeking new clients? Are their organizations certified or accredited in any way?

Clearly, SRC will need to overcome the entrenched positions that some of its competitors apparently enjoy. But SRC may already have channels that will facilitate access to corporate clients.

Overall Cost Structure of Programs and Services.   Although profit is not the driving force in public and nonprofit organizations, executives should of course be aware of the overall cost structure (or *profitability*) of various lines of programs and services in which their organization has a stake. The cost structure in any strategic environment is a dynamic phenomenon. The profitability of health care, for example, has eroded dramatically as a result of overcapacity, tighter controls on reimbursement in the managed care environment, and new government policies on Medicare reimbursements. The cost structure of health care will change even more dramatically when additional reductions in Medicare reimbursements become effective as part of the federal Balanced Budget Act. Similarly, in the 1980s the American Red Cross watched the profitability of the business of collecting and distributing human blood plummet as the government and the general public demanded significant investments in new technology and safety procedures to ensure the purity of blood and blood products.

Profitability in any context is a function of expected unit costs in relation to expected selling price. Obviously the greater the difference between production cost and price, the greater the average profitability of those programs and services. Maximum selling price is driven largely by supply and demand, factors over which individual executives have little control. However, you do have some control over profitability to the extent that you can rigorously control your fixed and variable production costs on a per unit basis.

Cost analysis would have helped Bill Markov answer these questions posed by Alice Green:

- What would be our fixed costs if we entered the EAP business? What would be our variable costs associated with each EAP client we serve?

- What is the industry standard in terms of pricing EAP services? Would we essentially try to meet this standard or could we undercut this price?

- Given the per unit price and per unit cost structure, how many clients or contracts would we need to recover our fixed costs and begin turning a profit? Have you done a rigorous break-even analysis?

These questions have important implications not only when you are contemplating a new line of programs and services but also when you are regarding your organization's ability to continue providing its existing portfolio. Many nonprofit hospitals apparently did not anticipate the dramatic changes in their cost structures that would occur with the advent of managed care. School districts have seen their cost structures change as tax revenues fail to keep pace with increased costs.

Public and nonprofit organizations are now beginning to use techniques like break-even analysis and financial ratio analysis to more closely monitor the cost structures of various parts of their service portfolio. Even if you have no intention of making a profit on a given service or program, a technique like break-even analysis can help you understand how heavily that service will need to be subsidized by other revenues or other programs in your portfolio in order to be sustainable (Young, 1994). Ratio analysis can help you compare your organization with others in your strategic environment on the critical factors of profitability, efficiency, liquidity, and the like (Anthony and Young, 1994).

Step 2: Describe the Level of Competition in Your Strategic Environment

The second step in an environmental scan is to assess the type of competition (if any) in your organization's strategic environment. Having outlined the general economic characteristics and parameters of your strategic environment in step one, you are now ready to ask more specific questions about the players and their strategies. The following questions, as they apply to private sector firms, are discussed extensively in Porter (1980). Our focus, of course, is on their application to public and nonprofit enterprises.

- How many organizations actively compete in our strategic environment?
- On what basis do these organizations compete? Cost? Quality? Market niches?

- How intense is the competitive rivalry among them?
- Are there opportunities for collaboration rather than competition?
- What are likely to be the next moves of our major competitors?
- What is the threat that new programs and services will emerge that can substitute for those in our portfolio?
- What is the bargaining power of our consumers, donors, taxpayers, and other stakeholders?

Understanding the competitive environment is important for several reasons. First, you must understand the nature of the competition before deciding if you *want* to play the competitive game. Therefore this step in the environmental scan can help you clarify your own management values. For example, you, others on the management team, and the board of trustees or the responsible elected officials might be philosophically opposed to engaging in intensely competitive behavior, and therefore you might steer a course away from lines of programs and services requiring a high level of competition, or you might look for opportunities to collaborate with other organizations in these lines.

Second, an understanding of the competitive environment will help you decide whether you are realistically able to compete with other organizations. If, for example, other organizations in your strategic environment compete largely on the basis of product differentiation, tailoring their programs to meet consumer needs, and your organization offers a bland, generic line of programs and services, then you may decide that your organization will never be able to compete effectively in that particular environment.

Let's examine some of the factors that are particularly important when assessing the competition in your strategic environment.

Number of Competing Organizations. The number of competitors in your strategic environment is a function of several factors we have already discussed such as the life cycle stages of your organization's programs and services, the cost structure of your organization's line of business, and the strength of entry and exit barriers. There is no absolute number of competitors that makes a strategic environment crowded or open. Some environments can easily accommodate many competitors, whereas others are crowded with only three or four.

Basis of Competition. In the private sector, organizations compete with each other in several ways: cost leadership, product differentiation, and focus (Porter, 1980). These same competitive elements are present in many public and nonprofit contexts.

If you decide to compete on the basis of *cost leadership*, then you must be confident in your organization's ability to keep operating costs to a minimum and to pass these savings along to consumers, donors, taxpayers, and other stakeholders. Organizations pursuing a cost leadership strategy take advantage of economies of scale whenever possible. They adopt new techniques for producing and distributing programs and services. They use their knowledge and experience to maximize efficiency and effectiveness. They minimize administrative overhead, labor costs, and any other costs associated with operations.

A cost leadership strategy can be appropriate even when goods and services are not sold in the traditional sense of that term. Certainly nonprofit and public organizations try to keep operating costs down even when they do not sell services to the public. Your organization may be able to boast, for example, that its fundraising costs are the lowest in the industry or that its road paving program has the lowest costs per lane mile of any city in the region. Keeping administrative costs down also means that more money can be allocated to direct services.

The second type of competition, *product differentiation*, occurs when organizations compete through tailoring, or differentiating, their programs to meet specific consumer demands and preferences. Differentiation may take the form of:

- Offering unique service designs, such as vocational training curricula tailored to the individual needs of students and offered in place of one curriculum with a one-size-fits-all philosophy

- Using innovative applications of technology, such as translating devices to help novice opera patrons understand foreign language dialogue

- Supplying additional customer services, such as taxpayer hot lines and ombudsman's offices

- Offering unbundled services, such as school voucher programs allowing parents to mix and match public and private educational programs to meet the needs of their children

- Finding unique distributor networks, such as the workplace network that United Way campaigns rely on

- Publicizing exceptionally high performance as indicated by objective outcome measures, such as awards for outstanding financial management given by organizations like the Government Finance Officers Association

It is traumatic for organizations to be forced to compete on the basis of product differentiation when they have never done so before. Public schools, for example, are scrambling to adapt to the new competitive environment in which charter schools are tailoring their curricula and programs to meet student needs and are competing with public schools for a share of tax revenues. Similarly, many United Way chapters around the country have had to work hard to respond to consumers who demanded more voice in how their contributions were spent.

The third competitive strategy described by Porter, *focus*, requires organizations to attend closely to specific segments of the marketplace. If your organization follows a focus strategy, it is not interested in dominating the entire market. Rather, it is trying to serve specific niches and market segments very well. For example, a neighborhood economic development corporation focuses all its energies on a relatively small geographical market. Historically black colleges focus on serving the educational needs and preferences of African Americans. Community colleges focus their efforts on commuting students and other market segments. Government organizations often cannot follow a focus strategy because they must serve all citizens without preference. Still, many government programs target people in particular circumstances or with particular needs.

It is important to note that a focus strategy usually employs differentiation and cost leadership strategies as well. If your organization were to use a *focus-differentiation* strategy, it would tailor its products to market segments that had very specific needs and preferences. Arts and cultural organizations, for example, tend to design programs and services to appeal to market segments composed of people who share certain artistic tastes and preferences. In contrast a *focus–cost leadership* strategy requires your organization to appeal especially to market segments for whom cost (rather than product differentiation) is a primary concern. Credit unions, for example, target their services to particular populations *and* compete on the basis of interest rates and other cost factors. Table 3.3 provides a few examples of dominant competitive patterns in selected public and nonprofit contexts.

Alice Green had several questions for Bill Markov that related to the dominant mode of competition in the employee assistance program business:

- On what basis do EAP providers compete with each other? Are their programs and services highly differentiated to appeal to particular types of customers, or do they offer generic programs that compete largely on price?

- Can SRC compete on the basis of cost leadership? It seems that this would be pretty hard to do, given that other providers have refined their cost structures. Can SRC compete on the basis of differentiation?

- Are there any market segments that are not adequately served by existing EAP providers? Could SRC establish a foothold in these niche markets?

TABLE 3.3 Basis of Competition by Type of Organization.

Dominant Basis of Competition	Selected Public and Nonprofit Organizations
Cost leadership	• Public utilities • Public transportation • Correctional facilities • Public works agencies • Sanitation agencies • Tax collection agencies
Product differentiation	• Public safety agencies • Parks and recreation programs • Private schools • Special education programs • Child welfare agencies • Churches • Social services agencies
Focus–cost leadership	• Community colleges • Credit unions • Economic development organizations • Public housing agencies
Focus-differentiation	• Arts and culture organizations • Advocacy organizations • Black colleges • Job training programs • Residential care facilities • Recreational clubs and organizations • Public radio and television services

- Are new markets emerging in which SRC might focus its efforts?

- Are there certain corporate buyers for whom the SRC "brand name" has particularly high credibility and appeal? Should SRC focus its efforts on that segment of the market, if it cannot compete on a cost leadership basis in the broader market?

These are very important questions for Bill Markov and his staff as they contemplate a foray into EAP programs and services. If on the one hand the dominant mode of competition plays to SRC's inherent strengths, then SRC might be able to establish itself as a major player even though it is obviously a late entry into the EAP business. If on the other hand the competitive patterns in the EAP market play to SRC's weaknesses, Markov would be well advised to look for other venues in which to diversify SRC's revenues.

During this phase of the environmental scan, it can be very helpful to plot the strategies used by your major competitors in a matrix like the one presented in Table 3.4.

You could easily add information to Table 3.4 by not only listing the major competing organizations in each of the four cells but also drawing circles of different sizes representing their respective shares of the total marketplace. This approach will provide a convenient visual display of not only your competitors' strategies but also their respective levels of leadership or dominance.

This type of matrix can help you clarify who your organization's *true* competitors are and can provide valuable information on how they are clustered in certain segments of the marketplace. Recently, for example, I and other members of my own academic department constructed such a matrix of our competitors at other colleges and universities, built around the factors of price (tuition minus financial aid) and quality (national ranking of comparable schools). We found that our market segment included competitors we had never before considered, and conversely, in some cases our presumed competitors were not really competitors at all!

TABLE 3.4 Sample Mapping of Competitors: SRC's EAP Competitors.

		Strategic Advantage of SRC's Competitors	
		Product Differentiation	Cost Leadership
Target Markets of Competitors	Total Marketplace	• One Way Out, Inc.	• AcuCare, Inc.
		• Fresh Start, Inc.	• Productive Employees, Inc.
	Various Niche Markets	• St. Joseph's Hospital • Workers Assistance League	• Back on Track, Inc. • TruCare, Inc.

Source: Adapted from Porter, 1985, p. 12; Thompson and Strickland, 1992, p. 87.

Intensity of the Rivalry. Although it is important to know how many competitors your organization must deal with, an even more important consideration is the intensity of the rivalry among them. How hot is the competition in your strategic environment? In business the rivalry among competing organizations may be manifested in many ways, such as price wars, advertising skirmishes, invasion of established markets by newcomers, introduction of "new and improved" products, investments in research and development, and hostile takeovers.

Generally, competitive rivalries among public and nonprofit organizations, if they exist at all, tend to be on the "polite" end of the continuum. After all, most organizations in the public and non-profit sectors share a fundamental purpose—to provide a public good and to advance the public's welfare. It is not only unseemly but often counterproductive for these organizations to engage in cutthroat competition. Nonetheless, competitive rivalries can occasionally be intense in the public sector, just as they are in business. For example, in higher education there is lively competition for the best students. Some colleges and universities have used clever marketing and pricing schemes that rival anything seen in the for-profit world. Schools offer increasingly complex financial aid packages, including "early bird specials" for parents who make a commitment to a college before the prospective student has even learned to walk. They engage in bidding wars for top faculty and researchers. They offer compensation and benefit packages to the best and the brightest students. They engage in aggressive advertising and product differentiation to lure midcareer professionals back to school. And they lobby legislators for earmarked research funds. Sometimes nonprofits compete with businesses. For many years, small businesses have claimed that some nonprofit organizations offering goods and services also supplied by for-profit companies have enjoyed an unfair competitive advantage due to their tax-exempt status. They claim that nonprofits have ruthlessly used this advantage over small businesses.

Also, local governments have been known to engage in their own unique price wars, in which the weapons are tax breaks and other incentives to attract large firms to their community. Some have engaged in remarkably sophisticated marketing strategies, segmenting the market of potential residents and tailoring their marketing message accordingly. A suburban community near Pittsburgh has developed a special marketing campaign directed specifically to millionaire professional athletes who play for the city's major league baseball, football, and hockey teams. Videos, brochures, and testimonials from other pro athletes portray the community as an outstanding place to live, convenient to the stadium but secluded, secure, and private.

So it is worthwhile examining the intensity of competitive rivalries among public and nonprofit organizations, even if these rivalries are, on the whole, less confrontational and less hostile than those in the for-profit sector.

The intensity of competitive rivalries has been studied by Michael Porter (1980) and others in the business world. A few of Porter's propositions (pp. 17–23) seem to have relevance for government and nonprofit organizations as well as business. Extracted from Porter's list, the following conditions are likely to intensify among public or nonprofit organizations:

- The market for particular programs or services has many players of roughly equal size and power.

- The pace of growth in the marketplace for these programs or services has slowed or stopped altogether.

- The marketplace is characterized by relatively low product differentiation.

- Consumers of programs and services incur minimal switching costs when they switch providers.

- Competitors are diverse and do not necessarily play by the same rules.

- Competing organizations face high exit barriers.

Using these six criteria, we can see why the health care field is so intensely competitive. First, there are many competing hospitals and health care systems. In fact, throughout the 1970s and 1980s, the health care infrastructure was built far beyond the needed capacity. Second, as smaller neighborhood hospitals are absorbed within larger multihospital health systems, the competing organizations are becoming more and more comparable in size, capability, and products. Third, under managed care, demand for health care facilities is diminishing and thus growth has slowed. Fourth, without strong allegiances to a family physician, people incur relatively low switching costs in moving from one hospital to another. Fifth, there is great diversity among competing organizations—nonprofit, for-profit, and public—which pursue vastly different objectives and function under different operating philosophies (or rules of the game). Finally, there are high exit costs for health care organizations. Huge capital investments in highly specialized facilities and equipment make it difficult for them to convert assets to other uses.

Opportunities for Collaboration. For public and nonprofit organizations, one of the most important questions regarding rivalries concerns the opportunities for collaboration rather than competition with other organizations. Many philanthropists and public policymakers have grown weary of the proliferation of nonprofit organizations and what they perceive as duplication of effort. They have urged nonprofit organizations to seek out collaborative activities, including mergers, joint ventures, consolidation of administrative functions, and information sharing.

In the nonprofit sector, collaborative strategies are most likely to be successful when organizations share a common mission, when they are committed to innovative and flexible approaches to fulfilling their mission, when they have strong and visionary leaders, and when they want to grow in size and influence (LaPiana, 1998).

Alice Green posed several questions to Bill Markov about opportunities for collaboration:

- Have you consulted with some of SRC's major supporters, like the United Way, to ask how they feel about SRC entering the competitive EAP business?

- Have you thought about finding a partner in this venture who could bring certain attributes and skills to the table that SRC does not have? Does SRC, in turn, have certain capabilities that might be attractive to one of the existing competitors? Could SRC be a subcontractor on certain EAP programs and services, rather than jumping in with both feet as a full service provider?

Predicting the Next Moves of Dominant Competitors. The most awkward moment in Markov's luncheon meeting with Alice Green came when she informed him, in almost an off-hand way that St. Joseph's Hospital was planning to divest its drug and alcohol rehabilitation programs because they were no longer holding their own in the managed care marketplace. Though it had not been officially announced, Green had reliable information that St. Joseph's planned to sell that component of its portfolio to Fresh Start, Inc., thereby giving Fresh Start a dramatically enhanced competitive position in the EAP market.

When she asked Markov how he interpreted this move, he was speechless. He had not heard about the impending sale, and the revelation caught him completely by surprise. "It would have been nice," Green mused, "if we had known of St. Joe's desire to get out of the field of drug and alcohol recovery. We might have made a bid for that portfolio so that we could hit the ground running rather than try to punch our way into an already crowded market."

In the business world the term *competitive intelligence* refers to the practice of keeping a watchful eye on competitors in order to accurately describe their current strategy and, if possible, predict their future strategies. Many firms spend millions of dollars trying their best to understand and anticipate the next moves of their major competitors. In some business industries the rivalry is so intense that firms try to disguise or mask their strategic objectives in order to fool the competition and maintain the advantage of a surprise market attack.

For the most part, public and nonprofit organizations do not and *should not* devote substantial resources to competitive intelligence. Still, keeping an ear to the rail is simply good, commonsense leadership. Following are some things to think about when anticipating the competitive strategies of another organization in your industry. These factors are extracted and adapted from a long list developed by Porter (1980, pp. 49–74).

The competitor's goals and operating philosophies. Does the competitor seem to operate according to certain core values or philosophies that have remained reasonably consistent over time? Do these philosophies hint at the organization's future strategies?

The competitor's current strategy. Is the competitor in a growth mode, is it in a retrenchment mode, or is it merely trying to hold its own in a competitive marketplace? Is the competitor trying for a cost leadership position or a product differentiation strategy or some combination of these strategies? Does it tend to focus on certain market segments or is its perspective broader than that?

The competitor's assumptions about its position in the strategic environment. Look at the competitor's public statements and marketing materials. Does it seem to have any assumptions about the distinctive advantages it brings to the marketplace? Does the competitor seem to embrace conventional wisdom, or does it often challenge the assumptions of others in the marketplace? Is the competitor usually an early adopter of innovations, or does it tend to wait till a new approach has been tried and proven?

The competitor's capabilities. Objectively, what are the competitor's strengths and weaknesses? What comparative advantages does it seem to enjoy in terms of its programs and services, its distribution network, its access to resources, the skill and knowledge of its workers, and so on? In what respects, if any, is the competitor especially vulnerable to environmental trends or competitive threats?

These questions can give you a better picture of the kinds of competitive forces, if any, your organization will need to overcome if it is to be successful in a particular line of programs and services. Again, the strategic environments of some public and nonprofit organizations are intensely competitive, whereas other organizations have little or no competition.

Threat of Substitute Products. Sometimes the most significant threat is the one we do not immediately see or the one we would rather not see. Regardless of your organization's mission, the chances are that it produces goods and services that are vulnerable to obsolescence. We all are familiar with this phenomenon in technological fields. Vacuum tubes, for example, were replaced by transistors, which in turn were replaced by microchips, and so on. Thus the threat of substitute products is driven in part by the product life cycle and the inevitable emergence of new products that make older products obsolete.

But sometimes the appearance of substitute products does not mean that existing products are obsolete but that suppliers in different but related industries have perceived an opportunity to invade a market. As an administrator and in effect product manager in the field of higher education, I have to worry primarily about other schools of public management and policy because they are my principal competitors for students, research grants, and other valued resources. But occasionally I also have to worry about competition from graduate schools of business, social work, public health, law, and economics, all of which offer educational programs and services that are comparable to and even substitutable for my own.

Many public school leaders seem to have been caught off guard by the sudden emergence and growing popularity of charter schools, which have become a significant substitute product. Similarly, many of my colleagues in higher education look down upon "upstart" institutions that permit students to earn college degrees entirely by means of distance learning technologies. But these fledgling institutions might be the start of a wave of product substitutes that will substantially challenge the ivory tower concept of higher education.

Bargaining Power of Key Stakeholders. Finally, in the competitive environment we must acknowledge that competitors are not the only relevant stakeholders. For public and nonprofit organizations, two additional very important groups of stakeholders are (1) those who consume the organizations' programs and services and (2) those who supply the organizations with money and other important resources so that they may continue to serve their consumers. These two groups of stakeholders can exert dramatic influence on the competitive environment. Consumers can make demands on public and nonprofit organizations to change the design or delivery of goods and services. Donors, taxpayers, and elected officials can grant or withhold money and other resources until their demands are met.

Mary Tschirhart (1996) has found that nonprofit arts organizations respond to stakeholders in different ways depending on the perceived power and legitimacy of these stakeholders. Oster (1995, pp. 38–39) suggests that stakeholders wield more power when the following circumstances are true: they control concentrated resources that are valued by the organization, they have access to substitute products or are able to produce the product themselves, and they are capable of organizing themselves into an interest group or block.

Sometimes we see these various types of stakeholder power interact in dynamic and unpredictable ways. Several years ago the United Way responded to the expressed wishes of contributors by allowing contributors to designate their donations for specific United Way member agencies, rather than having United Way officials allocate gifts among competing needs in the community. These *donor option*, or *contributor choice*, plans have been remarkably successful from the consumer satisfaction standpoint. But they have also constrained the discretionary authority and flexibility of United Ways around the country to direct the money as they see fit. Moreover, certain United Way member agencies have wondered privately, if not aloud, why they should continue to participate in United Way fund drives when they could appeal directly to prospective donors and skip the middleman. Thus a strategy designed to enhance consumer choice has had at least a modest impact on the bargaining power of some very important stakeholders.

Step 3: Identify and Assess Key Driving Forces in Your Strategic Environment

The third step in an environmental scan is to determine what forces have the greatest impact on organizations that produce programs and services like yours.

To return to the SRC case, Alice Green asked Bill Markov the following questions:

- What changes have taken place among organizations that provide EAP programs or services over the past five years? What factors caused those changes?

- It seems that EAP programs and services are heavily affected by social and political attitudes toward substance abuse. Are these attitudes relatively stable, or are they volatile?

- What are the latest trends in human resource management among the large corporations in this region? How do HRM practices affect the priority given by employers to EAP programs and services?

- The philosophy of *lean and mean* seems to be spreading like wildfire among large corporations in this region. I haven't seen much interest in humane treatment of employees who have drug or alcohol problems. How important are these intangible factors?

Here are a few generic forces that have varying degrees of impact on most types of organizations:

Demographic Forces. Demographic factors represent perhaps the strongest single set of driving forces for most organizations. For example, nearly everyone in the nonprofit world is trying to figure out how to raise money from members of the affluent baby boomer generation as they approach retirement (Hall, 1997). In health care, experts are predicting a shortage of skilled nurses due to demographic factors. These demographic factors may easily have ripple effects throughout the entire health care industry, affecting the rivalry among competitors, the bargaining power of various stakeholders, and the fundamental structure of the industry itself.

Although all organizations are affected by demographic trends, some are more heavily influenced than others. On one hand, any organization that provides its programs or services *directly* to consumers is likely to be strongly affected by significant demographic shifts in the number of consumers in certain age groups, income levels, geographical locations, educational levels, and so on (Porter, 1980). On the other hand, organizations that supply goods and services to other organizations rather than directly to the public might be buffered slightly from the impact of demographic shifts. Bill Markov, for example, is contemplating the sale of EAP services to corporations, not directly to end users. Thus the EAP field is only indirectly (though powerfully) affected by demographic trends in society at large. Certainly, demographic trends in the corporate workplace, such as the number of women and minorities in managerial positions, will affect the EAP field. It is likely, for example, that the clients SRC receives through corporate EAP programs will have a demographic profile different from the profile of clients from direct referral programs.

Societal Attitudes and Values. Most organizations in the public and nonprofit sectors can be greatly affected by changes in societal attitudes and beliefs. Employee assistance programs, for example, have become important as a result of several sets of beliefs and values that have coalesced over the past few decades such as the belief that addiction is a *disease* that can be treated and that employers have an *obligation* to offer their workers the chance to benefit from various treatment methodologies before the employer takes more drastic action such as termination of employment. If this belief system should ever change, the affects on the EAP field will be dramatic.

Consumer Experience and Knowledge. An important driving force in any line of business, whether profit or nonprofit, is the knowledge and sophistication of consumers. When programs and services are in the early life cycle stages of emerging and growing, consumers probably have little knowledge about them and thus may not be able to make informed or discriminating choices. Then, as consumers collectively gain greater experience with the programs and services, they become increasingly demanding and discriminating in their choices.

Economic Forces. All organizations are affected to some extent by economic forces, but some are especially vulnerable to economic fluctuations, which might be manifested in interest rates, access to venture capital, energy costs, labor costs, transportation costs, and so on. The key is to isolate the economic factors that have the greatest impact on the overall health and direction of your organization's line of programs and services and do your best to forecast how these factors will play out in the future.

Technology and Product Innovation. Although some organizations are relatively impervious to technological innovation, others are strongly driven by changes in technology. The field of job training, for example, is heavily influenced by technological innovation both in terms of the skills that are conveyed to trainees to help them compete for jobs and also in the way the training in those skills is delivered. In other industries, like parks and recreation management, for example, technology has somewhat milder impacts. Techniques for grass mowing, flower planting, and snow removal change gradually. Even in this domain, however, advanced technology has played a role by developing ways to make playgrounds safer for children. Cities are now facing significant capital expenditures to upgrade and replace playgrounds that are unsafe by contemporary standards.

Another important driving force stemming from technology is the rate at which product innovations and proprietary knowledge spread or diffuse among organizations engaged in similar activities. Most public and nonprofit organizations do not use patent protections, and they have a higher inclination to share knowledge than do organizations in the more intensely competitive for-profit world. Thus, when one organization develops a new methodology for, say, evaluating social programs or providing family counseling, there is a likelihood that this specialized knowledge will not remain proprietary for very long. Still, the spread of proprietary knowledge can vary significantly from one domain to another, and thus it may have differential effects on the viability of product differentiation strategies and on the very structure of an industry.

Public Policy and Regulatory Influences. Some organizations are more sensitive to government policy changes, or hints of policy changes, than others. During President Clinton's first term in office, he promised to introduce legislation for comprehensive reform of the U.S. health care system, because costs were running out of control and many poor people were uninsured and badly served. Although his legislative proposal ultimately failed in a narrowly political sense, the national debate on the topic spurred accelerated development of the managed care philosophy and its spread across the nation.

Regulation can sometimes work to the benefit of some organizations and to the detriment of others. Growing interest in regulating the conversion of nonprofit organizations to for-profit status, especially in the health care field, will likely have systemwide impacts on the for-profit hospital industry.

International Forces. Some public and nonprofit organizations are significantly affected by international forces. Obviously, international aid and relief organizations are driven directly by trends in international economics, politics, and conflict. But domestic public enterprises are also affected by international forces. Many public schools, for example, have been criticized for their performance compared to the performance of schools in Europe and Japan.

International monetary forces, like exchange rates, can have powerful effects on entire industries. Such factors can, for example, affect the flow and direction of international philanthropy and have important consequences for the structure of international nonprofit organizations.

Step 4: Assess Threats, Opportunities, and Prospects in Your Strategic Environment

The final step in an environmental scan is to synthesize and interpret all the information you have gathered in order to identify the opportunities and challenges in your organization's strategic environment. Table 3.5 illustrates a mechanism for organizing this information. To illustrate its application, I have invented hypothetical responses to the questions posed by Alice Green. Because the responses (in the "Brief Description" column) are hypothetical, the judgments offered in this table are also entirely hypothetical and to some extent arbitrary. They should not be used as the basis for any analysis of the EAP industry.

A chart constructed like Table 3.5 would provide Bill Markov and Alice Green with a lot of information on the opportunities and challenges in their regional EAP marketplace. In this hypothetical analysis the threats and opportunities are relatively equal in strength but not evenly distributed. It suggests that SRC's greatest opportunities might lie in niche markets and with the emerging high-tech and multinational corporations in the region. Also, there might be some opportunities for collaboration, especially with like-minded nonprofit organizations.

Comprehensive Environmental Scan Versus Trial and Error

At the end of this description of a comprehensive assessment of SRC's strategic environment, you might wonder whether all this work is justified. Couldn't SRC simply probe the EAP marketplace with a small trial venture, making greater investments only if the preliminary results looked promising? After all, by the time this comprehensive analysis is complete, SRC's strategic opportunity to enter the EAP field might be past. Also, it is pretty clear that this analysis is not entirely objective; there are many subjective

TABLE 3.5 Hypothetical Assessment by SRC of EAP Industry's Overall Attractiveness.

Key Economic Factors	Brief Description	Opportunity	Threat	Comments, Questions, Important Assumptions
Size and growth rate of EAP programs in SRC market area	Fifty corporations in the regional market spent a total of $4 million in 1998 on EAP programs. Average annual growth rate of 2% and flattening. 1,200 employees sought assistance through EAPs in 1998, a decrease of 1% from the previous year. The regional pattern seems to mirror national trends. Greatest growth is in high-tech industries that have recently emerged in the region.	Although growth is slow to stagnant, there are opportunities for penetration of niche markets, especially among high-tech firms, service industries, and larger nonprofit organizations.	The overall market is modest in size, and most competitors have established strong positions.	The corporate profile of the market area is in transition, with traditional manufacturing industries and large employers of all types giving way to smaller service industries and high-tech firms. The size of the EAP industry will likely mirror fluctuations in the regional economy.

Life cycle stage of EAP programs and services	Mature.	The EAP business is not likely to attract new competitors. In fact, there appears to be some consolidation, manifested in mergers and acquisitions among existing competitors.	Advanced levels of market segmentation and product differentiation have resulted in relatively entrenched patterns of market share among major competitors.	SRC has other mature products and services in its portfolio.
Barriers to entry or exit	Modestly high barriers based primarily on reputation.	SRC has an excellent reputation and high regional visibility in the field of addiction recovery.	Established EAP administrators have built up strong comparative advantages in cost control, marketing, and networks of access to related organizations and individuals like HMOs, human resource managers, and hospitals.	SRC should try to find out how many employers have switched EAP administrators over the past few years in order to assess level of customer loyalty and switching costs as entry barriers.

TABLE 3.5 Hypothetical Assessment by SRC of EAP Industry's Overall Attractiveness, *continued.*

Key Economic Factors	Brief Description	Opportunity	Threat	Comments, Questions, Important Assumptions
Overall profitability	Profit margins per EAP participant are volatile. Capitated contracts provide incentives to keep operating costs to a minimum.	SRC has excellent patient tracking capability, established through its residential treatment programs. This could be modified to assist in cost control.	The profitability of EAP programs and services seems to in anticipated changes in the supply and demand curves.	SRC should attempt to do a break-even analysis under different assumptions and conditions of non-linearity to determine the number of clients and the selling price that would allow SRC to recover its costs and make a profit.
Key Competitive Factors				
Number of competitors	The regional market now (with the divestiture of St. Joseph's)	The total number of EAP competitors has probably peaked and	The regional EAP market seems to be characterized by	There are early signs of market consolidation, as indicated by

	has seven EAP administrators.	will likely decline in the future.	overcapacity at this time.	divestments and mergers, joint ventures, and other consolidating mechanisms.
Rivalry	The rivalry is intense at the present time, with EAP administrators struggling to retain market share in a volatile market.	SRC is financially stronger and more visible in the region than most of the competitors.	SRC could be entering a hornet's nest of competition where it has little experience in the rules of the game.	SRC's board of directors is not averse to competitive strategies.
Collaboration	Collaboration among EAP administrators is strictly business and manifested in mergers, joint ventures, and subcontracting.	SRC would be an excellent partner for an established EAP administrator because of its stellar reputation and proven capabilities.	Collaboration diminishes the benefits of entering the EAP industry as well as the risks.	One of SRC's major donors has suggested that SRC look more carefully for opportunities to collaborate.
Basis for competition	Competition among existing EAP administrators seems to be on the basis of either price or product	There may be lucrative opportunities to carve out a *focus* strategy, targeted toward particular	Still, SRC is largely an unknown quantity in the EAP field, and therefore the risks of failure are high.	SRC cannot compete effectively solely on price.

TABLE 3.5 Hypothetical Assessment by SRC of EAP Industry's Overall Attractiveness, *continued.*

Key Economic Factors	Brief Description	Opportunity	Threat	Comments, Questions, Important Assumptions
	differentiation. There seems to be less competition for niche markets.	types of industries for example, those with knowledge workers) in which SRC can claim to have greater experience than others do.		
Dominant competitors	The dominant competitor from the standpoint of total market share is AccuCare, Inc., which also dominates from the standpoint of cost leadership. Workers Assistance League is	There currently is no competitor that is focusing attention on industries dominated by knowledge workers.	AccuCare's dominant position in the market will be difficult to attack.	SRC might be able to compete for niche markets.

	now the only competitor focusing on niche markets with specialized products.			
Next moves of competitors	AccuCare is likely to pursue a strategy of horizontal growth by absorbing other competitors and vertical integration by expanding its portfolio into human resource benefits administration. Workers Assistance League seems content to focus on manufacturing industries and blue-collar workers.	Workers Assistance League seems to be leaving the door open to the newly emerging high-tech industries.	AccuCare's strategy of aggressive horizontal and vertical integration increases the stakes for new entrants like SRC.	If AccuCare is successful in its vertical integration strategy, it could enhance its dominance in the market.
Substitute products	Potential substitutes include self-help programs like Alcoholics	SRC's historical alliances with substitute programs like AA might give it a slight	Substitute products are gaining in popularity as employees fear corporate backlash	Substitute products do not pose a major threat to EAP programs at the present

TABLE 3.5 Hypothetical Assessment by SRC of EAP Industry's Overall Attractiveness, *continued*.

Key Economic Factors	Brief Description	Opportunity	Threat	Comments, Questions, Important Assumptions
	Anonymous (AA), private counseling and family therapy, and corporate sponsorship of wellness programs that might temporarily combat the symptoms of substance abuse.	buffer against these substitutes.	against employees with substance abuse problems.	time but should be monitored closely.
Bargaining power of stakeholders	The bargaining power of corporate customers is increasing due to apparent overcapacity in the system.	The added bargaining power of customers over the current suppliers of EAP services might reduce the entry barriers for SRC.	The entry of SRC into a crowded marketplace will only increase the bargaining power of customers.	If the bargaining power of customers focuses only on price, then SRC will be at a disadvantage.

Driving Forces				
Demographics	A growing number of women and minorities in the workforce.	This demographic shift widens the market of potential clients, which may create opportunities for SRC. SRC has always been respected within the minority community.	There is one other competitor that has focused much of its attention on the needs of women and minorities.	What demographic trends are apparent in the emerging high-tech firms that may be SRC's niche market?
Societal values	Social attitudes toward addiction can be volatile. The news and entertainment media play a significant role in shaping public attitudes. Even professionals such as physicians and psychologists are sometimes not well informed.	There may be special opportunities for EAP providers that offer a full range of services from general education about substance abuse to direct intervention and follow-up.	Corporations may be less tolerant of substance abusers and may feel less obligation to help them toward recovery.	SRC is respected in the community as both an educational resource and a treatment center.

TABLE 3.5 Hypothetical Assessment by SRC of EAP Industry's Overall Attractiveness, *continued.*

Key Economic Factors	Brief Description	Opportunity	Threat	Comments, Questions, Important Assumptions
Consumer knowledge	Both corporate clients and employees themselves are far more intelligent and discriminating consumers of EAP and other treatment protocols than they were ten years ago.	There may be special opportunities for EAP providers that have proven track records of performance.	Many EAP providers are competing for the attention of informed consumers, leading to increasingly exaggerated claims of performance.	Marketing strategies for EAP programs must be sophisticated to reach intelligent consumers.
Economic forces	Structural changes in the local economy have had profound effects on the corporate profile.	New companies in the local marketplace will be establishing their human resource management systems and will be open to offers from EAP providers.	Volatility in the consumer marketplace will lead to more intense competition.	Niche markets may be appearing as new organizations enter the region.

Technology and innovation	No significant influence at this time.	No significant opportunities.	No significant threats.	
Public policy	Will public dissatisfaction with the managed care philosophy lead to the reemergence of traditional residential treatment programs for substance abusers?	Public dissatisfaction could lead to more liberal reimbursement policies for substance abuse recovery programs.	Efforts to balance the federal budget will continue to have adverse effects on federal and state reimbursement policies for health care.	SRC should watch policy developments closely and perhaps intensify its advocacy efforts.
International forces	The region has attracted a growing number of multinational corporations and foreign-held companies. More employees are from abroad or have had significant exposure to cultures other than U.S. culture.	SRC has a staff that is knowledgeable about different cultural attitudes toward addiction.	None.	SRC might find a market niche with certain international companies.
Summary	The EAP industry could be a moderately attractive investment for SRC if it pursues selected niche markets with carefully designed products and services.			

judgments in the cells of Table 3.5. Perhaps this type of comprehensive environmental scan is just a fancy (and time-consuming) way of classifying our subjective judgments. Finally, there is the question of data availability and our ability to do the analysis based on facts versus impressions.

There are several responses to these questions. First, a trial-and-error approach to market analysis might indeed be entirely appropriate under conditions of extreme uncertainty. Bill Markov could simply make some *cold calls* on a few prospective corporate clients to see whether SRC has any prospect of winning an EAP contract. Or SRC could set up an EAP division with a skeleton crew and minimal investment to test the market. But without at least some preliminary analysis, Markov's calls are likely to be random and perhaps very misleading. Say the hypothetical analysis in Table 3.5 is correct and that whatever opportunities exist in the EAP market are in niche markets. If Markov spent a few weeks making cold calls only on the traditional manufacturing industries in his region, he might get a misleading fix on the strategic environment.

Second, the advisability of employing a trial-and-error approach rather than an in-depth environmental scan depends also on the risks associated with making a wrong decision. For SRC, even a trial-and-error strategy is likely to be costly, both financially and in terms of organizational image. These costs will quickly add up. SRC could likely not probe the EAP market quietly. Soon competitors would know that SRC was exploring opportunities. Many stakeholders, especially prospective clients, would want assurances that SRC was serious about its commitment. SRC would need to build consumer confidence by making more than a trivial investment in EAP programs and services.

Third, subjectivity in an environmental scan might be considered one of its benefits, not a reason to criticize it. A formal environmental scan like the one illustrated in this chapter can help bring to the surface some of the subjective assumptions and values of key decision makers, as well as the data and facts that are available.

Fourth, there are many circumstances under which you might choose to conduct only selected steps of the comprehensive environmental scan presented in this chapter, making the process much less daunting. You might decide, for example, that you have acquired sufficient information for your purposes after assessing only the key economic characteristics or the competitive environment of your organization's line of business. Or you might focus on selected questions from each of the steps presented here, foregoing the ones less relevant to you.

Any successful corporate executive will tell you that it is difficult to succeed in business when you do not know what business you are in or what business you *want* to be in. Whether your organization's business is treating addicts and alcoholics, providing funding to artists, paving roads and bridges, collecting garbage, or regulating utility companies, your organization operates within an strategic environment composed of comparable organizations that provide related, similar, or substitutable programs and services. Perhaps this strategic environment is changing in terms of its size and growth patterns, the number of competing organizations, the intensity of the competition, and the types of strategies competitors are using to achieve their objectives. Failure to monitor and adapt to these changes is a recipe for organizational failure.

Conducting an environmental scan is absolutely essential when you are contemplating an addition to your organization's portfolio of programs and services and when, like Bill Markov, you are thinking about expanding the mission of your organization into a new line of programs and services. And even when you are not considering such major changes, it is imperative that you continually monitor trends affecting your organization's current portfolio.

Finally, a thorough industry analysis can help you identify the businesses you are *not* in and *should not* be in. As public and nonprofit organizations try to diversify their revenue streams, they run the risk of trying to compete in lines of programs and services in which they have little experience and no comparative advantage whatsoever.

Sometimes the consequences are disastrous. In the summer of 1998, the health care community in Pennsylvania and nationwide was rocked by the $1.3 billion bankruptcy of the Allegheny Health, Education and Research Foundation (AHERF), the Pittsburgh-based parent of a far-flung health care empire that included not only an extensive network of nonprofit hospitals in Pittsburgh and Philadelphia but dozens of physician practices, for-profit subsidiaries, and even a medical college. The chief financial officer of the organization blamed the financial collapse on AHERF's decision to assume medical risks for certain HMO enrollees (Shelly, 1998), a strategy that essentially put the hospitals in the business of providing insurance instead of the business of providing health care. Other observers have noted that AHERF took its strategy of horizontal and vertical integration too far by trying to penetrate new geographical markets where it had no "local knowledge." Although aggressive acquisition strategies are used by many health systems in today's increasingly consolidated health care environment, they sometimes lead these hospitals far astray from their primary mission and from their core competencies.

Conclusion

Summarizing the previous discussion, here are the reasons for doing an environmental scan:

- To clarify for management and for key stakeholders what "business" the organization is in, whether there are other organizations competing with the organization for customers or resources, and whether there are organizations that provide programs or services that are substitutable for the organization's own programs or services

- To clarify what businesses the organization is *not* in by alerting management to the risks of entering domains of activity that could put the organization's assets and its mission at risk

- To identify organizations that are leaders in a particular line of programs and services and to understand what practices and strategies make them so successful

- To compare the performance of the organization with that of other organizations

- To understand and perhaps anticipate the strategic issues and driving forces that have the greatest impact on all agencies in the organization's strategic environment

- To identify and diagnose opportunities and potential threats in the organization's strategic environment

- To help management design and implement an organizational strategy appropriate for the organization's environment

- To help management decide whether or not to enter a new line of programs and services or to enter a new market with the organization's existing portfolio

The framework of analysis presented here has been a staple of strategic management for generations of business professionals, but it has had far less exposure in the public and nonprofit sectors. The objective of an environmental scan is to stimulate your initial thinking about what types of organizational strategies will likely be necessary to succeed with a given line of programs and services. Later chapters offer a fuller understanding of these strategies and means of taking stock of the distinctive competencies of your organization and any comparative advantages it might have in light of current and anticipated industry trends.

Getting Started

1. How would you advise Bill Markov to proceed with SRC's interest in the EAP business? Should SRC try to penetrate this line of programs and services? Are the potential benefits worth the cost?

2. What parts of the environmental scanning template presented in this chapter need to be modified for application in your organization?

4

Analyzing Your Organization's Portfolio

Once you have assessed the opportunities and challenges in your organization's strategic environment, the next step is to determine whether or not your organization's programs and services are well positioned to prosper in that environment. Many strategic management texts recommend that managers develop an exhaustive list of internal strengths and weaknesses that they then compare with the opportunities and challenges in the environment. This is a useful approach, but it tends to produce general information about an organization's strategic position. Portfolio analysis is a more focused technique that requires management to examine each of the organization's programs and services in relation to the environment. Portfolio analysis produces very specific information that is helpful in determining whether management ought to grow, retrench, or stabilize these programs and services.

The Curran Opera Theater

At first glance the Curran Opera Theater (COT) appears to be a small (and sometimes struggling) nonprofit arts organization with a modest mission and limited resources. Closer inspection, however, reveals that COT is a multiproduct firm with a relatively large portfolio of programs and services and an ambitious but focused organizational strategy.

Founded in 1980 by retired opera star Rose Curran, COT's mission is "to provide a workshop for the recruitment and development of opera talent, and to enhance community access to and appreciation for opera as a musical and theatrical art form." In the early days, Curran did virtually everything. She visited music instructors in area high schools and colleges in search of young people who might be interested in opera. She talked to parents, community groups, and kids all over town. She provided voice lessons in her home and staged recitals and tiny productions in church basements and fire halls. She and her husband constructed stage sets and even made many of the costumes for the performers.

Curran also recruited a talented and resourceful group of volunteers, including a very effective board of trustees. Together they began to build an impressive organization that has grown and flourished. Today COT's portfolio of programs and services is as follows:

COT performs an annual program of three traditional opera productions, staged at the College Theater (which COT leases) from October through March. These productions are targeted toward traditional and relatively sophisticated opera enthusiasts. Sets and costumes are minimized to reduce production costs and to focus attention on the music and the acting, which traditional opera patrons most admire. Musical accompaniment is provided by the college orchestra, which cosponsors the annual program. Tickets are expensive, but patrons are happy to pay the price because COT is clearly the best of several opera companies in the vicinity. Patrons also enjoy the psychological reward of knowing they are supporting the development of young talent. Additional revenues are secured via an annual fundraising campaign to which the region's wealthiest patrons and corporations have gladly contributed.

COT sponsors an annual parks tour with a contemporary or light opera production that is staged outdoors on four successive weekends in June and July. These outdoor productions are designed to stimulate appreciation for opera among young people, adults, and families who have never been opera patrons. These tours may feature the popular work of contemporary composers like Andrew Lloyd Webber or traditional light opera classics such as those by Gilbert and Sullivan. The atmosphere is informal, and families are encouraged to bring picnics. Each tour is heavily subsidized by the Smith Foundation, allowing COT to stage relatively sophisticated productions while keeping ticket prices affordable for families. Set designs and costumes for the tour are more elaborate than those used in the traditional opera productions, because COT knows that a bit of "flash" is attractive and entertaining for these audiences. Still, attendance at these programs has never been high, and recently it has dwindled slightly. COT competes with other summer entertainment events such as the Symphony Under the Stars program of the local philharmonic orchestra.

COT operates a summer opera camp for two weeks. The camp offers a mix of educational and recreational programs for young people aged thirteen and over who have musical talent and aspirations. Admission to the camp is competitive, and the curriculum includes opera history, individual and group voice lessons, orchestration, and acting. The camp session culminates in a recital featuring the camp participants. Tuition and fees for the camp are set at a rate high enough to generate a modest profit. This program does not face direct competition from other summer programs. Some of COT's supporters believe that COT should admit more and more participants to the summer camp in order to subsidize other parts of its portfolio.

COT and the local school district are developing and will deliver a performing arts curriculum targeted toward elementary school students. They joined forces to win a grant from the Midwest Arts Council for this program. The curriculum, which will introduce students to many types of performing arts, earned the attention of the Arts Council because of its innovative features. It is designed to appeal to a broad range of students.

COT recently completed a strategic planning process in which the board of trustees strongly endorsed an overall organizational strategy that includes elements of both horizontal growth and vertical integration (see Chapter Five). Specifically, the trustees want to leverage COT's growing reputation by offering more programs and perhaps even replicating them in other cities. Also, COT wants to gain greater control of its production and distribution processes, perhaps by acquiring its own performance and teaching facility or by entering a long-term lease for an existing facility.

How should this organizational strategy be reflected in the program strategies for each of the four parts of COT's portfolio? Are the existing program strategies consistent with and supportive of this organizational vision?

Program and Service Strategies

Your program strategy describes how you intend to position each of your organization's programs and services in its respective market. If your organization produces only one program or service, then your organizational strategy and your program strategy will be very nearly the same. However, if your organization has a portfolio of several or many programs and services, then all of them should work in concert to support the organizational strategy.

For example, the Curran Opera Theater wants to grow horizontally and vertically. It can accomplish this overall strategic goal with any or all of the four principal programs in its portfolio. But each program will play a slightly different role as the drama unfolds (pardon the pun). The organizational strategy will be based in large part on how these various programs are positioned in their respective markets. In effect, COT's organizational strategy will be derived from the amalgamation of the various program strategies.

Thus we should not draw the distinction too sharply between organizational strategy and program strategy, because these levels of strategy are mutually interdependent (see Figure 4.1).

Portfolio Analysis

Portfolio analysis refers to the employment of a set of tools by multiproduct, multiservice organizations to help them understand how

FIGURE 4.1 Interaction Between Organizational Strategies and Program Strategies.

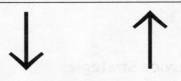

Organizational Strategy

Overall vision of growth, retrenchment, or stability derived from assessment of industry trends and organizational strengths and weaknesses

Program Strategy

A specific plan for advancing the organizational strategy by positioning each product or service within its respective market based on assessment of product attributes in relation to market forces

their respective programs and services support their overall organizational mission and strategy. It is a powerful means of visualizing and understanding how each of your organization's programs and services contributes to organizational strategy. As one of the most widely used strategic management tools in the business world, portfolio analysis can be used to

- Assess whether your organization's portfolio of programs and services is in sync with external opportunities and challenges
- Assess the contribution of each program or service to your organization's overall strategic position and competitiveness in the marketplace
- Assess the contribution of each program or service to organization-wide objectives and strategies

• Determine whether all parts of the portfolio are working in concert to achieve strategic goals

Typically, portfolio analysis is accomplished through the construction of a matrix that allows you to examine the points of *intersection* (represented by the cells in the matrix) between internal and external forces. Portfolio models have been developed for industrial giants as well as small nonprofit organizations.

Business Model of Portfolio Analysis: Boston Consulting Group's Growth-Share Matrix

Let's examine a prominent business model of portfolio analysis first in order to view the basic concepts.

One of the seminal models of portfolio analysis is the Growth-Share Matrix, developed by the Boston Consulting Group (BCG) (Hedley, 1977; Day, 1977; Wensley, 1981) to help corporations plot their products and services on two dimensions: (1) the observed growth rate of the market in which their product or service is sold and (2) the relative market share of the product or service in that market (see Table 4.1).

According to the logic of the Growth-Share Matrix, every business should have some *cash cows* that can be milked to feed the products that are *stars* and that are the most promising *question marks*. Conversely, this framework suggests that the firm should divest its weakest *question marks* and especially the products that are *dogs*, because they do not add value to the organization's overall portfolio.

The Growth-Share Matrix has several attractive features. First, it allows managers to visualize and understand the cash flow relationships among the various products and services in their portfolios. For example, many multipurpose nonprofit organizations have certain services that generate unrestricted revenues that can be moved from one part of the organization to another. These revenue streams can be used to subsidize the truly charitable programs in the portfolio, which consume more resources than they generate.

TABLE 4.1 Boston Consulting Group Growth-Share Matrix.

		Your Organization's Market Share	
		High	*Low*
	High	**Stars**	**Question Marks**
		Product strategy. Use revenues from other product lines to solidify the comparative advantages of stars and to ward off current or potential competitors.	*Product strategy.* Either invest in question marks to build their market share or consider eliminating these product lines.
Market Growth Rate of the Program or Service	*Low*	**Cash Cows**	**Dogs**
		Product strategy. Build market share of cash cows if possible. Otherwise, maintain current market share and use revenues from these product lines to build stars or question marks.	*Product strategy.* These product lines are targets for divestment.

Source: Adapted from Hedley, B. "Strategy and the Business Portfolio." *Long Range Planning,* 1977, *10*(1), 10–11. Copyright © 1977 by Elsevier Science. Reprinted with permission from the publisher.

Second, the Growth-Share Matrix is a useful communication tool. As public and nonprofit organizations become more and more involved in revenue generating ventures, they need to illustrate to donors, trustees, and other constituencies the increasingly complex relationships among the various parts of their portfolios. Because of its simplicity, the matrix is easily understood by these diverse constituencies.

Third, the Growth-Share Matrix can provide managers with an overall picture of the *balance* in their portfolio. The general objective is to have a sufficient number of cash cows to maintain current revenue flows and also to have some promising rising stars on which to build the organization's future. A portfolio dominated by too many cash cows, however, may signal that the organization needs to invest more in research and development for the future.

Despite some attractive features, the Growth-Share Matrix has only marginal utility for government and nonprofit organizations. Its emphasis on cash flows and its cavalier attitude toward divestiture are simply incompatible with the missions and core values of government and nonprofit organizations. One of the reasons that these organizations exist is to fill voids for services left in the market by for-profit firms. Therefore your organization's portfolio likely contains programs and services that businesses would consider to be dogs. These dogs that businesses would be so quick to divest may indeed be the heart and soul of your organization's public service mission. They cannot be casually shed in search of more fertile financial opportunities.

The matrix has also been criticized even within the business world for the fact that it considers only two factors in the analysis, market growth and relative market share. Sophisticated planners and analysts know that many factors besides market growth and market share must be considered when formulating organizational strategy. For example, the Growth-Share Matrix does not address many of the factors included in the comprehensive environmental scan discussed in Chapter Three. Thus, if you relied exclusively on this matrix, you might be seduced by high growth rates in an industry and overlook negative factors that would be uncovered if you conducted a comprehensive industry analysis. Also, the Growth-Share Matrix does not provide for an in-depth analysis of your organization's internal strengths and weaknesses. It forces you to focus attention only on the relative market share of your organization's programs and services, which may distort or hide serious organizational inefficiencies and other weaknesses.

Moreover, the notion of market share itself is problematic for many public and nonprofit organizations. Police departments, for example, are in effect multiproduct firms because they offer a range of services, from criminal investigations to community education. But most of the services offered by a typical police department cannot be analyzed in terms of market share because the department may have a virtual monopoly with respect to many parts of its portfolio. Even nonprofit organizations that compete directly with other nonprofits may have difficulty using the concept of market share as a principle ingredient in their strategic planning.

Finally, the cell labels themselves of the Growth-Share Matrix can cause problems of perception both inside and outside an organization. The late Harold Geneen (1984), former chairman of ITT, once quipped, "Who would want to work for a company or a division labeled a 'cash cow' whose earning were ladled out to someone else and which had no hope of future growth?" (p. 27). The labels are especially problematic in public and nonprofit organizations. Imagine referring to a program to assist the homeless as a dog simply because it does not generate sufficient revenues to support itself? Envision the kind of tension that would exist among your employees if some of them were given big budget increases to support high-profile star projects while those who worked on question mark projects were constantly waiting for the axe to fall on their budgets, their jobs, and their clients. Imagine how the press (or the Internal Revenue Service) would react to a government or nonprofit program that was labeled a cash cow.

For all these reasons, the Growth-Share Matrix is not very well suited to public and nonprofit organizations. But as one of the earliest portfolio analysis models, it provides a useful illustration of the basic concepts and approaches.

Portfolio Analysis Models for Public and Nonprofit Organizations

Several variants of portfolio analysis have been developed specifically for public and nonprofit organizations. They are based on the same fundamental principles as the industrial models but modified slightly to reflect the unique missions and contexts of public service organizations.

Gruber and Mohr Framework. Gruber and Mohr (1982) developed one of the first portfolio models specifically for nonprofit organizations. It has applicability in multipurpose government agencies as well as nonprofit organizations. Their model is a four-cell matrix that allows decision makers to plot the various programs in an organization's portfolio on two dimensions: (1) the social benefits or value of the program and (2) the financial returns generated by the program in terms of fees, philanthropic support, grants, contracts, and so on. Table 4.2 summarizes the Gruber and Mohr model as it might be used to classify the four programs in the portfolio of the Curran Opera Theater. The emphasis on social value and financial returns makes the Gruber and Mohr framework somewhat difficult to apply to an arts and cultural organization like COT. For example, I am not sure that one can say that COT's parks tour is of lower "social value" than its summer opera camp. Both programs advance the central mission of COT, which is to introduce young people to opera and nurture their interests and skills.

The Gruber and Mohr framework is based heavily on the BCG Growth-Share Matrix, and suffers some of the same shortcomings when applied to public and nonprofit organizations. First, the emphasis in the vertical axis on financial returns is too narrow and limiting. It ignores, for example, the prospect that a program might offer substantial financial returns but be wholly incongruent with

TABLE 4.2 Gruber and Mohr Portfolio Analysis Matrix for Nonprofit Organizations.

		Social Value of the Program	
		Low Social Value	*High Social Value*
Financial Returns of the Program	Positive Financial Returns	Sustaining Programs (Necessary Evil) Maintain these programs and use their revenues to support worthwhile programs. *Summer parks tour?*	Beneficial Programs (Best of All Worlds) Expand these programs and use the revenues they generate to subsidize worthwhile programs. *Traditional opera program* *Summer opera camp* *Summer parks tour?*
	Negative Financial Returns	Detrimental Programs (No Redeeming Qualities) Prune these programs from the portfolio. *Summer parks tour?*	Worthwhile Programs (Satisfying, Good for Society) Carefully nurture these programs with aggressive fundraising and subsidies from other parts of the portfolio. *Curriculum development project*

Source: Adapted from Gruber, R. E., and Mohr, M. "Strategic Management for Multipurpose Nonprofit Organizations." *California Management Review*, 1982, 24(3), 17–18. Copyright © 1982 by The Regents of the University of California. Reprinted by permission of The Regents.

your organization's mission, the skills of its employees, and the other programs in its portfolio. Moreover, this simplistic dimension does not allow you to consider the prospects for improving the financial returns from a program or service. Thus, although the COT summer parks tour is not generating substantial revenue at present, it might produce a profit if given the necessary attention.

Second, the emphasis on social benefit on the horizontal axis of the matrix does not allow the organization to assess its own strengths and weaknesses in delivering the socially desirable program. An organization might do a very *bad* job of delivering a *good* program, one that is socially desirable. Despite the program's social value, should the organization continue to provide that program if other providers are doing a much better job? Also, the framework does not assess whether competing organizations are engaged in the production of the same programs and services that are in your portfolio. Thus the Gruber and Mohr framework might lead you to invest in *beneficial* programs (the upper right cell) for all the wrong reasons. It is quite conceivable that programs in this cell of the matrix would be wholly incompatible with your organization's mission and capabilities. Investing in them would only place your organization in direct competition with more qualified organizations, thereby putting it in the position of being little more than a drain on scarce community resources.

Finally, the Gruber and Mohr framework assumes an unrealistically high level of flexibility in transferring funds between nonprofit programs. True, earned revenues might be transferable from one part of the portfolio to another, allowing one program to subsidize another. But grants, contracts, philanthropic contributions, and similar sources of revenue often are restricted in their use, which prevents the subsidization and cross-fertilization advocated by Gruber and Mohr.

MacMillan Framework. MacMillan (1983) developed a far more sophisticated approach to portfolio analysis, specifically designed for nonprofit organizations. MacMillan's recommended approach to portfolio analysis contains three dimensions to consider for each program or service in the portfolio. The first dimension is *program attractiveness*, which is a measure of the degree to which a particular program or service is attractive to the nonprofit organization in its deployment of scarce resources. This dimension is similar to, though not quite as comprehensive as, the environmental scanning criteria discussed in Chapter Three.

The second dimension is *competitive position*, which is the extent to which an organization can legitimately claim to have a superior ability to support the program.

Finally, *alternative coverage* refers to the number of other agencies that can, or are inclined to, provide the program. Exhibit 4.1 summarizes the variables that make up these three dimensions of MacMillan's framework. MacMillan's criteria result in an eight-cell matrix, as shown in Table 4.3 For the purpose of illustration, I have plotted the programs of the Curran Opera Theater in this matrix.

Here is a distillation of the types of strategies that MacMillan recommends for programs in each of the eight cells of the matrix.

Cell I: aggressive competition. The situation described in this cell is one in which other agencies are competing for one or more highly attractive programs in which your agency has clear superiority. If your organization is truly superior, you should engage in aggressive competition to ease other providers out of this particular market. You might build up your strengths in this part of your portfolio to enhance your competitive position or negotiate with other organizations to convince them to yield this part of their portfolio to you. COT's traditional opera program is in direct competition with the programs of several other opera companies. But its clear superiority might justify a competitive strategy, especially as COT seeks funds to support its strategy of vertical integration.

Cell II: aggressive growth. This cell describes an open market for your organization, a situation in which you have a demonstrated comparative advantage in providing certain very attractive programs and there are few if any competitors. MacMillan argues that

EXHIBIT 4.1 Dimensions of MacMillan's Portfolio Analysis.

Program Attractiveness

- *Congruence with mission.* Without stretching the imagination, is the proposed program or activity congruent with the formal mission of the organization?

- *Congruence with existing skills.* Does the organization have people who are skilled in undertaking the proposed program or activity?

- *Synergy.* Can the program activities be shared by other programs in the organization's portfolio?

- *Support group appeal.* Does the program appeal to the values and interests of major support constituencies?

- *Fundability.* Is the program likely to attract sufficient and stable funding from the community?

- *Size and concentration of the client base.* Is the client base sufficiently large and growing to sustain the program?

- *Volunteer appeal.* Will the program attract able and enthusiastic volunteers?

- *Measurability of results.* Does the program lend itself to outcome measurement?

- *Prevention versus cure.* Does the program have a preventive component, or is it exclusively ameliorative?

- *Exit barriers.* How difficult would it be to abandon the program once the organization has committed resources to it?

- *Client resistance.* To what extent do clients resist participation in similar programs?

- *Self-sufficiency orientation.* To what extent will the program build self-sufficiency (versus dependency) in the client?

Competitive Position

- *Location and logistics.* Does your agency have logistical advantages such as location and delivery systems that are especially attractive to clients?

- *Stakeholder loyalty.* Does your organization have a large reservoir of community support that gives you a comparative advantage?

EXHIBIT 4.1 Dimensions of MacMillan's Portfolio Analysis, *continued*.

- *Prior funding history.* Do you have a successful track record of fundraising that might offer special access to donors and grantmakers?
- *Track record.* Do you have a track record of service delivery that is relevant to this type of program?
- *Market share.* Does your organization already serve a large portion of the target clientele?
- *Quality.* Are your services widely recognized for their quality?
- *Fundraising ability.* Do you have proven ability to raise funds, especially for this type of program?
- *Advocacy.* Does your organization have a track record of advocacy related to the program?
- *Technical skills.* Does your organization have special technical capabilities related to the program?
- *Organizational skills.* Does your organization have superior support services and organizational infrastructure to sustain the program?
- *Local contacts.* Does your organization have superior networks of contacts and relationships related to the program?
- *Research skills.* Does your organization have a superior ability to conduct research on the issues related to the program, including root causes of problems and testing of solutions?
- *Communication skills.* Does your organization have a superior ability to communicate and report results of the program?
- *Cost effectiveness.* Does your organization have any advantages in delivering the program in an efficient and effective manner?

Alternative Coverage

- *Large agencies.* Are there no other large agencies delivering programs like the one under consideration?
- *Small agencies.* Are there very few small agencies delivering programs like the one under consideration?

Source: Compiled and adapted from MacMillan, I. C. "Competitive Strategies for Not-for-Profit Organizations." *Advances in Strategic Management.* Vol. 1. Greenwich, Conn.: JAI Press, 1983. Copyright © 1983 by JAI Press. Reprinted with permission from the publisher.

TABLE 4.3 MacMillan's Portfolio Analysis Matrix.

		Program Attractiveness			
		High		Low	
		Alternative Coverage		Alternative Coverage	
		High	Low	High	Low
	Strong	I	II	V	VI
		Aggressive competition	Aggressive growth	Build up best competitor	Soul of the agency
The Competitive Position of Your Programs and Services		COT's Traditional opera program	COT's opera camp		COT's curriculum development program
	Weak	III	IV	VII	VIII
		Aggressive divestment	Build strength or sell out	Orderly divestment	Joint venture
				COT's summer parks tour	

Source: Adapted from MacMillan, I. C. "Competitive Strategies for Not-for-Profit Organizations." Advances in Strategic Management. Vol. 1. Greenwich, Conn: JAI Press, 1983, p. 65. Copyright © 1983 by JAI Press. Reprinted with permission from the publisher.

the appropriate strategy for this part of your organization's portfolio is to consolidate your strong position by expanding the program as rapidly as possible, thereby discouraging other organizations that might contemplate a market penetration strategy. MacMillan suggests that every nonprofit organization should have at least one program in this cell of the matrix on which to build its future. COT's summer opera camp seems to fall in this category because it has little or no competition and it seems to have high potential for future growth. Following MacMillan's logic, COT would want to solidify its position in this program through a strategy of aggressive growth. Perhaps it could achieve economies of scale through a strategy of horizontal integration that would discourage prospective competitors from entering this attractive program area.

Cell III: aggressive divestment. This part of your organization's portfolio represents your least defensible position. Your organization has a weak position relative to other providers and is little more than a drain on scarce community resources. Therefore you should consider conceding your position to others who are more qualified to meet the need. Even though these programs are highly attractive, MacMillan recommends aggressive divestment, allowing the superior providers to serve the clientele. Obviously, the decision to walk away from these attractive (and potentially lucrative) programs requires vision, leadership, and moral courage.

Cell IV: build strength or sell out. With a program in this cell, your organization is providing an attractive program for which there is little or no competition. The unusual feature of this cell is that your organization is in a weak position despite the absence of strong competition. For example, this cell might contain a new program initiative for which the organization has not yet mastered the operational and administrative techniques to establish a true leadership position, even though it is nearly alone in blazing the trail. If your organization has slack resources and if the program is compatible with its mission, MacMillan recommends that you build the needed skills to establish a leadership position as quickly as possible, before other organizations erode your fragile comparative advantage. If resources are not available, you should identify and even assist other organizations that are better positioned than yours to take over responsibility for these programs.

Cell V: build up best competitor. In this part of its portfolio your organization finds itself in competition with other providers in delivering programs that are not very attractive. Normally, you would want to exit these markets as quickly as possible, allowing other organizations to provide these services. But your superior position in this unattractive program creates the obligation to transfer the skills that are providing your comparative advantage to the best of the other competing organizations.

Cell VI: soul of the agency. The programs your agency offers in this cell may be the only hope for clients who desperately need services not provided by other agencies. You must try to find ways to support these programs in your organization's portfolio even though they are not very attractive from a financial standpoint or perhaps even from the standpoint of community visibility. COT's curriculum development program may fall within this category. It is a program that will never generate excess revenue and, in fact, will likely need to be subsidized by other programs in COT's portfolio. But the curriculum development program represents the essence of COT's original mission. It represents the soul of Rose Curran's original vision for COT. MacMillan says that the strategic imperative is to find creative ways to use programs in the other cells to support, leverage, or promote the programs in this cell. Still, your agency will find it difficult to survive if its portfolio is dominated by programs in Cell VI. If nothing else, you must constantly search for innovative ways to guide clients in this cell toward self-sufficiency.

Cell VII: orderly divestment. This cell describes unattractive programs that already are provided by many other organizations. Your organization's weak position in this competitive environment makes the strategic choice quite clear: MacMillan suggests that you should concede these programs to the most competent competitors. But the concession should be carefully managed so as to minimize disruption to the clients. COT's summer parks tour might be classified in this cell. It seems that COT no longer is able to compete in the crowded summer entertainment marketplace. Still, it has sunk costs invested in this program and a small but loyal constituency, including the Smith Foundation. Thus, it should not simply abandon the parks tour but phase it out gradually, perhaps in cooperation with one of its competitors and certainly in close coordination with the Smith Foundation.

Cell VIII: joint venture. MacMillan notes that programs in this cell are rare. They may involve serving a very small number of clients with a very specific short-term need, such as helping a group of immigrants with transition services. Because your organization is in a weak position in this cell, the recommended approach is to seek assistance from another organization, so that both organizations jointly take responsibility for addressing the problem as effectively as possible, then move on to other activities that are more congruent with your organization's mission.

MacMillan notes that the matrix presented in Table 4.3 can be used to interpret *patterns* in your organization's portfolio, not just isolated programs in each of the eight cells. For example, if your organization's programs are concentrated in the four cells on the left side of the matrix, that is likely an indication that your organization has drifted away from the most difficult, hard-core social problems in favor of highly attractive programs that are easy to support. If your organization is ostensibly dedicated to the delivery of charitable social services, it will be open to the charge that it has abandoned its mission in favor of other performance objectives. Organizations that have all their programs and services on the left side of the matrix may face significant challenges to their accountability and ethics (see Kearns, 1996).

Conversely, if your organization's portfolio concentrates on the right side of the matrix, this may be the result of its having been repeatedly enticed into programs that offer the promise of temporary funding. When funding eventually disappears, you may find your organization locked into the program by significant exit barriers.

The ideal balance in MacMillan's matrix is a portfolio of programs of both high and low attractiveness in which the organization has a demonstrably strong position. In other words, the bulk of your programs and services should be in the upper half of the matrix with a balance between the more and the less attractive programs. MacMillan notes that this balance is achieved only with sustained strategic thinking and highly disciplined leadership. A balanced portfolio is achieved through these actions:

- Conceding attractive programs when your organization is in a weak position relative to other providers

- Constructively easing less capable providers out of attractive programs when it is clear your organization has a comparative advantage

- Ensuring that all programs in the portfolio are congruent with your organization's mission

MacMillan's matrix has several benefits as a tool for portfolio analysis in public and nonprofit organizations. First, the criteria for *competitive position* and *program attractiveness* are far more appropriate to public and nonprofit organizations than are those used in models of portfolio analysis for for-profit organizations or those used in the Gruber and Mohr model discussed earlier.

Second, the recommended strategies in the cells of MacMillan's model reflect the fact that public and nonprofit organizations often must collaborate with other organizations in fulfilling their missions. Even when organizations try to ease weaker competitors out of certain program areas, MacMillan recommends doing so in constructive ways, through negotiation and collaboration.

Third, MacMillan's framework is sensitive to the difficulty of shedding or divesting programs on which clients have become dependent. Public and nonprofit organizations simply cannot walk away from programs merely because they no longer contribute to the organization's performance objectives.

Finally, MacMillan's framework can alert executives to the dangers of *mission creep* in public and nonprofit organizations. The comparative advantages of nonprofit organizations are threatened when they succumb to the temptation to chase attractive programs simply because they offer financial stability or when they get locked into unattractive programs because of temporary funding streams.

Despite its many strengths, MacMillan's model suffers from some of the same weaknesses that plague all methods of portfolio analysis. In sum, these models create an illusion of certainty and objectivity by imposing artificially clear boundaries between parts of the organization's portfolio. Program attractiveness, for example, is a highly subjective construct that defies precise measurement or classification into roughly defined high and low categories.

Similarly, it is not easy to define the discrete program categories that form the parts of the portfolio. Even in multipurpose nonprofit organizations and government agencies, the programs and services that make up the portfolio often are not as discretely defined as, say, the product lines in a business. Personnel, for example, may be assigned to more than one program, and programs may share other resources as well. Moreover, different programs and services may serve the same client base, making it difficult to ascertain whether one program is more attractive than another to that group of clients.

Strengths and Weaknesses of Portfolio Analysis

Portfolio analysis can be a very helpful tool when you need to understand how well your programs and services are positioned to respond to challenges and opportunities in the external environment and how well they support your overall strategy of growth, retrenchment, or stability. But the greatest danger of portfolio analysis is a propensity to use it unreflectively. If you do, it may lead you to adopt predetermined strategies in an enthusiastic but overly hasty and blind effort to conform to whatever the matrix recommends. It is easy to be seduced by the apparent objectivity of portfolio analysis and to allow the "recipes" it presents to select strategies for you. In a way, the simple matching exercise advocated by portfolio analysis relieves decision makers of the responsibility to challenge assumptions, ask probing questions, and ultimately use their own imagination and skill to develop a strategy that is best for their organization.

Portfolio analysis is most valuable when it is used as a heuristic device, not as a cookbook for strategy development. In other words, when portfolio analysis helps us ask the right questions about our organizations, then it has taken us 90 percent of the way to the right solutions.

In the early 1990s, I (Kearns, 1992a) developed a framework for strategic issue analysis based on the principles of portfolio analysis presented earlier. The major difference is that this approach is designed to help decision makers identify and clarify *strategic issues* and *choices* rather than leap directly to the selection of strategies to address those issues. The matrix presented in Table 4.4 lends itself to the classification of four types of strategic issues and choices facing the organization.

Each cell of Table 4.4 highlights a different set of strategic choices facing the organization. Note that the cells do not contain recommended strategies. Rather, they lead participants in this analysis process to ask questions and make strategic choices that are best for them. This represents a fundamental departure from the methods of portfolio analysis presented earlier.

This approach to strategic issue analysis addresses some of the inherent problems associated with portfolio analysis. Specifically, strategic issue analysis does not try to *fit* a particular strategy to a particular mix of internal and external conditions. Instead, it stimulates dialogue and assumption-challenging interactions among participants in the strategic planning process. Although it provides a familiar framework (the matrix) in which to classify strategic issues, it also encourages analysis participants to think creatively, outside the box, when clarifying and ranking those issues.

Conclusion

Portfolio management in the public and nonprofit sectors is a more subtle art form than it is in the private, for-profit sector. In multiproduct firms, especially conglomerates, the various components of the portfolio are thought of as profit centers that can be bought and sold with relative ease, according to objective criteria related to profitability and the parent corporation's strategic objectives in the marketplace. In the public and nonprofit sectors, organizational mission must drive the overall approach to portfolio management.

TABLE 4.4 Strategic Issue Analysis.

Internal Factors	External Factors	
	Community Opportunities or Needs That Your Organization Can Meet	Threats to Your Ability to Fulfill Your Mission
Strong Programs or Services in Your Portfolio	**Comparative Advantage** *Strategic issue.* How can you leverage your strongest programs and services to build or enhance your organization's comparative advantage?	**Mobilization** *Strategic issue.* Can you mobilize your strongest programs and services to avert a threat or to minimize its negative impact?
Weak Programs or Services in Your Portfolio	**Comparative Disadvantage** *Strategic issue.* Should you invest in your weak programs to turn them into strengths? Should you divest weak programs in order to redirect your scarce resources? Should you seek a partner organization to compensate for your weaknesses?	**Damage Control** *Strategic issue.* Your weak programs and services make your organization extremely vulnerable to external threats. How can your organization minimize the damage likely to be inflicted?

Portfolio analysis, when used intelligently, can be a powerful tool for your public or nonprofit organization, especially when you want an overall view of your organization's products and services and how they work together to achieve organizational strategy. The greatest value of portfolio analysis may be as a heuristic device, a method for surfacing assumptions about and visualizing relationships among various parts of your organization. As is often the case with such tools, the real value of portfolio analysis is not in the answers or prescriptions it provides but in the questions it forces you to ask about your organization.

Getting Started

1. Is it useful to think of your organization as a multiproduct firm?

2. Are all your products and services contributing to your organization's mission and to its strategy? Are all your organization's products and services subject to the same competitive forces and pressures?

3. Is there any synergy among the parts of your organization's portfolio? Is that portfolio reasonably balanced, and does it provide a solid foundation for the future of your organization?

4. Does your organization really need to provide all the products and services currently in its portfolio?

5. How should COT position its programs and services to support its overall strategy?

PART TWO

Choosing the Right Strategy

5

Growth Strategies

I might have subtitled this chapter "opportunity and seduction," except that that has a rather ominous ring to it, perhaps implying that I have a bias against growth as an organizational strategy in the public and nonprofit sectors. To the contrary, I believe that growth is a desirable goal to which many organizations should aspire. Growth, when achieved in a responsible way, is a sign of an organization's success in anticipating and meeting the needs of citizens and clients (Corbin, 1999). Growth signifies progress, astute management of resources, and visionary leadership.

But for these very reasons growth may also be seductive and perhaps destructive (Ward, 1994). An organization may choose to pursue a growth strategy for the wrong reasons, such as advancing the professional ambitions of its managers instead of the organization's mission and goals. Or growth may be used to divert attention from problems lurking just beneath the surface. External impressions can be deceptive. Like a freshly painted home that is infested by termites, a growing organization may hide inefficiencies, waste, and even corruption.

In any consideration of growth strategies, executives should keep one thought at the forefront. In the public and nonprofit sectors, growth should never become an end in itself. Rather, growth is only a means to an end, one way among many to improve services and accountability to the publics these sectors serve.

Barbara Jenkins and the Lakeview Women's Center and Shelter

The Lakeview Women's Center and Shelter (LWCS) offers short-term shelter for female victims of domestic violence. The women who come to the shelter also are provided with counseling and referrals to other social service providers, law enforcement agencies, and legal assistance organizations. In addition, LWCS engages in public education programs and advocacy of public policies designed to combat domestic violence. LWCS is fifteen years old and has just completed the search for its third executive director.

Jenkins's Credentials

The trustees of LWCS were thrilled when Barbara Jenkins accepted their offer to become the new executive director. In addition to impressive management credentials, Jenkins brought with her a growing national reputation for her high-profile advocacy and educational activities. In her home state she had chaired a governor's task force on domestic violence, which pushed through several important legislative initiatives that subsequently served as models for other states. She was invited to a White House conference on domestic violence, and as a conference subcommittee spokesperson, she attracted some very favorable national publicity. Jenkins was far and away the most qualified and enthusiastic applicant for the job. Consequently, the trustees were unanimous in their support of her candidacy.

For Jenkins, too, the Lakeview job seemed to be the perfect fit for her skills and ambitions. LWCS was a moderately large and growing nonprofit organization; with a $3.7 million annual budget, it was much bigger and more complex than the agency she previously managed. It owned its main shelter facility and central offices in downtown Lakeview and leased several smaller branch facilities in outlying neighborhoods. LWCS enjoyed an excellent reputation among local philanthropies and corporations. Thus its funding was secure. Just as important to Jenkins, LWCS had made significant progress in its ancillary missions of public education and advocacy, and the trustees seemed receptive to the prospect of doing even more in that domain. Jenkins had secured approval from the trustees to earmark funds to hire a director of research, who would conduct research and publish findings on the various issues related to domestic violence—causes, effects, intervention strategies, and public policies. Jenkins wanted LWCS to do its own research and maintain its own databases, thereby becoming less reliant on secondary data sources.

The Emergence of the Growth Strategy

Soon Jenkins had LWCS on a trajectory of dramatic growth. She increased LWCS's budget by more than 50 percent, securing grants from local foundations to purchase the satellite shelters that LWCS had previously leased. She added several high-profile programs for clients' children and family members. The growing research and development (R&D) staff began to run workshops and seminars for social service professionals, charging tuition and fees for materials that gave a helpful boost to the budget. These workshops attracted participants from around the state and even from neighboring states. The staff were busy preparing for a summer workshop, which they planned to advertise nationally. They also had plans for distance learning workshops, teleconferencing, video productions, and interactive learning on a very sophisticated Web site. They even were considering a proposal from a Russian social service agency to organize and host an international teleconference on domestic violence.

The Proposal to Diversify LWCS

Despite this significant progress, Jenkins began to worry that LWCS would stagnate unless a new growth strategy was mobilized. After much thought, she came to the trustees with an idea. She proposed a radically new structure for LWCS, the centerpiece of which was the creation of a nonprofit foundation, or *holding company*, that would be the parent corporation for three organizations: (1) the existing LWCS, which would continue its charitable service to the Lakeview regions; (2) a new for-profit subsidiary organization that would provide consulting and educational products to a national audience; and (3) a new 501(c)(4) organization that would engage exclusively in political advocacy. With her characteristic thoroughness, Jenkins backed up her proposal with a detailed environmental scan (see Chapter Three) and portfolio analysis (see Chapter Four) that demonstrated beyond a reasonable doubt that the new ventures would be highly successful. In fact, within five years the income from the consulting arm of the organization would generate sufficient profit to subsidize nearly 25 percent of the two nonprofit entities. From a management standpoint, each subsidiary organization would have its own chief operating officer (COO). Jenkins would preside as president and chief executive officer (CEO) of the parent foundation, allowing her to focus her enormous talents on the "bigger" strategic issues, and three full-time managers would handle the daily details of each of the subsidiaries.

Despite the obvious merits of the plan, some trustees had serious reservations about it. They decided to schedule a retreat to give Jenkins's proposal a careful review. During the retreat they broke up into several discussion groups to generate a list of the pros and cons of the proposal. Here is a synopsis of their discussion.

The Arguments Against the Proposal

Drift from the original LWCS mission. A few of the current trustees had helped found the Lakeview Women's Center and Shelter and could remember the time, not all that long ago, when it struggled to keep itself afloat. In the early days the community offered minimal support and was highly skeptical that LWCS would survive to see its first birthday. Gradually, however, with an enormous investment of time and energy, LWCS began to carve out a legitimate place in Lakeview. It built its reputation on client services, not education and advocacy, demonstrating positive outcomes for women and their children.

Clash of cultures in LWCS. The original LWCS staff and volunteers were proud to provide a safe haven for women who had lost all hope, many of whom were also in grave danger. LWCS filled a gaping hole in the social service infrastructure of Lakeview. Several of the trustees sensed that some of the early passion that had pervaded LWCS had gradually been drained from the organization. They noted the apparent tension between staff who worked in the shelters and staff who traveled all over the country giving speeches and planning seminars. There seemed to be some jealousy, jockeying for position, and competition for Jenkins's attention and also more blatant budgetary battles than every before.

Loss of motivation among the trustees. Despite Jenkins's enthusiasm, several trustees were not very motivated by the prospect of developing a "strategically positioned portfolio of services." They had joined the board of trustees because they felt passionately about the LWCS mission. Several trustees were themselves survivors of domestic abuse. These trustees found themselves feeling isolated and out of their depth as board meetings were increasingly dominated by market forecasts, pricing strategies, reports of earned revenue, and legislative agendas in Washington. They found the new strategy, which Jenkins described as "horizontal and vertical integration" to be numbing and far removed from the organization's original mission to provide safe shelter to abused women in Lakeview. They noted that there were very few volunteers at LWCS anymore. Nearly all staff members were full-time paid professionals. In sum, they simply felt the organization was drifting too far from its roots.

Bad timing for growth. A few of the trustees softened their negative statements by saying that they were not against growth in principle but that now was simply the wrong time to take on a set of new initiatives. They noted that LWCS had just weathered three years of explosive growth under Jenkins's leadership. Now, they suggested, was the time to consolidate some of these gains and focus inwardly. They said, "It's time to get our own house back in order."

Too much reliance on Jenkins. Finally, one of the critics of the plan put on the table the issue that was on many minds in the room, "This plan seems too dependent on the vision and skill of Barbara Jenkins. I have no doubts about her ability to carry this out successfully. But should we base our strategy so completely on the skills and capabilities of one person? What if Barbara decides to take another job, or what if something dreadful happens that prevents her from continuing in this job? What on earth will we do then after making such a major commitment to this national agenda?"

The Arguments Favoring the Proposal

Stabilization and support of the original mission. Some trustees argued that LWCS could ensure its future with Jenkins's strategy. Gone were the days of living from hand to mouth, chasing grants, and worrying about paying the rent. "We can't romanticize those early difficult days in LWCS," said one veteran trustee. "Let's not forget that those days were stressful and exhausting. We couldn't meet our payroll some months! We had to turn away women who needed us! Today we are serving more clients in Lakeview with better services than we ever dreamed of at the beginning. We can't turn back now." Supporters of the plan said that the proposed portfolio of services was "perfectly consistent" with the original mission and chartered mandate of LWCS.

A *moral obligation to use organizational strengths.* One of the trustees surprised everyone by saying that LWCS had a "moral obligation" to grow, sharing its expertise with other communities and expanding the "cause" of protecting abused women to a national, even international, scale: "As long as we do not neglect the needs right here in Lakeview, I believe we must share what we have learned with other communities."

A *need to address causes, not just symptoms, of domestic violence.* The envisioned plan, the supporting trustees suggested, would help LWCS play a role in *prevention* of domestic violence, not just in providing temporary shelter to victims of that violence. They argued that foundations and donors were increasingly demanding that LWCS provide evidence of outcomes, not just outputs. The new strategy, they argued, would focus on solutions and remedies without abandoning the urgent needs of women and children who needed temporary shelter.

Opportunities for collaboration. The growth strategy presented by Jenkins contained several opportunities for LWCS to collaborate with other agencies locally, nationally, and even internationally. "We live in a global society," said one trustee. "We can't have a parochial attitude and focus only on Lakeview." Some trustees noted that many foundations and grantmaking organizations had adopted policies demanding collaborative efforts as a condition of funding. The new proposal would bolster the fundraising efforts of LWCS in Lakeview as well as around the country.

Perfect timing for growth. Although acknowledging that the staff and volunteers of LWCS had been "stretched pretty thin" over the past three years, the supporters of Jenkins's plan said emphatically that now was the *perfect time* to launch this new strategy: "We are riding the wave of a growing national reputation. If we stop now we will lose momentum and send a very confusing signal to the external constituencies who are waiting for us to make a decision. We have to strike now while the opportunity is hot!"

The trustees deliberated the proposal well into the evening. We'll return to the case throughout this chapter. But let's step back now to examine the strategic options and issues illustrated by LWCS.

Types of Growth Strategies

An organization can grow in two ways. First, it can focus on delivering more of the programs and services that are already in its portfolio, essentially doing more of what it already does. This is called a *concentration growth* strategy, because the organization *concentrates* its efforts on expanding the impact of its current portfolio, not on branching out into new programs or services. There are several types of concentration strategies. An organization follows a strategy of *horizontal growth* whenever it tries to expand the geographical scope of its portfolio or reach out to new markets that it is not now serving. An organization follows a *vertical growth* strategy whenever it tries to gain greater control over its supply or distribution channels. I illustrate each of these strategies and their costs and benefits in the subsequent discussion.

The second type of growth occurs when an organization adds new programs and services to its portfolio. This is called a *diversification* strategy. An organization engages in *concentric diversification* when it adds programs or services that are similar or fundamentally related to its existing portfolio. An organization follows a *conglomerate diversification* strategy when it adds programs and services that are not related to each other.

Whether your organization concentrates on its current portfolio or diversifies into other products and services, it can choose between two ways to implement these growth strategies. First, it can use its existing resources. This is called *internal growth*. Or it can acquire the resources it needs from another organization through collaboration, acquisition, or merger. This is called *external growth*.

Taken together, these parameters create a rather wide variety of growth strategies, as depicted in Table 5.1.

Concentration Strategies

Concentration strategies, presented in the top half of Table 5.1, are the most popular growth strategies in the public and nonprofit sectors because they do not require a change in an organization's core mission or its portfolio of programs and services. When you embark on a concentration growth strategy, you are, in effect, expressing strong confidence in your organization's existing portfolio of programs and services. You simply want to reach more people with these programs or enhance your efficiency in their production and distribution. If you choose a concentration growth strategy, you should have a high level of confidence in your organization's comparative

TABLE 5.1 Dimensions of Growth Strategies.

Growth Strategies	Concentration (build on current portfolio)	Horizontal integration (expanding geographical market and production capacity)	Accomplished internally (with own resources)
			Accomplished externally (via collaboration, acquisition, or merger)
		Vertical integration (gaining control of supply and distribution channels)	Accomplished internally
			Accomplished externally
	Diversification (build new portfolio)	Concentric diversification (diversifying into related products and services)	Accomplished internally
			Accomplished externally
		Conglomerate diversification (diversifying into unrelated products and services)	Accomplished internally
			Accomplished externally

advantages and its ability to provide the necessary portfolio at least as well as other providers. With this approach to growth, your organization is making a renewed investment in the programs and services in which it already has a track record.

Here are some issues to think about when contemplating a concentration strategy:

- Does our organization have a strong comparative advantage over other organizations in the production and delivery of certain programs and services?

- Is the demand among citizens or clients for these programs and services likely to remain strong for the foreseeable future?

- If it seems that demand will be strong for the foreseeable future, how can our organization serve more people with its programs and services?

- Is it possible to strengthen our organization's already strong position vis-à-vis other providers?

- Would it be helpful for our organization to gain greater control over the supply of raw materials and other inputs it needs to produce its programs and services?

- Would it be helpful for our organization to gain greater control over the distribution channels for its programs and services?

- Is it desirable for our organization to extend the boundaries of its service area to include people or regions it is not now serving?

These are relatively straightforward questions, not all that different from the ones you might have asked yourself after your first childhood experience with a commercial venture, say, selling lemonade: "How can I sell more lemonade to more people?" (concentric growth). "Should I set up a second stand at that busy intersection two blocks away?" (horizontal growth). "Can I convince Mom to give me more lemons?" (horizontal growth). "Could I get my lemons from a different source, or even buy my own lemon tree, instead of relying on Mom's patience and generosity, both of which seem to be running out?" (vertical growth). "Should I try to convince Jimmy, who also has a lemonade stand, to join forces with me?" (external growth).

Concentration growth strategies do not require a leap of faith or a stretch of the imagination in relation to the mission and goals of the organization. The goal is simple: get more people to use your organization's programs and services (sell more lemonade). But you may use various strategies to achieve this goal.

Horizontal Growth

When your organization is doing well with its current portfolio of programs and services, your first inclination may be to produce more of those programs and services and to provide them to a wider market. This strategy is known as horizontal growth.

Sometimes horizontal growth is essential to achieve sufficient economies of scale to make a program or service economically feasible or politically acceptable. A small municipality maintained a modest animal control program, using makeshift equipment (borrowed from the public works department) and cross-trained personnel from various departments. However, the fledgling program was in danger of being closed by the city council, and the city manager knew that the service would continue to be a drain on scarce resources and would never amount to a professional program unless she could somehow increase its coverage beyond the municipal borders. Over lunch with officials from two neighboring towns, the city manager struck a deal to provide animal control services to all three communities. With the larger coverage area and a substantial increase in service fees, the animal control program became a first-rate, professionally staffed service with state-of-the-art equipment and procedures. This example also illustrates one popular approach to horizontal integration, which is to increase the geographical coverage or scope of a program.

Benefits and Costs of Horizontal Growth

Horizontal integration is, in many respects, the most conservative and the safest growth strategy. After all, the organization simply continues to do what it currently is doing quite well, except on a larger scale and perhaps covering a wider geographical area. Here are the main benefits of horizontal integration.

A relatively flat learning curve. A horizontal growth strategy does not require you or your employees to master new skills except for learning how to expand the scale of the organization's operation without losing control and coordination. In the case of the Lakeview Women's Center and Shelter, Barbara Jenkins and her staff are already experts in the field of domestic violence. As they expand their educational and advocacy activities to a national and international scale, much of what they already know about their work will be transferable.

Modest entry costs. Once an organization has established a formidable presence in the marketplace, the costs of expansion within that industry are not as great as the costs of entering a new industry. LWCS, for example, will incur some legal expenses to arrange its new organizational structure, and of course operational expenses will increase as the scope of activities expands beyond Lakeview. But these expenses pale in comparison with what it would cost to enter an entirely new industry.

Continuity of mission and culture. Because horizontal growth typically does not have a significant effect on an organization's core mission, the continuity of the organization and its operating culture is not compromised. The trustees of LWCS are wise to worry about the changes in the LWCS culture. But the mission of LWCS will remain fundamentally unchanged under Jenkins's proposal.

High levels of employee commitment and morale. Horizontal growth is easy for all employees to understand, and for nearly all of them it signifies the organization's success in fulfilling its core purpose. Other types of growth, like diversification, can confuse employees and send the unintended message that the organization's core products are threatened.

Enhancement of comparative advantage. Producing larger quantities of a program or service for delivery to a larger market share can enhance your organization's comparative advantage by producing economies of scale not enjoyed by smaller providers. Horizontal growth can help you leverage your organization's bargaining power with vendors and other key stakeholders, thereby increasing the entry costs for prospective competitors. If LWCS embarks on this proposed strategy, it will set the pace for other organizations to follow. In effect it will raise the entry costs for any other organization that is contemplating a similar move.

In addition to these advantages to horizontal integration, there are potential pitfalls. Michael Porter (1980, pp. 324–338) notes that many of these pitfalls stem from a propensity for organizations to overbuild their production capacity during phases of horizontal growth, overshooting the mark in meeting consumer needs and being left with expensive excess production capacity.

Vertical Growth

A more aggressive approach to growth is known as vertical growth, often called *vertical integration* because the objective is to integrate input, throughput, and output processes. If your organization follows this approach to growth, it will try to seize greater control over (1) the supply of resources used to produce its programs and services (*backward vertical integration*) and (2) the distribution system and mechanisms used to deliver the programs and services to consumers (*forward vertical integration*). Typically organizations consider vertical integration when they have a strong comparative advantage or a dominant position in the marketplace.

There are several reasons to pursue a strategy of vertical integration. First, this strategy might solidify the organization's position as an industry leader. Second, you might feel forced to adopt a strategy of vertical integration because the supply channels or distribution networks for your organization's programs and services are threatened by forces beyond your control.

The case study at the beginning of this chapter provides an example of backward vertical integration. Barbara Jenkins added an internal research capacity to LWCS rather than relying on secondary research supplied by other organizations.

In the environment of managed care, many large hospitals are engaging in both backward and forward vertical integration. Some nonteaching hospitals have sought affiliations with, or even purchased, medical colleges. This backward vertical integration strategy gives the hospitals a steady supply of interns, residents, and other professionals and adds a teaching and research component to their portfolios of programs and services. Hospitals follow a forward vertical integration strategy when they purchase physician practices and groups. These medical practices become in effect a distribution network for the hospitals' portfolios of goods and services.

Benefits and Costs of Vertical Growth

Vertical integration is a more ambitious and aggressive growth strategy than horizontal integration. Consequently, the benefits can be substantial, but the stakes are high and the risks too are significant. Again, Michael Porter (1980, pp. 300–323) provides very useful insights into the benefits and costs of vertical integration in corporations. Some of the same benefits and costs apply to public and nonprofit organizations.

Vertical integration can have the following benefits:

Increased control and coordination. When an organization gains control of its supply and distribution channels, it is able to more fully coordinate related production processes. Thus the vertical integration strategy proposed by Barbara Jenkins may help LWCS to more precisely coordinate the processes of providing temporary shelter, conducting research, and leading advocacy campaigns. By gaining control of the research component, LWCS can coordinate research processes with advocacy and shelter activities, leading, in theory, to better outcomes all around.

Reduced transaction costs. When an organization relies on vendors for supply and distribution services, it incurs transaction costs for such processes as negotiation of prices, administration of contracts, quality control, and troubleshooting. When supply and distribution functions are performed in house, some of these transaction costs are reduced or even eliminated. Barbara Jenkins will reduce many of these transactions costs, though they may be trivial, by incorporating her own research and education costs.

Stability. Relationships with vendors can be inherently unstable. Vendors themselves exist in a competitive environment, and their prices can fluctuate wildly in response to market and competitive forces. Even the availability of their products can be threatened. A vertically integrated organization enjoys the luxury of being not quite so vulnerable to fluctuations in supply and distribution.

Ability to differentiate the final product or service. Vertical integration gives an organization more discretion and flexibility to tailor its programs and services to meet the needs and preferences of consumers because it gives the organization greater control over the supply of inputs at each stage of the production and distribution process. Thus the vertically integrated organization has greater latitude to make adjustments in design or delivery that will differentiate its programs and services from others in the marketplace. Barbara Jenkins and LWCS will be able to tailor educational and advocacy projects to specific audiences by virtue of having in-house research and educational capabilities.

Higher entry barriers for potential competitors. From a purely competitive standpoint, a fully integrated organization represents a more formidable target for potential competitors, often leading them to conclude that they cannot afford to enter the market.

The benefits of vertical integration are significant but so are the hidden costs. Here are a few costs of vertical integration that should be fully considered before employing this strategy:

High entry costs. Most obviously, vertical integration is expensive to achieve. Gaining control of supply and distribution channels often involves large investments in equipment, expertise, people, and facilities. Although Barbara Jenkins has effectively avoided high initial entry costs by building her research and educational capacities incrementally, her long-term financial outlay will be substantial. She has been gradually guiding LWCS toward the strategy of vertical and horizontal integration over several years.

High operating costs. In nonintegrated organizations many of the costs of supply and distribution are counted as *variable costs*, because they rise or fall in relation to production. In fully integrated systems, these are counted as *fixed costs*, because the organization owns and must support the infrastructure to maintain them regardless of fluctuations in production. Thus the fully integrated organization has high fixed costs that affect both its overall financial stability and the break-even point of any future venture. In other words, once Jenkins begins to build her staff to handle the expanded operations, then these resources will become fixed costs— part of the LWCS infrastructure. However, if she continues to rely on vendors for research, education, and advocacy consultations, then these expenses will be variable costs, which LWCS could increase or decrease depending on its needs.

High exit barriers, high mobility barriers, and reduced flexibility. A fully integrated organization makes a major commitment to its core product or service by taking control of supply and distribution channels. This sizable commitment can increase an organization's vulnerability to fluctuations in demand for the core product or service. Everything about an integrated organization is larger and more complex than it is in a nonintegrated one. They are like ocean liners in comparison with speed boats: not very maneuverable. Jenkins will be adding mass and volume to LWCS, making it less mobile. It is likely that LWCS will become more compartmentalized and bureaucratized as the growth continues. Jenkins already contemplates adding additional administrative layers between herself and the daily operations. She will need to work hard to combat this natural tendency.

Reduced flow of technology from vendors. We often forget that vendors give organizations access to new ideas and innovative technologies as well as a supply of goods and services. Integrated organizations are at least partially cut off from this flow of technological innovation because they have limited or even eliminated external vendors. Although vertically integrated organizations are more self-sufficient, they also are more insulated from the outside world. If Jenkins's plan is approved by the LWCS trustees, LWCS will assume almost total responsibility for research and development, essentially cutting itself off from the expertise previously provided by vendors.

High demands on managers. A vertically integrated organization demands particular types of managerial skill and technical expertise. Managing a full range of functions (supply, production, distribution) demands an extremely talented, even gifted, chief executive officer. The trustees of LWCS must have complete faith in Barbara Jenkins to manage the newly designed organization. But just as important, they must conclude that the restructured LWCS could be managed by someone else should Jenkins ever leave or be unable to perform her duties. In other words, they would be well advised to reject the proposal if they conclude that Jenkins is the only person in their hiring environment who is capable of pulling it off.

The vertically integrated organization is much more complex than the nonintegrated one. This complexity can be both a blessing and a curse. On the one hand, there are compelling benefits from controlling your own destiny and establishing your organization as the dominant player in the marketplace. On the other hand, integration carries the burden of added costs, reduced flexibility, and enormous demands on management.

Diversification Strategies

Diversification strategies might be appropriate for your organization, depending on how you answer the following questions:

- Is the demand for our organization's current portfolio of programs and services likely to shrink in the foreseeable future? If so, diversification might be necessary before the bottom drops out of the market for that existing portfolio.

- Does our organization have *spin-off* expertise; can it apply its skills to the delivery of programs and services that are not currently in its portfolio? If so, this expertise might be directed toward more fruitful activities as demand shifts away from the organization's current portfolio. Harold Geneen was fond of saying that the core expertise of ITT was "management," not telecommunications. He believed that management was a transferable skill that could be directed to a vast array of subsidiaries.

- Can diversification open new opportunities for synergy among the programs and services in our organization's portfolio or with other organizations?

- Can our organization diversify without losing sight of our core mission? Will diversification help to advance our core mission?

These are the questions to ask when you suspect that your organization's current portfolio of programs and services may be endangered or when its mission could be advanced more effectively with a more diverse portfolio. Perhaps demand for the current portfolio is waning because the programs and services have become obsolete. Perhaps other providers have penetrated the marketplace, leading to more intense competition. Perhaps the current portfolio has simply reached its maximum growth potential. These and other factors might justify diversification strategies.

Concentric Diversification

The most frequently used diversification strategy in the public and nonprofit sectors is concentric diversification, wherein an organization adds products and services to its portfolio that are fundamentally *related* to its current portfolio. This can be a very effective strategy for an organization that has acquired skills, resources, and competitive advantages that are readily applicable to the production of related (or at least comparable) programs and services. Similarly, in the LWCS case study, Barbara Jenkins proposed a diversification strategy that will add consulting services to the organization's existing portfolio of shelter, research, and advocacy programs. But the consulting services are directly related to the existing portfolio.

Typically, when looking for opportunities for concentric diversification, decision makers will try to enhance the synergy between the programs and services in the current portfolio and the new programs and services added by diversification. In other words, concentric diversification seeks to make the whole more than the sum of its parts. Thus a Red Cross chapter in a major city added to its portfolio a transportation program for the elderly and the handicapped, driving them to doctor appointments and assisting them with other essential transportation needs. This new service, even though diverging slightly from the mission of disaster relief, was a natural fit with the logistical expertise the Red Cross had acquired through its core business. Even more important, the visibility of the Red Cross chapter was greatly enhanced by the presence of many vans (all displaying the famous logo) driving around town providing a service that people can readily appreciate and even envision themselves using. The enhanced visibility has helped the Red Cross chapter shore up its image in the community.

Concentric diversification may also be the appropriate strategic response when an organization's core business is threatened. For example, an AIDS counseling program has acquired expertise in political advocacy and health counseling that can be transferred to other domains, even as demand for its core product has declined.

Conglomerate Diversification

Conglomerate diversification involves the addition of products and services that are unrelated to the organization's core mission. Conglomerate diversification is somewhat less prevalent in the public and nonprofit sectors than in the business world. The best examples are found among nonprofit organizations that engage in unrelated business ventures as a means of earning supplemental income to support a core mission (see Skloot, 1988).

Benefits and Costs of Diversification

Diversification is growing in popularity, especially in the nonprofit sector. The Internal Revenue Service reports, for example, that a growing number of nonprofit organizations are paying unrelated business income tax (UBIT) on the proceeds of income-producing ventures that are unrelated to their charitable, tax-exempt purposes.

Diversification in the public and nonprofit sectors can have the following benefits:

Revenue generation. Diversification into related or unrelated businesses can generate revenue to support the core mission of an organization.

Responsiveness to community needs. Diversification can be a way of responding to changing needs in the community. Even the most stable and conservative organizations must occasionally make changes in their portfolios to respond to new needs.

Increased adaptation and innovation. Diversification can, under the right circumstances, be a mechanism for continuous organizational renewal, innovation, and learning. In multiproduct organizations, knowledge and technology can be transferred from one product line to another.

Increased buffering against cyclical markets. A diversified organization might enjoy a margin of immunity from the market cycles that plague single-product organizations. Low demand for one part of its portfolio might be compensated for by high demand for other parts of the portfolio.

Survival. If demand for an organization's core programs and services decreases dramatically or ceases entirely, then diversification into related or unrelated products might be the only avenue to survival.

Conversely, diversification carries many costs that should be fully factored into any growth strategy. Even the corporate sector has become wary of diversification strategies, based on their own experience and on research suggesting that successful organizations tend to "stick to the knitting" (Peters and Waterman, 1982) by developing greater competence in their core businesses rather than diversifying into product lines in which they have no distinctive competence. Here are some specific concerns regarding diversification in the public and nonprofit sectors.

Potential for mission creep. Public and nonprofit organizations are more mission bound than their counterparts in the corporate world. The diversified organization runs the risk of losing sight of its core purpose and mission as it tries to simultaneously manage multiple programs and services.

Perceived need to be all things to all people. Similar to mission creep is the trap of trying to be all things to all people, adding a program here and a service there each time a new need arises in the marketplace. A diversified organization sometimes loses sight of its focus and its comparative advantages.

Increased management challenges. A diversified organization is more difficult to manage, due to the variety of consumers, markets, programs, and professional disciplines served by and embodied in the organization. Problems of vertical and lateral communication are accentuated in diversified organizations.

Threats to the organizational culture. Public and nonprofit organizations often have powerful organizational cultures, rooted in strongly held beliefs about the sanctity of the organization's core mission, its values and philosophies, and the people it serves (Young, 1988).

The addition of new programs and services to the portfolio, especially when they are not related to the core mission, may be perceived as a threat to the organization's implicit values, beliefs, and norms. In effect, diversification can threaten the core identity of the organization.

Questionable ability to perform accurate market analysis. Adding a new program or service to a portfolio requires having very clear objectives for the new enterprise, including a full and careful accounting of its costs and benefits (Skloot, 1988; Massarsky, 1988; Crimmins and Kiel, [1983] 1990). Does your organization want to make a profit, provide a community service, address an underserved population, or position itself for future opportunities? Although business firms are adept at conducting formal market analysis based on clear objectives, public and nonprofit organizations have little experience with techniques like portfolio analysis, cost accounting, and break-even analysis (see Chapters Seven and Eight).

Use of diversification to mask failure. Organizations that fail with one portfolio may be inclined to try their hand at yet another product or service. Chances are they will fail again.

Need to maintain accountability in the face of public scrutiny. The general public authorizes government and nonprofit organizations to pursue a relatively limited range of purposes as specified in law and, perhaps more important, as implicitly specified in the expectations of taxpayers, philanthropists, and citizens. When decision makers diverge from this implied agenda by diversifying into related or unrelated business ventures, they may become the target of criticism.

Thus diversification in the public and nonprofit sectors is risky for many of the same reasons that it is risky in the corporate sector. Government and nonprofit organizations, like their business counterparts, are more likely to succeed when they diversify into *related* products and services, where they can draw upon their expertise and remain true to their core missions.

Internal Growth Versus External Growth

Concentration and diversification strategies can be accomplished via *internal* or *external* growth. Internal growth occurs when an organization enhances its own capacity to produce more goods and services and to distribute them more widely. External growth is accomplished through mergers, acquisitions, consolidations, and joint ventures. Thus a hospital grows internally when it opens a neighborhood health clinic, using its existing staff or hiring new staff to run the facility. It engages in external growth when it purchases an existing neighborhood health clinic.

Typically, internal growth requires a substantial investment in infrastructure, new program development, and process control in order to increase the organization's capacity to produce more and more programs and services. For example, a hospital that opens a neighborhood health clinic may have no substantial expertise in the methods of comprehensive, community-based health care. All of its existing processes and skills may be oriented toward treatment of inpatients for acute illnesses and treatment of trauma cases in its emergency room. But when a hospital purchases an existing neighborhood clinic, with the stroke of a pen it instantly also acquires the capability of delivering the clinic's services to a relatively large population. Consequently, internal growth tends to be relatively incremental because of the need to build up internal capabilities and expertise, whereas external growth often circumvents the need for extensive research and development because capabilities and expertise are acquired from other organizations.

Thus, if your organization is trying to make the choice between growing internally or externally, you may want to address questions like the following:

- Assuming that growth is the appropriate strategy, can we grow on our own, or do we need the assistance of another organization?

- Does our organization have the necessary resources, skills, willpower, and time to grow on its own? What is preventing it from using internal growth strategies?

- What investment is our organization able and willing to make to expand its capacity? Is it possible to accomplish the growth objectives internally?

- Are there any targets of opportunity for external growth? Do we know of other organizations looking for a partner or a savior?

- Will the weaknesses of our organization preclude an external growth strategy? Or will other organizations find it an attractive partner?

External growth is accomplished through mergers, acquisitions, consolidations, and joint ventures. Each of these approaches is briefly described in the following sections.

Mergers

A *merger* is the "total absorption of one organization by another whose corporate existence is preserved" (Yankey, 1991, p. 2). Although a merger is a legally binding action, there is not necessarily an exchange of assets. In other words, the absorbed organization is not necessarily purchased by the absorbing organization. The absorbed organization is dissolved and its assets are transferred to the absorbing organization. The absorbed organization retains no legal status. A merger can help the absorbing organization diversify services, gain geographical market share, enhance economies of scale, or acquire new expertise (Yankey, 1991), while saving the absorbed organization from extinction or providing access to new resources to advance the mission.

Chief executive officers and boards of directors play a key role in all phases of mergers: making the decision to merge, selecting potential partners for the merger, planning and negotiating the merger, and implementing and stabilizing the new combined organization. Also, there are likely to be many technical experts involved in the process, including attorneys, financial experts, and management consultants.

Acquisition

An *acquisition* is the purchase of all or part of one organization by another in which the acquired organization becomes a subsidiary of the acquiring organization. In an acquisition, there is a transfer of ownership from one organization to another. Acquisitions serve many of the same purposes as mergers by advancing objectives related to horizontal and vertical integration. In addition, and because acquisitions involve a formal purchase and commitment of assets, they must be viewed as a financial investment that is expected to yield certain financial dividends for the acquiring organization. Consequently, the acquiring organization generally will have an explicit business strategy for the acquired organization that will contribute to its own grand strategy.

Although acquisitions are not frequent in the public sector, they have become increasingly prevalent (and controversial) in the nonprofit sector. Especially noteworthy has been the acquisition of nonprofit hospitals by for-profit corporations. These transactions, governed by state law, generally require that the assets of the nonprofit organization be fairly valued and used to capitalize a private foundation to carry on the charitable purpose for which the nonprofit hospital was originally chartered. There have been concerns, however, whether these assets have been fairly and completely valued. These are, after all, community assets that have been invested in the nonprofit organization over a period of many years by charitable donations, grants, and public contracts. Critics have noted that the assets are often undervalued, resulting in a windfall for the purchasing corporation. Also, many people have questioned the closed-door negotiations that lead up to the such acquisitions. There have been calls for greater openness and accountability in the process (Claxton, Feder, Shactman, and Altman, 1997).

Consolidation

A *consolidation* is a transaction involving the pooling of assets between two or more organizations and resulting in the creation of a third organization and the extinguishing of the original organization. Often the corporate identity of the resulting organization will be an amalgam of the identities of its predecessors. In the public sector, consolidations are sometimes imposed by the courts to achieve certain objectives, like school desegregation.

Joint Ventures

A *joint venture* is a cooperative activity among two or more organizations in which all parties retain their corporate identities and autonomy. In the corporate world a joint venture often involves the creation of an independent business entity to undertake projects that none of the partners could profitably undertake on its own. In the public and nonprofit sectors a joint venture is usually less formal, taking the form of a cooperative agreement among two or more organizations. Still, the joint venture, even if it does not result in the incorporation of a new organization, generally involves a contractual agreement in which each party agrees to certain obligations and holds certain rights over the other parties.

Joint ventures provide a mechanism for temporarily drawing upon the strengths of the participating organizations without sacrificing long-term organizational autonomy. Consequently, they are more popular than mergers or acquisitions in the public and nonprofit sectors.

Conclusion

The objective of any growth strategy is to improve the fit or alignment between your organization and its environment. Growth strategies make very good sense when your organization has a true comparative advantage, when its strengths and distinctive competencies allow it to benefit from capitalizing on existing or emerging opportunities.

Vertical integration is appropriate only for organizations that can demonstrate extraordinary strengths in a market that shows strong potential for continued growth into the foreseeable future. This of course is the ideal strategic situation—to which all organizations may aspire, but which only a few attain. Because of its high costs and high risks, however, vertical integration is not a wise strategy for an organization trying to hold its own in a declining line of business.

Horizontal integration, on the other hand, may be a viable growth strategy for a wider range of organizations. With its lower costs and lower risks, horizontal integration can be used by moderately strong organizations to solidify their competitive position or better serve the community.

In general, conglomerate and concentric growth strategies make sense only if your organization has *portable* competencies that can help it diversify its portfolio of programs and services. Diversification may strengthen the long-term prospects for your organization, especially if you foresee an eventual decline in demand for your current portfolio of programs and services.

Getting Started

1. If your organization is in a growth mode, does it have an explicit growth strategy, or is it simply growing opportunistically in response to changing needs and circumstances? What are the pros and cons of each approach?

2. In what ways has growth advanced the mission of your organization? In what ways has growth impeded the mission?

3. If you were a member of the LWCS board of trustees, would you support or reject Barbara Jenkins's proposal? What additional information would you want before making a decision?

4. Suppose the board of trustees votes to approve Jenkins's plan. What implementation issues will she need to address?

6

Retrenchment Strategies

A few years ago a friend invited me to join a casual Friday night poker game. We play about once a month for nickels, dimes, and quarters. "Even with the worst of luck," my friend assured me, "it is difficult to lose more than five dollars in a game. Not a bad price for an evening of entertainment." Quite true, but early on I developed a nasty habit of defying the odds by losing considerably more than five dollars. As a novice, I did not fully understand the strategy of the game. I had difficulty recognizing a bad hand when the dealing began and difficulty assessing the odds of improving on the hand as the game went on. I had only a vague idea of how strong a hand was needed to win a particular game. I was so focused on my own hand that I paid no attention to the cards held by my friends around the table, and I had no sense of the strategies they used in playing their cards. I tended to hang on to poor hands far too long in the naïve hope that I would improve my lot. Even when I recognized a bad hand at the outset, I sometimes tried bluffing and delaying tactics, but these only dug me deeper into the hole. Not surprisingly, my victories were few and far between and always due to pure luck of the draw.

There was also an emotional and psychological aspect to my early failures. Often I was in denial that my hand was truly bad and not likely to improve with subsequent draws. The thought of folding my cards seemed an admission of defeat. I thought it was bad form to fold early. Now I see it as a subtle form of vanity and arrogance. The winning strategy sometimes is to fold early and live to fight another day. Retreat, or retrenchment, can conserve critical resources and lay the foundation for later victories. Trivial as playing games of cards is in relation to running an organization, sometimes the same logic applies in management.

This chapter explores the strategy of retrenchment and the contexts in which retrenchment strategies are most appropriate. It discusses some specific tactics of retrenchment, and it also examines the costs and benefits of these strategies.

The Municipal Budget Crisis

The town of Clairsville is experiencing a fiscal crisis. After the town defaulted on one of its many loans, the state intervened by appointing an interim management team to recommend solutions to the problem. The team members gathered for a weekend retreat to assess the situation. First, they sketched the chronology of events and actions leading up to the crisis:

The years from 1980 to 1985 brought modest revenue growth to Clairsville as local industries invested cautiously in new equipment, personnel, and marketing. The population grew slightly and property values increased a little more than the rate of inflation. Interest groups and coalitions in the town were relatively fragmented and inactive. The elected officials made incremental investments in infrastructure, social services, and education.

The years from 1985 to 1992 began with flat revenues, which then showed a moderate but sustained downward trend as local industries divested and moved parts or all of their operations to other locations. Population in Clairsville declined gradually, and property values began to stagnate and then fall moderately relative to the rate of inflation. The mayor and other elected officials responded with a strategy of delay and denial. "The problem is cyclical," they said. "Things will improve when the economy takes off again." Operating revenues fell short of expenses, but this was easily handled by clever budget manipulation, deferral of expenses, and short-term borrowing. The town made no concerted effort to decrease its spending. Interest groups, though still fragmented, began to voice their self-interests. In particular, police and fire unions began seeking protection of positions and salaries. Various community groups started to mobilize around neighborhood issues.

The years from 1992 to 1997 brought more substantial decline as revenues fell faster. Initial denial gave way to several high-profile productivity and quality improvement programs throughout the Clairsville bureaucracy in an effort to stretch resources. Corporate executives were "loaned" to the town to identify cost-saving strategies. A major study, financed by a coalition of corporate CEOs, recommended strategies to attract new businesses to Clairsville. When these efforts failed to fill the gap between expenditures and revenues, the mayor took the "bold step" of initiating across-the-board cuts, but many of these were in the form of deferred expenditures and reductions in personnel by attrition. The town then sold its water treatment facility and used the revenues to help "balance" its 1997 operating budget. Wall Street responded by downgrading Clairsville's bond rating.

In 1998, the town's largest employer announced that it would phase out its operations over a three-year period. The company planned to close its plant completely in 2001 and move its headquarters to another city. Overall this would result in the loss of five thousand jobs.

Beginning in 1999, revenues dropped precipitously as the effects of the closure began to be felt. Many of the town's revenue sources were affected by the closure—property, occupation, and wage taxes; license and user fees; and so on. For the first time the mayor made deep and targeted cuts, focusing on social services, parks and recreation, public works, and general administration. Also, the town began divesting services (a public hospital, courts, a community college) to other organizations. The mayor asked the state to assume responsibility for maintenance of certain roads. In a controversial move, the mayor asked the state police to begin regular patrols in certain parts of Clairsville so the town could reduce the size of its police force. Previously fragmented coalitions, including the police and fire unions, joined forces with community groups to protect their turf. After years of covering operating losses with short-term and long-term borrowing, the town faced an increasingly hostile borrowing climate.

In 1999, Clairsville was in technical default on one of its bonds and the lending market was effectively closed to the city. The state's Municipal Fiscal Distress law automatically kicked in, and an interim management team was assigned to turn the situation around.

At this point, the options available to Clairsville are not very attractive. The town will need to brace itself for years of more cost cutting, service reductions, possible bailouts from the state, intricate loan arrangements, additional divestments of services to other providers, and concerted efforts to improve operating efficiencies. Taxes will likely increase, which might prompt more plant closures and lengthen the cycle of decline.

The best options for Clairsville likely were passed up, ignored, or not fully understood during the 1980s when growth began to stagnate and the early warning signs of fiscal distress appeared. Unfortunately, the mayor was in denial about the bad cards he had been dealt. Later, denial evolved into clever delay and budget manipulation strategies designed essentially to mask the problem. Such strategies are akin to bluffing strategies in poker. They do not work for long. Even when the problems were recognized, the initial efforts to cut costs were not strategic and certainly based on no vision for a viable outcome. The mayor made across-the-board cuts which, although politically palatable, did little to address the root cause of the problem. Deep cuts came too late, and by then the town had become dependent on the bond market to finance short-term operating expenses. The stage for the technical default in 1999 was likely set fifteen years earlier when the elected officials ignored the signs of impending trouble.

In their classic study of municipal fiscal distress and the politics of retrenchment, Levine, Rubin, and Wolohojian (1981, pp. 31–32) suggest that governments may go through several phases of retrenchment, similar to those displayed by the Clairsville government:

Denying and delaying. Public officials either do not or cannot recognize the signs of fiscal distress. Once they do realize there is a problem, they try to delay retrenchment through artful budget manipulations, funding operations from the capital budget, or issuing short-term notes to cover operating expenses.

Stretching resources. Public officials finally acknowledge that there is a revenue-expenditure gap, yet they do not address the gap strategically. Instead, they try to stretch their resources with various efficiency initiatives designed to save money. When retrenchment becomes essential, they make across-the-board cuts instead of targeting their reductions according to strategic priorities. Capital improvement projects are deferred or canceled.

Making deeper cuts. Finally, but often after it is too late, public officials begin to make deep cuts in selected services, and they begin in earnest the search for additional revenues. They divest some municipal responsibilities, looking to other levels of government or to the private sector to take over certain obligations and services.

Levine, Rubin, and Wolohojian point out that these phases of retrenchment are not necessarily fixed in their sequence. Some of the municipal governments in their study seemed to follow two of these strategies or all three of them simultaneously, whereas others seemed to lock onto one of the approaches and stick with it throughout the fiscal crisis. The way a government unit responds to fiscal distress seems to depend not only on the extent of the revenue-expenditure gap but also on the political system (for example, the degree of formal authority of the decision makers) and the power and energy of the various groups who lobby for protection of their interests. Although there has not been much research on retrenchment strategies in nonprofit organizations, it is reasonable to expect that they too are subject to many of the same pressures as government organizations.

Let's step back from the Clairsville example to examine some general issues related to retrenchment and some research findings from private and public organizations.

There is a continuum of retrenchment from modest to extreme. On the modest end of the continuum are efforts to reverse the fortunes of troubled organizations with concerted *turnaround* strategies. A more aggressive approach to retrenchment involves *divestment* of selected programs or services provided by the organization. Finally, at the extreme end of the retrenchment continuum, are the strategies of *liquidation*.

Turnaround Strategies

A turnaround strategy focuses on improving an organization's operating efficiencies and overall performance, without changing its core mission or its portfolio of programs and services. Turnaround strategies are used when the organization's performance has eroded, but prospects for revitalization are good or at least plausible. Turnaround strategies are appropriate for organizations that although slipping in performance are at least in the right business—they serve a demonstrated community need in a line of business that is reasonably viable. Their prospects for long-term survival are good if they can only improve their performance (Wheelen and Hunger, 1992). Thus the following questions are often asked when contemplating a turnaround strategy:

- Is there a strong demand for the portfolio of programs and services our organization produces? If there is, why has performance eroded?

- Does the environment offer prospects for long-term sustainability of our organization's mission? Are other organizations in our strategic environment succeeding, or are they too trying to get out of the market?

- If the demand seems to be essentially sound, why has our organization's performance slipped? What contributing factors are within our control?

- Even though our organization's performance has seriously eroded, is there a foundation upon which to rebuild? That is, if we take corrective action now, is there a good chance that our organization will once again be competitive? Or has our organization permanently lost any comparative advantages it might have once enjoyed?

John Murray and the Turnaround of Duquesne University

Early in 1988, the situation could not have been much worse for Duquesne University. This medium-sized Catholic university was reeling from a series of missteps, controversies, and management blunders. Wallowing in debt, with decades of a growing negative fund balance, the institution was in deep trouble. Its aging buildings were crumbling and woefully out of date. The inner-city campus was a mess and not a comforting environment for prospective students and their parents. Its faculty, significantly underpaid and demoralized, had issued a vote of no confidence in the university administrators. Enrollments were declining, quality was diminishing, and the university was in real danger of losing its accreditation. An operational scandal involving a university-sponsored folk dance troupe threatened to be the straw that would break the university's back.

All of this was recorded by a watchful and ravenous local media, which dutifully (and at times gleefully) reported every new controversy as it unfolded. The faculty revolted, the trustees bickered, and the administration clung for its life to what seemed to be a sinking ship.

Today, strolling across the pleasant and fully renovated campus, it is difficult to imagine the dark scenario of 1988. Duquesne University is alive with energy, activity, and optimism about the future. The physical plant has been nearly completely overhauled, with new classrooms, a new basketball arena, new research labs, and new or revamped dormitories, all hardwired for the latest in telecommunications technology. Both enrollments and admissions standards are up, and the university is on the verge of completing its second capital campaign in the last ten years, for a total of nearly $300 million. Its faculty are active in research as well as teaching, capturing an especially high proportion of funding from the National Institutes of Health. The budget is balanced, new programs are being planned and launched, and the future once again looks very bright for this venerable institution.

What happened at Duquesne to turn the situation around so dramatically in a little over ten years? The answer is of course multifaceted, but the single most important event was the appointment of John E. Murray Jr. as the first lay president of Duquesne in its then 111-year history.

John Murray had several things going for him the moment he stepped onto the Duquesne campus in 1988. First, he is a professional academic administrator who has spent his entire adult life in and around universities. Some troubled universities have tried to dig themselves out by hiring a "turnaround specialist" who moves from one failing organization to another. Some have looked to the business sector or to government for a "hired gun" to shake things up. Others have hired a retired politician or another celebrity give a quick infusion of visibility to their fundraising. Murray, in contrast, came up through the ranks as a teacher, scholar, and academic administrator.

A brilliant and internationally acclaimed legal scholar, Murray immediately enjoyed the respect of the disgruntled and demoralized faculty. As former dean of two respected law schools, with leadership and corporate relations experience, he immediately earned the confidence of the trustees. He knows all aspects of the business of higher education—teaching, research, public service, fundraising, community relations—as well as anyone in the country.

Second, Murray understands and embraces the distinctive Roman Catholic mission of Duquesne University. Murray previously served as dean at Villanova's School of Law and so is entirely comfortable with the combination of a spiritual and educational mission. He has lived firsthand with the Catholic tradition in higher education, in which rigorous science, diversity, and spirituality coexist. Few people who have not had personal experience with this tradition can understand the subtleties of managing in a Catholic university.

Third, Murray has several managerial qualities needed to set priorities for Duquesne and to help engineer its remarkable turnaround. He focused first on the problems that were at the heart of the organization's poor performance—the threat from the accrediting agency to withdraw accreditation, the demoralized faculty, and the crumbling campus. Murray had the sense of timing needed to understand that his window of opportunity for making significant change was very narrow indeed. The accrediting organization had given the university two years to take steps to improve from its probationary status. But Murray's timetable was even more urgent. "We did not have two years, two months, or even two weeks," he says. He needed to move immediately.

One of his first actions was to demand the immediate return of the accreditation site visit team and the removal of the probationary status, pending another review in several years. Murray knew that probationary accreditation would be the kiss of death for the institution. The probationary accreditation was removed.

Second, Murray began negotiations and fundraising to increase faculty salaries to be in line with salary standards at other universities. Although this was a risky move for an institution already in deep financial trouble, Murray knew that low faculty morale was one of his major problems. A productive and content faculty was a prerequisite for the university's rebirth.

Next, Murray took steps to improve the campus environment, marginally at first and then more dramatically as funds became available. He knew that he could not recruit students to a crumbling inner-city campus. He knew that an attractive and well-maintained facility sent a symbolic message to everyone who visited the campus.

While all these short-term steps were taken, Murray plotted his longer-term turnaround strategy, which was based on a remarkably clear but effective philosophy with these tenets.

A very lean administrative infrastructure. Murray says, "Basically four people run the place, and we do not have large support staffs. We try to maintain direct contact with faculty, staff, students, and the community."

A focus on the core mission, programs, and services. Murray says, "There are four questions we ask before undertaking anything: (1) Does the proposed program or initiative meet our mission? (2) Does it enlarge opportunities for students? (3) Can we do it extremely well? (4) Can we afford it?"

A focus on product differentiation. Murray says that he constantly asks his staff and faculty to focus on what is distinctive or should be distinctive about Duquesne. "What is different about Duquesne? What is unique? We must base our future on these distinctive characteristics. We can't try to imitate other institutions."

An opportunistic management philosophy, responding to felt needs in the community. "We try to be market driven," Murray says. But he is not a reckless entrepreneur. In 1999, he decided to cancel further investigation into opening a medical school, recognizing that it would be difficult and probably counterproductive to compete with the existing program at the University of Pittsburgh.

The turnaround of Duquesne University has not been a solo show. It has been a collective effort, involving the Pittsburgh community and national constituencies as well. Nevertheless much of the credit must be given to John Murray. His approach of focusing on core programs and services, striving for product differentiation, and serving needs in the community is quite consistent with some powerful evidence on how organizations reverse their declining fortunes (Zimmerman, 1989). We will examine those generic turnaround strategies below.

When to Consider a Turnaround Strategy

As its name implies, a turnaround is a change in direction, but not necessarily a radical change in mission, goals, or portfolio of programs and services. A turnaround strategy presumes that there is a core foundation within the organization that although damaged is still strong enough to build upon.

A turnaround strategy may be appropriate when major indicators of financial performance are declining, there are a growing number of complaints about the organization's products and services, there is a noticeable decrease in productivity and morale, the organization has been criticized for ethical issues, or the organization has experienced a steady erosion of public confidence and trust and of the public's sense of the organization's legitimacy (Zimmerman, 1991). Even though these perceptions are not precisely quantifiable, the general opinion among knowledgeable people is that the organization has "slipped" in terms of its contributions to the community.

Often these indicators of trouble are subtle and are either ignored or easily rationalized by managers who do not want to admit that the organization is in need of an overhaul. The decline may be gradual, and thus changes in these indicators may not even be noticed by key decision makers. Even when the problems reach crisis proportions, executives may be more inclined to blame the market, the funders, the government, or seemingly any source other than the organization itself.

Successful and Unsuccessful Turnaround Strategies

Frederick Zimmerman (1989, 1991), an expert on turnaround strategies, has compared successful and unsuccessful turnarounds throughout the modern history of U.S. industry. His research suggests that the following characteristics distinguish organizations that reversed a decline from those that continued their downward spiral.

An Ability to Reduce the Cost of Production. Successful turn-around strategies are based on intensive and *sustained* efforts to reduce all costs associated with the production of goods and services, including administrative and overhead costs (see Angelica and Hyman, 1997). The organizations that succeed in their turnaround efforts tend to stay with their cost-cutting programs longer and with greater discipline than unsuccessful organizations, continuing the cost cutting until total operating costs are well below revenues. Organizations that fail in their turnaround efforts may make initial efforts to reduce operating costs but then let costs creep upward again after the initial crisis passes. Thus vigilance toward costs and sustained efforts to reduce costs seem to be important tactics in successful turnaround strategies.

Here are some cost-cutting strategies recommended by Zimmerman (1989, 1991):

- Strive for efficiencies by reducing costs or increasing outputs per unit of cost. Address indirect costs (for inventory and utilities, for example) as well as direct costs.

- Bring costs down at least to current levels of revenue, even lower if possible, and keep them there. Do not base your turnaround strategy on trying to increase revenues to meet current costs. Do not allow costs to creep upward after initial reductions.

- Be disciplined and evenhanded in your cost reduction program. Management must accept its share of cost reductions along with the operational units. Evenhandedness does not necessarily mean across-the-board cuts. Some programs might necessarily suffer deeper cost reductions than others, but all parts of the organization should focus on cost reductions.

- Build cost consciousness into the culture of the organization. Use orientation programs for new employees, incentive programs for staff and managers, and continuous involvement of overseers and trustees to build a culture of cost consciousness.

This advice designed for profit-making companies must be tempered when applied to public and nonprofit organizations. At Duquesne University, John Murray spent more (not less) on production by immediately increasing faculty salaries in order to bring them closer to national standards. He knew that the university had to make an investment in quality in order to turn around its dismal fiscal prospects. Significantly, the community was willing to help him do this. The increased costs of production at Duquesne were covered not only by increased earned revenue (tuition) but by contributions from alumni and other sources. Obviously, private sector firms cannot rely on contributions to bring their costs and revenues in line. But Murray made strategic use of an unusually high rate of faculty attrition during the early years of his presidency to both control costs and to renew the faculty.

A Focus on Product Differentiation. Zimmerman suggests that successful turnarounds are more likely to happen when the organization can truly differentiate its program or service in the minds of consumers and other stakeholders. Thus cost cutting alone may not be sufficient for a successful turnaround. You need to be able to convince people that your organization has something uniquely valuable to offer. Perhaps you can base your organization's turnaround strategy on bringing new, highly differentiated programs and services to the market or on making incremental improvements in older programs that differentiate them from other providers' programs. Zimmerman recommends making small, incremental improvements rather than trying to hit a home run with a single, high-risk technological improvement. Turnarounds do not happen over night. They must be nurtured and sustained over the long term. Thus, if you were turning your organization around, you would strive to improve quality during the production process, not just the end product quality. You would not make dramatic jumps or abrupt changes in the positioning of your products. And you would not go fishing in unfamiliar markets. These tactics will only confuse your organization's existing customers.

Here are some product differentiation strategies found in successful turnaround organizations:

- Stay with existing programs and services; do not diversify beyond the core competencies of your organization. Successful turnarounds seem to occur more frequently in organizations that seek to improve their competitiveness in their existing lines of programs and services rather than to acquire new lines through diversification, mergers, or acquisitions. This of course assumes that the demand for these existing program and services remains viable. If the bottom has dropped out of your organization's market, you may have no choice but to diversify into more promising programs and services.

- Make steady, incremental improvements in the quality of existing programs and services. Focus on quality in the production process, not just in the final program or service.

- Stay the course. Do not make sudden or abrupt moves to reposition programs and services in the marketplace.

- Look for new ways to differentiate programs and services in the minds of consumers and other important stakeholders. Improvements in quality, accountability, responsiveness, customer service, and accessibility are ways to differentiate your organization's programs and services from those offered by other providers.

At Duquesne, John Murray's actions illustrate this approach. First he focused attention on areas in which Duquesne had demonstrated strengths and comparative advantages—the sciences, business, and health care. His product differentiation strategy focused on Duquesne's distinctive mission, its Catholic heritage, the small size of its campus, the loyalty and dedication of its faculty. Murray also made an organization-wide commitment to Total Quality Management (TQM), making Duquesne one of the first universities to systematically apply TQM to its own operations.

Technically Competent Leaders. For a turnaround to work, an organization needs people at the top and in key line positions who have specialized knowledge and experience relative to the organization's mission and the people it serves. Outsiders, especially hired guns from other industries, are not typically associated with successful turnarounds. Here are some specific strategies:

- Foster the development of leaders at all levels of the organization who are able to accurately gauge the organization's ability to meet its strategic objectives. Do not set wildly high turnaround benchmarks that cannot be attained. It is better to set modest objectives that are attainable than high objectives that are consistently missed.

- Focus the turnaround strategy on getting your own house in order. Do not try to buy your way out of difficulty through expansion, acquisitions, or mergers.

- Strive for managerial stability as you implement turnaround strategies. If possible, avoid high turnover in key managerial positions.

- Hire managers and top executives who know your organization's environment. Do not look for saviors (turnaround specialists) from other public or nonprofit environments. Managers who have direct line experience seem to be more successful at implementing turnaround strategies than are managers who rose through the ranks from support functions like marketing, public relations, and legislative affairs.

The latter strategy was followed by Duquesne when the trustees decided to hire John Murray, a proven academic leader. He in turn hired a small but highly experienced team of proven leaders who had extensive experience in academic leadership.

Note that Zimmerman does not recommend radical changes in direction or drastic actions as turnaround strategies. Rather he suggests a rigorous and disciplined effort to (1) focus on the organization's core mission and avoid straying from its comparative advantages, (2) make steady and continual progress to improve efficiency and quality in core programs and services, and (3) place people in leadership positions who have direct knowledge and experience of the portfolio of programs and services and refrain from searching for a savior from another industry who might offer "fresh" perspectives that will only lead the organization astray.

Two Phases of a Turnaround Strategy

Turnaround strategies generally occur in two phases. The first phase, *contraction*, consists of the initial efforts, sometimes in crisis management mode, to halt the decline of the organization with reductions in expenditures and improvements in operating efficiencies. The second phase, *consolidation*, is the longer-term process of stabilizing the "new" organization with redesigned structures, policies, procedures, and ways to continuously involve employees in the retrenchment process (Wheelen and Hunger, 1992).

Both phases are crucial to the retrenchment process. Contraction must be accomplished relatively quickly, although not recklessly or in any way that does more harm than good. For example, the former executive director of a large nonprofit organization has candidly lamented his decision to cut the communications department during the contraction phase of that organization's turnaround strategy. In retrospect he believes that this decision created more problems than it solved because it impeded communication with the many community volunteers whose services are essential to the organization's mission. The volunteers interpreted the lack of communication as a sign that the organization no longer valued their services, when in fact it was trying to involve even more volunteers. The lack of communication also diminished the visibility of the organization in the community, leading people to think of the organization as withdrawn and isolated.

The consolidation phase is critically important if the organization is to retain its best employees and adapt its operating policies and procedures to the new environment. The nonprofit organization just mentioned downsized its operation by consolidating jobs and responsibilities, asking people to do more with less. This approach proved effective, and employees even supported many of the cost-cutting tactics. Subsequently, however, the organization was slow to develop new job descriptions, organizational charts, communication protocols, and other policies to stabilize the new, leaner organization. Thus four years later the organization was still recovering from its initial round of contraction. Employees did not know the parameters of their jobs, how to report through the modified communication structure, or what performance criteria would affect their evaluations.

Bankruptcy as a Turnaround Strategy

When an organization files for bankruptcy, it admits that it is at least temporarily insolvent, and it petitions the courts to protect it from creditors while it makes one final attempt at reorganization and recovery. The hope is that court protection from creditors will allow the organization time to get back on its feet. The most famous recent case of a public sector bankruptcy involved an unlikely organization, affluent Orange County, California, where County Treasurer Robert Citron's risky investment strategies backfired, leaving the county's investment fund technically insolvent (Kearns, 1995). Three years later, following a court-supervised recovery plan, the county is once again fully solvent and operational.

Bankruptcies in the public sector are relatively rare. When they do occur, the recovery plans are fairly straightforward. Unlike businesses, governments have a steady and guaranteed stream of revenue in the form of taxes. Thus the primary task in a public bankruptcy is to get control of program expenditures and operational costs. Private organizations, whether nonprofit or for-profit, do not have a guaranteed source of revenues. Thus bankruptcy proceedings are complicated by efforts to accurately predict and, if possible, enhance the organization's revenues while simultaneously reorganizing to gain greater control over costs.

Pros and Cons of Turnaround Strategies

Turnaround strategies, especially those that follow a philosophy like Zimmerman's, can have many positive benefits for your organization. First and foremost, a turnaround strategy will, if properly executed, help get your organization back on a solid footing and regain public confidence. These are the ultimate objectives of any turnaround strategy. But along the way several indirect benefits may also accrue.

Refocusing of the Organization on Its Core Mission. A turnaround strategy can rivet attention of you and your employees on ways to protect your organization's core mission, the essence of your organization. Perhaps over the years your organization has accumulated a variety of ancillary functions, products, and services. Perhaps these have gradually distracted attention or drained resources away from its core purpose and its most important constituencies. A turnaround strategy will force those in the organization to refocus their attention on ways to protect that core mission at all costs. This can be a useful exercise for organizations that have strayed from their comparative advantages.

Reenergizing of Employees. Although turnaround strategies can be painful, even wrenching, they also pose an intellectual and managerial challenge that some employees find stimulating and energizing. If handled properly, a turnaround strategy can build a sense of common purpose and camaraderie as all employees and departments are encouraged to focus on their core purpose and to find ways to better serve their clients.

Development of Leadership. It is relatively easy to be a good manager during good times. The real management challenge is to lead effectively during difficult times. Turnaround strategies can help you discover the employees in the middle and even lower ranks of your organization who have latent leadership skills or potential. Heroes are sometimes born out of organizational crises, and a turnaround is an opportunity for your future leaders to emerge and demonstrate their abilities to control costs, establish priorities, and keep their focus on the core mission and how best to protect it.

Building of Public Confidence and Legitimacy. Turnaround strategies can, if handled properly, focus positive public attention on your organization. The general public likes a comeback story. We love to see sports heroes make a valiant comeback, and similarly, we admire organizations that overcome adversity and once again make a positive contribution to the community.

However, there are also potential pitfalls with any turnaround strategy, even one that is brilliantly conceived and executed. Here are a few issues to consider.

Threat of Introversion. By necessity a turnaround strategy forces you to look inward in search of cost-cutting opportunities and ways to refocus on the organization's core mission. The risk is a turnaround strategy that focuses exclusively on inner operations, ignores important trends and events in the external environment, and isolates the organization from the community on which it ultimately relies for support. The world does not stop while your organization is immersed in cost cutting and refocusing. Client needs continue to change, political trends produce new priorities, and other providers and competitors are busy mobilizing their resources to respond to these changes. Therefore, during a turnaround process your organization must intensify its connections with the outside world, informing important stakeholders of its strategy, providing progress reports, building networks of support for its efforts, and generally staying in touch with its strategic environment. Isolation is perhaps the most dangerous side effect of a turnaround strategy.

Vulnerability of Young and Small Organizations.   Organizational mortality rates are highest among relatively young and small organizations (Bielefeld, 1994; Galaskiewicz and Bielefeld, 1990). The turnaround process can be especially traumatic for young and small organizations that have very little fat in their budgets. Moreover, these organizations lack the knowledge and experience to weather a fiscal storm and overcome hard times. They are often highly dependent on a few revenue sources, or perhaps even one source, and when those are jeopardized, the entire organization is threatened. Resources that are normally devoted to the operational core are diverted to address the crisis or are cut entirely. Thus the heart of the young organization is immediately in danger. Cost cutting alone will generally not work as a turnaround strategy for young and small organizations. They must also become adept at broadening their base of community support, perhaps searching for new revenue sources or seeking strategic alliances that will help them survive during their most vulnerable periods.

Tension Between Mission and Costs.   In the midst of a turnaround strategy every employee in the organization is going to feel the tension between controlling operational costs and fulfilling the organization's mission. The leader of a turnaround strategy must be extremely skilled at providing a clear picture of the organization's mission, directing everyone's attention to that vision, and resolving the constant conflicts of values and perspectives that result from this tension.

Likelihood of Burnout.   Turnaround strategies take a tremendous toll on leaders and employees. Sometimes progress is slow and motivation drains away. Sometimes organizational politics gets the upper hand and employees grow cynical and disillusioned. The prospects for burnout are high, and they increase if the turnaround strategy drags on with few observable benefits.

Divestment Strategies

Turnaround strategies are called for when you are convinced that your organization is offering the right mix of programs and services to the community but needs to be transformed into a more efficient and effective provider of those services in order to retain the public's trust and confidence. Occasionally, however, you will come to the conclusion that your organization is *not* offering the right portfolio of programs and services. You may discover, for example, that one of your programs is a financial drain on the others, jeopardizing the financial performance of the entire organization. Perhaps the quality of services in one part of your organization is far below public expectations, and you cannot turn it around. Or community needs may have changed, making one or more programs far less attractive as a part of your organization's portfolio.

These problematic parts of your portfolio are candidates for *divestment*, a strategy that may take several forms. First, you might spin off or transfer the problematic program or service to another organization. Second, you might simply eliminate this part of your portfolio. Third, you might find a way to incorporate this line of business into another part of your portfolio. The town of Clairsville, as described earlier in this chapter, apparently tried all three of these divestment strategies.

The most important question you can ask about any part of your organization's portfolio is this: If we were not providing this program or service today, would we want to get into it now? If the answer to that question is no, then a divestiture strategy should be considered (Thompson and Strickland, 1992). There are other questions as well that might lead you to consider a divestment strategy:

- What are the weakest programs and services in our portfolio? Why are they weak? Are other providers succeeding where we have failed?

- Have we done all we can to turn these programs and services around? Do these programs have viable prospects?

- Are any of these problematic programs and services in the mature or declining stage of the product life cycle? If they are, do we have a realistic prospect of turning them around?

- Is it acceptable for us to be among the least effective providers of these programs and services? Are these weak programs diverting attention and resources away from our core mission?

- If we divest these programs and services, what will be the implications for the communities we serve? Will they have access to alternative providers? Can we help create or strengthen other providers of these programs and services? Can we help clients make the transition?

- What are our moral or legal obligations to continue providing all the existing services in our portfolio? Will retrenchment significantly affect our core mission and fulfillment of our fundamental goals?

- What are the exit costs associated with divestment in both the short term and the long term? How much will it cost us to phase out a program or service?

- What will be the true savings resulting from the divestment, and when will these savings actually accrue to our organization?

- What are the political and organizational forces that will likely resist a divestment strategy?

Divestment strategies are far more traumatic than turnaround strategies. Although turnaround strategies, on the one hand, may involve reductions in personnel and overhead expenditures, the fundamental mission of the organization and scope of its activities remains unchanged. Divestment, on the other hand, involves a reduction in the scope of the organization's activities by eliminating entirely certain programs, services, or activities that have heretofore been part of the portfolio. Thus divestment strategies affect the mission of an organization by changing the array of goods and services it offers to the community. Divestment affects the purposes served by the organization, not simply its production processes.

Of all the retrenchment strategies discussed in this chapter, divestment may be psychologically the most difficult strategy for decision makers to embrace. Turnaround strategies, although painful and difficult, can actually be energizing for leaders and workers because they challenge them to do more with less. Also, turnaround strategies offer the prospect that the organization may emerge even stronger than before. At the other end of the continuum, liquidation (discussed later in this chapter) is the culmination of a long and exhausting struggle that can leave people resigned to (and perhaps even relieved by) the ultimate demise of the organization. Divestment is an extremely painful intermediary step that admits the futility of traditional turnaround strategies for the organization but, in the minds of some, also portends the ultimate death of the organization.

Reasons to Consider Divestment

Divestment strategies may be appropriate under several circumstances (Schmidt, 1990, p. 9).

Changes in the Organizational Life Cycle.   Organizations progress through stages, just like the programs and services they produce. As your organization goes through these stages, organizational priorities typically change accordingly (see Table 6.1). The organizational life cycle can change your attitude toward programs and services in your portfolio. During its growth phase, for example, your organization might be willing to take some calculated risks on new programs

TABLE 6.1 Organizational Priorities at
Each Stage of the Organizational Life Cycle.

Stage in the Organizational Life Cycle	Typical Organizational Priorities
Development	Nurturing ideas for new products and services. Discovering and capturing a niche in the community. Anticipating and meeting emerging community needs. Building a track record of performance. Building credibility and legitimacy.
Growth	Securing resources and expanding scope and volume of services. Diversifying into related programs and services. Improving operating efficiencies and carving out a stable market. Pursuing financial stability. Institution building.
Maturity	Adding programs and services and increasing the scope of operations. Continuing to diversify. Refining production processes. Finding economies of scale. Defending the organization's position in the community. Investing in new techniques for producing and delivering services.
Decline	Adjusting to shrinking demand. Defending market share. Trying to diagnose problems.
Turnaround or renewal	Cutting costs. Refocusing on core mission. Improving quality of programs and services. Rebuilding credibility and trust. Divesting programs and services that do not add value.
Demise	Confronting the prospect of organizational failure. Negotiating transfer of functions to another organization. Ensuring that client needs are met.

or services. But when your organization is in the mature or declining stage, its appetite for risk and its ability to carry nonproductive programs and services in its portfolio may diminish substantially. During the later stages of the organizational life cycle, your organization may be more inclined to divest weak programs than to risk the draining scarce resources to revitalize them. The stakes are higher during the later stages of the organizational life cycle.

Changes in Community Needs and Preferences. A change in demand for a product or service will significantly affect your attitude toward keeping it in your portfolio. Why invest in a program if, after substantial effort, the community is not willing to support it? The trick, of course, is to determine with some confidence whether the change in demand is temporary or permanent and within or beyond your control. For example, it seems reasonably safe to assume that welfare reform is here to stay, a fact that will likely permanently diminish the need for some types of social and public services although dramatically increasing the need for others such as day care for dependent children and adults.

When you notice any significant change in demand for certain programs and services, you should assess whether this is likely to be a permanent change. If the change is likely to be permanent and beyond your control, can you survive by emerging as the dominant provider of this service in a shrinking market? If the chances are not good, then divestment may be an option.

Increasing Competition. Any significant change in the competitive environment in your industry will affect your attitudes toward staying with certain programs or divesting. Divestment may be the appropriate retrenchment strategy if you come to the conclusion that your organization simply cannot compete effectively with others even though the service or program in question remains highly attractive or appears to be on the rise in its life cycle. Government agencies, for example, are beginning to realize that their portfolios may be laden with certain services that can be more effectively and efficiently provided by the private sector. Continued direct provision of these services may simply drain the organization's resources and distract its attention away from its core mission or the programs and services in which it has a true comparative advantage. When the rules of the game change significantly and when the intensity of competition grows, you may decide that the timing is right to fold your cards in part of your organization's portfolio in order to conserve resources or direct them elsewhere.

Obsolete Technology and Facilities. A nonprofit organization owns its headquarters building in the central business district of its town. Once a vibrant and bustling center, the building has been the victim of decades of neglect as well as shifting demographic patterns. Clients of the organization no longer live near the headquarters building and therefore must travel, find parking, and suffer other inconveniences to visit its offices. Also, the building is in need of a complete (and very expensive) facelift. As the board members contemplated the unpleasant prospects of investing a lot of money to upgrade the facility, the new executive director challenged them to ask the most important question of all, a question to start them thinking about divestment: "If we were starting this organization from scratch, would we want to own a building in the downtown area?"

New Organizational Goals. Divestment may become an option when there is a significant change in organizational goals or priorities. For example, if a municipal government decides to follow the philosophy endorsed by Osborne and Gaebler (1992), its leaders may conclude that the government does not need to *directly provide* all public services to municipal residents. But the government must ensure that these services are provided by someone, perhaps a for-profit firm or a nonprofit organization. This would represent a fundamental change in the goals of this public organization, making divestment a major part of its strategy as it spins off selected services to other providers and assumes the role of overseer or contractor.

Substitute Products. When clients and other stakeholders conclude that they can substitute another product or service for those your organization produces, then you must seriously consider divestment as an option. Just as plastics and aluminum became substitutes for steel in auto manufacturing, public and nonprofit programs and services may be vulnerable to substitutions as well. As we saw in Chapter Three, Bill Markov and the Shadyside Rehabilitation Clinic are facing the prospect of product substitution as outpatient drug and alcohol rehabilitation programs replace the old twenty-eight-day inpatient programs.

Changes in Government Policy. A significant change in government policy may affect your organization's attitude toward divestment. For example, a nonprofit organization might decide to shed one or more of its profit-making activities if the federal government decided to hold nonprofit organizations accountable to stricter regulations regarding earned revenues and unrelated business income. Stricter state or federal regulations regarding environmental protection might prompt a municipal government to contract out activities like hazardous waste disposal that have high compliance costs and potential liabilities. Certainly, government policy has a dramatic impact on any investment portfolio your organization might have.

Types of Divestment Strategies

Once your organization has decided to divest part of its portfolio, it has four options.

Transfer of Responsibility to Another Provider. Although divestment is never easy, the pain may be reduced if you can find another suitable provider who is able and willing to meet the needs of your organization's clients.

There are two types of program transfer you might consider. First, you can *contract* a program to another organization. Under this scenario, your organization retains ultimate responsibility for the program, which is delivered by a subcontractor. Strictly speaking, this is not really a divestment because your organization retains financial and legal responsibility for program delivery. The subcontractor is equivalent to a vendor, retained by your organization and under its authority to provide its clients with a service.

The second form of transfer involves *ceding* total responsibility for a program to another agency, thereby eliminating your organization from the equation altogether.

The key to both of these approaches is "orderly divestment" (MacMillan, 1983, p. 72), so that clients and services are not abandoned but responsibly transferred to another provider. When considering a transfer of responsibility, you should consider these issues.

Willingness and capability of the acquiring agency. Obviously the agency that assumes responsibility for your organization's program must be willing and able to assume this additional responsibility. The divesting organization develops and circulates bid specifications that require the acquiring organization to meet specified performance criteria. Even when the transfer is not handled via a bidding process, the divesting organization has a moral obligation to do everything in its power to identify the most capable organization willing to assume responsibility for the program. The acquiring agency must be fully aware of the scope and demands of this responsibility, with full access to all information necessary for making an informed decision about its ability to take on the responsibility.

Skill building and skill transfer. The divesting organization has the obligation to assist the acquiring organization in building the skills necessary to handle the added responsibility. The transition might occur in several stages. For example, the first phase of the transition might allow the acquiring organization to passively observe and monitor how the divesting organization provides the service. In the second phase, the acquiring agency might provide assistance in the delivery of the service while the divesting agency retains control and accountability. In the third phase, the acquiring agency might assume control and accountability while the divesting organization continues to provide substantial technical assistance. In the fourth phase, the acquiring organization might assume complete control and responsibility for the program.

Shared values and philosophies. It is not enough simply to transfer a program to another agency that is comparably equipped to deliver the services. Ideally you should look for an acquiring organization that shares your organization's values and beliefs about the program and the clients it serves.

Client preparation and participation. Consumers of public and nonprofit services have the right to be involved and fully informed about decisions to transfer services that affect them. Public hearings, citizen advisory committees, written notices, hot lines, ombudspersons, and other such mechanisms allow clients to be involved in the process and to express their concerns.

In the public and nonprofit sectors, transfer of authority and responsibility for a program should be contemplated only when there is powerful evidence that continuation of the program is in the best interests of the community. If the community has demonstrated a continuing need for the program or service, yet it has become apparent that your organization is not the most viable provider, you may seriously consider a transfer of responsibility.

Collaboration with Another Organization.   Collaboration spans several types of organizational strategies. It can be part of a growth strategy, for example, if the partnership leads to geographical expansion or addition of new services. It can be part of a retrenchment strategy if it results in sharing responsibility for services your organization can no longer afford to deliver (Angelica and Hyman, 1997). Because collaboration is such an important part of public and nonprofit organizations' strategic landscape, I discuss this approach at much greater length in Chapter Eight. However, in sum, the following characteristics should be present in any collaborative endeavor.

Mission advancement. The missions of both organizations must be advanced by the collaborative effort, and this advancement must be the driving force of the collaboration. It must not be driven by fear, complacency, convenience, or mere concern for survival.

Strategic alliance. The collaborative effort must enhance the comparative advantages of both organizations as each tries to respond effectively to its own unique environment. Cost savings alone provide a powerful rationale to form a collaborative effort, but there should be more. The collaboration should add resources, capabilities, or visibility that each organization values in its own way and perhaps for its own unique reasons. What opportunities will the alliance allow your organization to pursue that it would not otherwise be able to? What resources are leveraged and enhanced by the alliance? How does the alliance strengthen your organization's position with respect to threats and challenges in the environment?

Explicit expectations and outcomes. As with any relationship, the partners must enter the collaborative effort with a shared understanding of their respective responsibilities and expected outcomes. Each organization must be clear about what resources, strengths, and competencies it brings to the alliance and, in turn, what it expects from its partner. If these expectations are vague at the start, they are likely to produce conflict later.

Trust. Naturally the partners to any collaborative effort must trust each other to nurture and protect the partnership as well as self-interests. The partnership, like a marriage, will never be devoid of self-interested motives. Indeed, self-interest is part of what holds any relationship together. But there must also be a shared commitment to the partnership and to making sacrifices as necessary to keep the partnership viable. Above all, the partners must trust each other to fulfill the expectations as laid out at the inception of the agreement.

Agreed-upon methods of conflict resolution. No relationship, personal or organizational, can sustain itself if the parties lack effective and constructive ways to resolve inevitable conflicts.

Continual dialogue and adjustment. Like a successful marriage, a successful collaborative effort relies on continual communication. The partners must keep each other informed of key developments, progress, and setbacks. Initial expectations that are too high or too low must be modified, and if new responsibilities emerge, their distribution among the participating organizations must be immediately discussed and resolved.

Agreed-upon form of governance. Collaborative arrangements exist along a continuum of formality. Some collaborations are organizations in themselves, with their own staffs and governing bodies selected from each of the participating organizations. Other collaborative ventures are more informal, involving little more than a handshake and, perhaps, the formation of an ad hoc coordinating team.

Attention to growth. Once relationships among people stagnate, they often falter and die. So it is too with collaborations among organizations. When a collaboration is healthy, the purposes of the collaboration and the relationship among the parties will continually evolve and change.

Consolidation. Another approach to divestment is to consolidate a weak or endangered program into another part of the organization's portfolio. Strictly speaking, this is not a true divestment strategy because the program will continue serve the community, albeit at a reduced level and with less autonomy and visibility than before. In fact, consolidation may be part of a turnaround strategy as well as a divestment strategy. Consolidation might be a viable option when you can give positive answers to these questions.

- *Synergy and transferable skills.* Does the program that is the candidate for divestment have natural synergies with other parts of our organization, so that it might be folded into a stronger and more viable program?
- *Adding value.* Will the consolidation actually add value to both programs, not merely hide a weak program under the

skirts of a stronger one? Will the whole be more than the sum of the two parts?

- *Cost reduction.* Will the consolidation save us operating and overhead costs?

- *Morale and organizational culture.* Will this arranged marriage be successful from the standpoint of our morale and our organizational culture? Will the two program staffs be compatible and work constructively together?

- *Symbolism.* What symbolic message will we send to our employees and other stakeholders by trying to find a new home for this troubled program? Will the message be positive ("we are committed to continuing to serve the consumers of this service") or negative ("we can't summon the will to close down a marginal program").

Program Elimination. Under certain circumstances the appropriate strategy is simply to close down the program. You may come to this conclusion after discovering that there is no longer a strong justification for offering the program yourself and that no other agency is willing to assume responsibility for it. This is an extremely difficult step and should not be taken until your organization has investigated and answered the following questions.

- *Alternative coverage.* Are we absolutely certain that there are no other providers—nonprofit, public, or for-profit—who are willing and able to assume responsibility for the program?

- *Need.* Are we sure that the community support for the program is so small that it does not justify continuation?

- *Agency mission.* Is this program central to our mission? If so, does the diminishing community support for this program jeopardize the mission of our organization as a whole?

- *Fate of consumers.* What will be the fate of people who are currently using this program or service? To what extent are they dependent on it?

- *Moral obligation*. To what extent are we morally obligated to provide this product or service despite its apparent lack of community support?
- *Exit costs*. Will the exit costs, tangible and intangible, exceed the benefits of divesting this program?
- *Benefits*. What are the true benefits of divestiture, and when will they accrue to our organization?

For example, my academic department decided last year to close one of its three master's degree programs due to stagnant student demand, a shrinking faculty, and low national visibility. There were many compelling reasons to close the program. A turnaround strategy would have been quite costly, with uncertain returns on our investment. Still, the exit costs were quite high. Alumni of this program mobilized quickly to oppose the decision. State legislators wrote angry letters to the dean. Current students in that degree program felt betrayed, even though we vowed to wind the program down gradually, assuring them of the opportunity to graduate with an accredited degree. Moreover, the savings from eliminating this program will not accrue for years. Current faculty will not be fired but will be reduced by attrition. Meanwhile, they have less and less to do because they lack the subject-area expertise for teaching in other academic programs. In short, the exit costs for this strategy may be high, and the short-term marginal benefits modest.

Advantages of Divestment

Divestment strategies, although painful, can have beneficial outcomes for an organization. Here are a few positive aspects of divestment.

Renewed Focus and Redirection of Scarce Resources.   Even more than a turnaround strategy, divestment has the effect of riveting the attention of employees and other stakeholders on the core mission, purpose, and priorities of the organization. When a portion of an organization's portfolio is divested, peoples' lives are affected almost immediately. Jobs may be lost or redefined. Clients may be directed to other providers or turned away. These are not desirable circumstances, but they do have the derivative effect of capturing the attention of people who might otherwise believe that the overall retrenchment strategy is just a passing fad.

An External Perspective. As noted earlier, turnaround strategies tend to focus attention inward, in a search for cost savings and quality improvements. Divestment strategies tend to focus attention *outward* as well as inward. When following a divestment strategy, for example, you will try to discover as much as you can about the present and anticipated levels of community support and need for the various parts of your portfolio. You will also try to gain a clear picture of the competitive landscape, including the availability of other providers who may be interested in assuming responsibility for the programs and services you want to divest. Moreover, divestment forces you to consider community reactions to your decision. Who has a stake in the divested programs and services? Are these people likely to oppose divestment? Is it possible to work with them rather than against them? All these issues force you to look beyond the boundaries of your organization to assess the strategic environment.

Reduced Overhead. Divestment strategies can have ripple benefits with respect to the cost of operations. The shedding of programs may reduce overhead expenses in addition to lowering or eliminating these programs' direct costs. Offices are vacated. The need for secretarial support is relieved. Travel and administrative expenses are reduced.

Significant and Permanent Change. I noted earlier that turnaround strategies often falter after the financial crisis passes. The organization that has done a stellar job of cutting costs, finds that it simply cannot sustain the momentum, and it begins to slip back into its old ways. Divestment, on the other hand, has the effect of creating long-term and lasting change in the organization.

Certainly, new programs may eventually replace the divested ones, and ten years hence the organization might once again look just as it does today. Still, a divestment tends to alter permanently the profile of an organization. Once a program has been spun off to another provider or closed completely, it is difficult to retrieve. The positive effect of this is that the organization does not find it so easy to fall back into its old ways following the crisis. It is altered programmatically, structurally, and even psychologically and culturally.

Complications of Divestment

But for all its benefits, divestment is still one of the most traumatic events your organization will ever endure. In public and nonprofit organizations, divestment is complicated by many factors. Here are a few sobering thoughts.

Moral and Legal Obligations. Governments and nonprofit organizations produce public or quasi-public goods on which people have come to depend, creating powerful moral forces that resist program termination. When these programs and services are closed down, consumers in the public sector often cannot turn to alternative providers, either because alternative providers are nonexistent or because the consumers cannot gain access to them. For example, it may not be sufficient to find an organization twenty miles away that is willing to take responsibility for the program your organization wants to divest. If your clients cannot arrange transportation to that agency, they will not be able to use the services. In certain circumstances, even a modest change in location might as well be on the other side of the moon for clients who lack the resources or the will to seek out the new provider. Also, there are legal mandates that may bind an organization to pursue certain purposes and offer certain programs no matter how much it wants to divest them. Public and nonprofit organizations are often bound by legislation, charters, and articles of incorporation that prescribe certain purposes and, by implication, proscribe others. When part of the portfolio of services is divested, the entire mission and purpose of the organization may be affected, raising questions regarding its continued commitment to its legally authorized purposes.

Entrenched Interests and Constituencies. There are powerful political and budgetary forces in public sector organizations that *resist* termination of programs. Every program has constituencies, both within your organization and outside. When the interests of these constituencies are threatened, they mobilize to vigorously resist any significant divestment strategy. These constituencies are not likely to be persuaded by your organization's portfolio analysis or its assessment that another provider is more capable of providing the program or service. They have powerful motivations to see to it that the service continues to be provided by your organization.

Bureaucratic Inertia. The phenomenon of bureaucratic inertia is quite powerful in both the public and nonprofit sectors, resisting any efforts to substantially redirect priorities and resources. This is not just a resistance to innovation or change. The organizational cultures of public and nonprofit organizations often are premised on the very desirable values of stability and predictability (Salipante and Golden-Biddle, 1995). Citizens might expect to encounter change in other aspects of their lives, but they are relatively intolerant of change in government or social services. The company that provides their telephone service may change from month to month, but they want assurances that they will send their tax bill to the same location year after year. Public and nonprofit organizations make an implicit promise to the communities they serve: We will be there when others are not. The public may even have a relatively high level of tolerance for inefficiency and waste in return for predictability of service.

Deferred Savings and High Exit Costs. Divestments may not yield immediate financial benefits. The financial savings of divestment may be delayed and diffused. Termination of employees may be precluded or delayed by union contracts or job tenure. The shutdown of a program may take months or even years, especially when the organization is under a legal mandate to continue serving existing clients until their benefits expire.

Moreover, the exit costs of most public and nonprofit programs tend to be quite high. These costs are driven upward by political factors, legal factors, and the organization's sense of commitment to the community it serves.

Public Statements of Defeat.   Perhaps the most bitter pill to swallow when adopting a divestment strategy is that it may be interpreted as a public expression of defeat. Unlike turnaround strategies, divestments rarely take place behind closed doors. If your organization undertakes a divestment, at some point in the process, you will need to make a public statement of your intentions, which will appear to many (and may feel to you) like a very public admission of failure. The community will sit up and take notice when you announce that your organization is divesting one or more of its programs. This can be especially difficult to handle if your organization is not able to transfer the program or service to another provider. Opponents of the divestment will angrily accuse your organization of abandoning the community it is chartered to serve.

The pain may be lessened if you can legitimately claim that you are closing a program because it has achieved its mission. Divestments based on program success, however, are rare. And an organization will not fare well if it tries to bluff the community by declaring victory and retreating when everyone knows that the needs addressed by the program remain as strong as ever.

Often public and nonprofit officials will shift the blame when announcing the closure of a program. They may point out that a higher level of government cut off program funding or that the community never fully supported the program. Typically, however, the community will not be significantly persuaded by such arguments. There is no escaping the fact that they look to program providers to overcome funding problems and provide the advocacy and leadership needed to maintain program support.

In short, divestment is an extremely difficult move to make, even when fully justified by the most careful strategic analysis.

Liquidation

The most extreme measure of retrenchment is *liquidation*, or the formal termination of the organization, generally accomplished by selling as many assets as possible and distributing the proceeds to creditors and stockholders. Because public and nonprofit organizations do not have stockholders per se, the assets are redistributed to another public purpose or organization. In the nonprofit sector, the state attorney general may have a voice in how assets are sold and distributed back to the community. The assets of a nonprofit organization must be used in perpetuity for the charitable purpose for which they were donated. Thus, if a nonprofit organization goes out of business and has excess funds after all creditors have been paid, these excess funds are either transferred to another nonprofit organization that has a similar mission or used to endow a foundation that will carry on the charitable purposes.

Forces Promoting and Resisting Liquidation

Typically, liquidation is discussed as an option only when an organization is in the final stages of a chronic or acute financial crisis. But perhaps liquidation should be considered under less extreme circumstances as well. For example, liquidation may be the morally responsible choice when a nonprofit organization can no longer compete effectively and its continued existence merely drains scarce charitable resources from other more effective and more deserving organizations in the community. Noble as this notion sounds, most organizations are inclined to search first for self-preservation strategies, including radical modification of their missions, rather than close their doors. Self-preservation is a part of human nature and therefore the instinctive goal of most organizations.

Also, public and nonprofit organizations might consider liquidating their assets not only when they fail but when they *succeed* in accomplishing their missions. Ostensibly they were established to address a specific community need or problem. When that need is satisfied, why not declare victory and quit, thereby liberating scarce resources for other more pressing needs? But this too is rather rare in the nonprofit sector (Hager, 1997). Instead, the prevailing pattern seems to be to find another cause to pursue, another mission to serve.

Liquidations are rare in the public sector. Typically, liquidation of a government agency or jurisdiction requires approval by a higher legislative body. Cities and counties, for example, are creatures of state governments, which are effectively their parent organizations. Such extreme action is not likely to be taken, except perhaps in cases of extremely small hamlets that are no longer able to care for themselves. Of course there are many examples of government consolidations, such as city-county mergers and annexations in which one government jurisdiction essentially loses its organizational identity when it is absorbed into another, but these are not liquidations per se.

Some states have the option of placing a locality in a kind of financial receivership when it is no longer able to sustain basic public services with its tax revenues. In most of these cases the state will appoint a manager and perhaps an interim oversight team to help the municipality get back on its feet. Some of the powers of the elected governing body may be suspended or altered while the financially distressed community is under the oversight of the state government. This occurred in the town of Clairsville, as described in the earlier case study. This too is not a liquidation per se but rather a kind of enforced and strictly regulated turnaround.

Finally, there are organizations in both the private and public sectors that seem to be "permanently failing" (Meyer and Zucker, 1989). Despite chronic poor performance and widely acknowledged failure, these organizations somehow continue to exist for years, even decades. Meyer and Zucker contend that the number of people who have a stake in any organization's *survival* generally outnumber those who have a stake in its *performance*. Even in the face of chronic poor performance, the constituencies that favor liquidation will find it difficult to overcome the political forces favoring the continued existence of the organization. Thus organizations enter a kind of poor performance steady state that can last for a very long time.

Rose and Peters (1978) have addressed a similar phenomenon among governments, which they call *political bankruptcy*. Political bankruptcy occurs when a government loses its position of legitimate authority among citizens and consequently its ability to engender voluntary compliance with laws, regulations, and social norms. Still, even politically bankrupt governments can sustain themselves indefinitely.

Why Organizations Fail

Despite attempts to preserve themselves, some public and nonprofit organizations do indeed fail, die, and close their doors forever. A panel study of nonprofit organizations in the Minneapolis-St. Paul area showed a mortality rate of 20 percent over an eight-year period (Bielefeld, 1994). What factors contribute to organizational decline and death? Using data from the panel study, researchers have shed some interesting light on this important question (Galaskiewicz and Bielefeld, 1990; Bielefeld, 1994; Hager, Galaskiewicz, Bielefeld, and Pins, 1996).

Small and Young Organizations Are Most Vulnerable. Relatively young organizations have greater difficulty surviving a significant challenge than older organizations. Like young lion cubs in the jungle, they find the first months and years the most dangerous. It is logical to assume that older organizations have survived at least one, and perhaps many, significant challenges in their lifetime. Therefore they have accumulated a store of institutional memory and knowledge and perhaps even codified routines for responding to adversity and the ability to anticipate and then avoid challenges. Young organizations, however, must still successfully weather some storms in order to learn how to adapt. The dilemma of course is that they must get past the first few hurdles without the benefit of refined and sophisticated adaptive mechanisms. Thus many of them fail before they have the chance to learn these mechanisms from their experience.

Survival also seems to be related to the resources and personnel that an organization can mobilize when it encounters difficulties. Young nonprofit organizations often have no slack resources at all. They live from hand to mouth and count themselves fortunate if they balance their books at the end of the year. Unexpected expenditures or needs simply cannot be accommodated. Because their revenue streams generally are not diversified, they are extremely vulnerable to even temporary shifts in demand for their core programs and services. They are often highly reliant on one or two funding sources. If these dry up or are diverted to other needs in the community, the young organization simply may not be able to survive. Young organizations also often do not have a network of community contacts and alliances that can come to their aid during adversity.

Thus research in many different contexts seems to reach the same conclusion: young and small organizations are more vulnerable than older and larger organizations.

Single Purpose Organizations Are Vulnerable. As I discussed in Chapter Five, diversification of programs and revenue streams can be a buffer against financial adversity and market vagaries. If demand for one program in your organization's portfolio is down, demand for another may go up. Revenues from popular programs may temporarily subsidize struggling programs. Research on organizational mortality in the nonprofit sector seems to reinforce this notion. Organizations that have multiple and diverse funding sources to begin with seem to have a better chance of survival than those that are dependent on one or a few major funding sources. Moreover, and very significantly, organizations that survive seem to have had greater success than those that eventually die in continually *increasing* the diversification of their funding sources (Bielefeld, 1994). In other words, they continually add new sources of funding, making themselves progressively stronger for the times when they must face of adversity.

Obviously this may be a circumstance in which success breeds more success and failure breeds more failure. As an organization succeeds in its mission, more and more funders will be interested in supporting it. Conversely, an organization that is struggling will have difficulty attracting interest from diverse funding sources, making it more and more reliant on a single funding source and, consequently, more vulnerable. Thus efforts to diversify funding and expand the mission will be easier for organizations that have a track record of success than for those that are on the margins.

Organizations Without a Strategy Are Vulnerable. Bielefeld (1994) found that organizational survival in the nonprofit sector seems to be at least mildly related to the types of adaptive strategies used by the organization. He found that nonprofit organizations that died tended to use fewer adaptive strategies and tended to rely more heavily on retrenchment strategies alone than did the cohort of organizations that survived. Surviving organizations seem to rely more heavily on strategies that would generate new sources of revenue or enhance the reputation of the organization in the community.

Again, there may be a dilemma inherent in these findings. It is reasonable to assume that failing organizations will find it harder to attract new revenues or to enhance their image in the community. Thus their only real recourse is to retrench and hope to gradually turn the situation around. Meanwhile, however, their competitors are out in the community following more proactive and constructive strategies that further enhance their comparative advantages over the weaker organizations.

Managing Organizational Demise

It may seem odd to discuss termination as an organizational *strategy*. After all, once the organization has been closed, there is essentially nothing left to manage and the concept of strategic management becomes moot. Thus, in a sense, closure is not a strategic action because it presents no long-term vision for the organization. But closure *is* a strategic alternative, especially in the private nonprofit sector, and it must be seriously considered when one or more of the following conditions apply:

- When an organization is clearly incapable of contributing sufficient value to the community in proportion to the resources it consumes.
- When an organization has fulfilled its mission and a new purpose cannot be formulated.
- When liquidation might be a precursor to forming a new organization out of the ashes, as is the case with many nonprofit conversions.

When closure is inevitable, there are management issues that should be addressed to ensure that the closure goes as smoothly as possible. Robert Sutton (1983, 1987) has conducted research on how management can facilitate the process.

Sutton (1983) notes some special management challenges that arise after an organization has announced its intention to close. The best employees tend to jump ship unless they are either exceptionally loyal or assured of equal or better positions in an acquiring or spin-off organization. Rumors of all types run rampant, especially when information is not shared with employees. Employees often display anger toward management, which they blame for the decline of the organization. But more often, sorrow and fear are their dominant emotions. Finally, employees have trouble accepting that closure is actually going to occur. They hold out hope of being saved or spared by some dramatic turn of events. Their lack of acceptance is often quite logical, occurring because management has given them poor information.

Sutton (1987) suggests that management must master skills in these areas related to termination of the organization.

Dismantling. Once executives decide to close the organization, they must lead it through the delicate process of severing its links with its employees, supporters, clients, suppliers, creditors, and affiliated partners. During this process, they must be extremely skilled at communicating the closure to all affected stakeholders. They should document the efforts that have been made to save the organization, explain to employees and others the criteria and the process used to make the decision to close the organization, provide information on how and when the closure will take place, and be explicit that nothing more can be done to save the organization (Sutton, 1987).

Reconnecting. This is the process of creating links between members of the dying organization and other support systems, building bridges to other organizations for clients, and distributing net assets to another organization (Sutton, 1987).

Sustaining. Typically, organizational closure does not happen overnight. Instead, the organization winds down gradually, completing the terms of existing contracts, negotiating the transfer of functions to other organizations, disposing of assets, and so on. During this process, management must still take responsibility for ensuring that the fundamental tasks of the organization are accomplished and the mission continues to be pursued. Difficult as it is, executives must simultaneously attend to the contradictory tasks of closing the organization while maintaining (as much as possible) its standards of performance and its obligations to key stakeholders. Sutton (1983) found that a good predictor of how well an organization will manage its demise is how well it did its work when it thrived.

Information sharing. Management must walk the very thin line between providing too little and too much information to key stakeholders during the process of organizational closure. Sutton (1983) finds that some amount of secrecy is justifiable, even advisable, during the earliest phase, when the decision has not yet been officially made to close the organization. During this crucial phase, decision makers need to be able to consider all options without the glare of public scrutiny. Secrecy might also be called for when news that an organization *might* close would hasten its demise. Such news contributed to the run on the banks that helped launch the Great Depression. Information that the financial collapse of Orange County, California, was impending hastened that county's bankruptcy as nervous investors began to call options on bonds and notes faster than Orange County could pay them. However, even though there are a few instances where secrecy might be justified for a short period of time, managers must quickly master the art of informing key constituencies of decisions affecting the future of the organization. Without adequate information, rumors abound, and they may be far more destructive than even the most unpleasant truth.

Delegating. The death of an organization places huge demands on managers. They must attend simultaneously to administrative, legal, political, and public relations challenges. The enormity of the task will quickly take its toll on even the most gifted and energetic leader. Moreover, throughout the process, valued employees will be leaving the organization to take jobs elsewhere. Because they will not be replaced, the workload must be spread among the employees who remain, and managers must quickly master the art of delegating and reassigning. This is among the most challenging tasks for managers because they are in effect shooting at a moving target. Every time tasks are reassigned to compensate for the loss of some employees, other employees leave, and the reassignment continues (Sutton, 1983).

Inventing. Organizations typically do not have a procedures manual for their own demise and closure. Managers must make up the rules as they go along, inventing policies and procedures to ensure that the essential work of the organization continues to be accomplished as they gradually dismantle the infrastructure. Even if certain procedures and policies governing the closure have been promulgated, most people in the organization will be participating in an organizational death for the very first time. Thus, they will lack the experience they would need to follow the procedures without a hitch (Sutton, 1983).

Coping. The process of organizational demise is probably the most stressful that any manager will ever experience. There is simply no escaping the fact that this stress will take its toll and manifest itself in many ways—hasty judgments, crisis management, distortion of information, group conflict, errors, and even illnesses. Astronauts, test pilots, deep sea divers, and other professionals who work under extreme conditions are trained to recognize when their judgment is affected and possibly impaired by the physical demands of their job. Managers may not have the benefit of this type of training, but they must at least understand and try to prepare for the inevitable stress that will follow them like a shadow throughout the process of closure. Impromptu systems of checks and balances might be installed to ensure that important decisions are reviewed by several people. Employees might be given opportunities to discuss and cope with their emotions, gaining some tools to deal with these feelings rather than simply pressing on with the dreary task. Other strategies as well might be employed to help the organization cope with the stress of closure (Sutton, 1983).

The Benefits of Organizational Closure

For the organization and the people who work in it, there are few if any benefits from organizational closure. Still, it may be useful to look for some silver lining to this cloud.

Reallocation of community resources. The closure of a public or nonprofit organization frees up community resources that can then be reallocated to other purposes, perhaps ones more beneficial to the community as a whole.

Opportunity to tell a success story. If closure is brought about by the successful accomplishment of the organization's mission, then there is the opportunity to tell that story to the world. Case studies of successful mission accomplishment are rare and extremely valuable.

Lessons to be learned. The demise of an organization presents a relatively rare opportunity for all of us to learn from our mistakes. Perhaps the organization should not have been created in the first place. Perhaps its original mandate and structure were too limiting. Perhaps it suffered from poor leadership or lackluster staff performance. Or perhaps it was simply a victim of changing times, needs, and community priorities. Whatever the reason for closure, there are lessons to be learned by the organizations that survive and by the employees who toiled in the failing organization. Perhaps these lessons can be applied to other contexts with more constructive outcomes.

Development of management talent. Like all of the retrenchment strategies discussed in this chapter, the demise of an organization can develop the skills of talented managers. During the process of closure, managers must master many of the most challenging tasks they will ever face, including defining priorities; sustaining operations in the face of extreme adversity; managing crises, political issues, public relations, and stress; arranging collaborations; networking; and delegating. While in the throes of this process, managers will be unable to view it as a learning experience. But when they emerge from this dark tunnel, they and those around them will likely be better managers than they were when they began this journey.

Motivations for Retrenchment

Hard-driving executives are conditioned to view retrenchment as a form of defeat, a sign of managerial incompetence, organizational decline and ultimate demise. They hold their cards for too long, hoping for a miracle, because the prospect of a tactical retreat is simply too unpleasant to contemplate. In the public and nonprofit sectors the reluctance to retrench often is institutionally and politically supported. The same taxpayers who denounce big government may be the first to write to their elected representatives when their own favorite program or service is cut. Government retrenchment often incurs the wrath of powerful groups like employee unions, vendors, lobbyists, and special interest groups who have high stakes in a program or service. Sometimes local politicians engage in denial and delay tactics in order to bolster investor confidence and to portray a dynamic image of their community (Levine, Rubin, and Wolohojian, 1981).

Retrenchment also is difficult in the nonprofit sector, where organizations are vulnerable to the fickle affections of foundations and other donors. Any substantial cutback can represent a serious threat to the organization's reputation and perceived legitimacy in the community. People are reluctant to donate their money or time to an organization that appears to be on the ropes. They want their donations to advance a noble cause, not to pay an overdue telephone bill for an organization that may close its doors tomorrow. Moreover, most nonprofit organizations operate on a bare-bones budget even in good times, meaning they have very little fat that can be cut before serious consequences are felt in program quality and quantity. Thus, except in the largest nonprofit organizations, retrenchment generally has immediate and painful consequences for clients, who may have no other service alternatives.

So there are powerful incentives in public and nonprofit organizations to delay retrenchment for as long as possible or avoid it altogether. Vast amounts of energy and resources are expended trying to avoid this strategy when in fact it is sometimes the best strategy to follow. Even liquidation, the ultimate and most devastating form of retrenchment, may sometimes be in the best interests of the community an organization serves. And yet organizations will generally follow their natural survival instincts to avoid closure at all costs, sometimes degenerating into "permanently failing organizations" (Meyer and Zucker, 1989). Levin, Rubin, and Wolohojian (1981) found that the cities in their study preferred a using variety of delaying tactics to terminating services. Even when these cities admitted they could no longer provide a service, they looked in earnest for another organization to assume responsibility rather than terminate the service altogether.

These findings are not surprising when you consider the power of various interests groups such as employee unions, vendors, neighborhood organizations, ethnic groups, political parties, and others who have a high stake in municipal budgeting and who are quite effective at protecting their respective interests.

There is another way. Retrenchment can be approached astutely, proactively, and energetically, leaving the organization's comparative advantages intact to continue to serve community needs and, perhaps one day, be rekindled in a growth strategy. Although never enjoyable, retrenchment can be intellectually stimulating and the ultimate test of executive skill.

Good Reasons to Retrench

When properly conceived and executed, retrenchment strategies can be a powerful tool in your arsenal. Here are a few circumstances in which retrenchment may be advisable.

To Revitalize a Financially Distressed Organization. When expenditures exceed revenues for an extended period of time, an organization must take affirmative steps to reduce its financial obligations. Unless revenues increase significantly and quickly, a financially distressed organization must retrench. Cutting programs or services is of course one way but not the only way to accomplish cost reductions. Work flows and processes can be reengineered to save steps, cut costs, and create efficiencies. Administrative overhead and perks can be cut. Travel allowances and other ancillary expenses can be reduced or eliminated. Exhibit 6.1 summarizes some of the cost-cutting strategies used by fiscally distressed municipalities.

As straightforward as this strategy sounds, many executives find it hard to follow. They will do nearly anything to avoid reducing costs. They will seek loans from banks, borrow from endowment funds, reallocate unrestricted funds, renegotiate payment schedules

EXHIBIT 6.1 Cost-Cutting Strategies
Used by Fiscally Distressed Municipalities.

- *Deferral of expenditures:* capital projects, maintenance, street cleaning, repairs to infrastructure, equipment replacement, training for staff.

- *Efficiency improvements:* energy saving streetlamps, temporary wage freeze, reductions of persons assigned to tasks, improved cash management systems, flextime, Total Quality Management, equipment sharing between departments, consolidation of overhead and administrative functions, reduced overtime expenditures, automation.

- *Application of management systems:* management by objectives, new cost-accounting techniques, benchmarking, development of priorities for making cuts, use of cost-benefit analysis, increased budgetary control by the executive.

- *Reduction of demand for services:* increasing user fees, reducing hours of operation, reducing number of service stations to create longer waits for service.

Source: Compiled from Levin, Rubin, and Wolohojian, 1981, pp. 183–187.

with vendors, hire a new development director, or chase grant proposals that are unrelated to their mission. All these strategies can be easily rationalized as short-term, stopgap measures that will keep the organization afloat until the revenues pick up again. Often these strategies are sold to trustees and other stakeholders as "investments" in the future of the organization. "We have to spend money to make money" may be the refrain heard in boardrooms where another deficit budget has just been reluctantly authorized by the trustees.

To Redirect Resources, Protect the Core of the Organization, and Refocus Energies. James Thompson's classic work on organizational strategy (1967) says that one of your primary concerns as a manager is to protect the core processes of your organization—the operational components that support the central mission. When the operational core is threatened, the organization itself is in peril. Thus it is highly justifiable to reduce or eliminate optional or ancillary parts of the organization in order to protect the core functions, processes, and activities.

The American Red Cross, for example, continually reminds its chapters around the country of the hierarchy of services provided by the Red Cross: *must* services are those that every Red Cross chapter must provide, according to its charter; *should* services are those that every Red Cross chapter should provide, assuming availability of resources; *may* services are those provided at the discretion of local chapters, perhaps in response to unique local needs.

Also, it is entirely justifiable to use retrenchment as a way to refocus an organization's attention and energy on its core mission, whether or not that mission is seriously in jeopardy. The natural process of organizational inertia may sometimes take your organization gradually down a path of diversification, adding more and more programs, services, personnel, and activities that are only marginally related to its core mission if at all. Then, suddenly it seems, you walk into work one morning and hardly recognize your own organization. A review of your organization's portfolio may reveal expendable programs or activities that are doing little more than distracting employees' attention. A periodic housecleaning is sometimes needed, regardless of the organization's financial condition.

To Shed Ineffective Programs. Weak and ineffective programs can be a drain on community resources and can damage the reputation of your organization. Sometimes, of course, as I have discussed, you have no choice but to continue to provide a service, even if your organization is not doing the best possible job of it, because there are no other providers to serve a clientele in need. You cannot simply abandon the recipients of the service, even though you are unable to make it a first-rate service. But when there are alternative service providers, and it is clear that your organization is in an inferior position relative to them, it makes sense to divest or transfer the service to the organization that is best able to meet the need. This is a way of concentrating resources in the hands of those who are most able to meet the need, thereby creating "public value" (Moore, 1995), which is akin to stockholder value in the private sector.

To Respond to Mission Completion.   Rarely does a public service organization shut down a program or close its doors feeling satisfied that it has fully accomplished its mission. It seems there are always more needs to fill, more people to serve. And after all, it is relatively easy to modify a program or even to adjust the mission of an entire organization in order to take it in a new direction once its original objectives have been achieved. Recognizing this natural tendency in government, legislators began to impose *sunset* legislation in the 1970s, placing time limits on selected government programs.

When a nonprofit organization closes its doors because it has accomplished its mission, it can create quite a stir. Observers were aghast when Peggy Charren matter-of-factly closed down the Association for Children's Television (ACT) shortly after it achieved its goal of national legislation regulating the content of children's programs and the advertising on those programs. Couldn't she redirect her efforts, they asked, toward state and local arenas where the issues of children's programming were just as intense? Her response was remarkably honest and simple. She stated that ACT had accomplished its mission and that there were other organizations more capable of carrying on the fight at the state and local levels (Moore, 1992).

Retrenchment or liquidation due to mission accomplishment is a completely justifiable strategy. Unfortunately, there is not much research on this phenomenon (Hager, 1997).

Bad Reasons to Retrench

Although retrenchment can be a bitter pill to swallow, it is not always undertaken for noble purposes. Here are some rather questionable reasons to retrench.

To Compensate for a Lack of Strategy. The executive who has no coherent strategy for dealing with difficulties might undertake a slash and burn approach in the hope that in the process some promising strategy will reveal itself. Typically this tactic takes the form of across-the-board cuts that are devoid of priorities or strategic direction. This was the approach followed by Clairsville. Often, the stated rationale is that "everyone in the organization must share the pain." Such exhortations are no substitute for a coherent strategy, and they will quickly wear thin among employees and other stakeholders. Management may be trying to buy some time until an appropriate strategy reveals itself. If so, this will soon become apparent to key groups of stakeholders, and the situation is likely to degenerate into turf wars, mass exodus, and erosion of organizational legitimacy.

To Make a Symbolic Sacrifice. Occasionally, retrenchment is nothing more than a symbolic gesture to pacify critics of the organization or to send a message to certain stakeholders. Suppose, for example, that there has been a rash of public news stories about "excessive" salaries and perks among top executives in certain local government agencies. In response, the mayor informs the local media that she is eliminating the practice of allowing top executives to take government cars home for their personal use. The intended message is that the mayor is making significant cuts to protect the taxpayers. In reality, the action may be little more than a symbolic gesture, with a minimal impact on the government's budget.

Another example of symbolic retrenchment may be found in the managers who are anxious to show "decisiveness" or "willingness to confront the tough issues." They believe that even an unreflective approach to retrenchment will demonstrate to their employees and to other observers that they are "in charge." It is true that retrenchment can send a powerful message to key constituencies, but if that retrenchment is not well thought out, that message will also not be the one desired.

To Use Retrenchment as a Political Weapon. As the winds of political fortune shift back and forth, those who have power will inevitably try to wield it over those who do not. When the Republican Party captured a majority in Congress in 1994, many of the pet programs of the Democrats were targeted for budget cuts or outright elimination. This is a natural, perhaps even desirable, part of our political process. But retrenchment is sometimes used for less noble political agendas like punishing political opponents, thwarting the power of potential political adversaries, and preventing access to services in a way that is discriminatory and fundamentally at odds with the ideals that an organization is supposed to advance. Retrenchment can also be used as a political tool to punish employees who have lost favor with management or who are on the "wrong" side of some internal dispute between coalitions in the organization.

To Use Retrenchment as Political Bait. A few years ago, the county in which I live experienced a political trauma of sorts. After more than sixty years of a Democratic majority on the three-person board of county commissioners, the Republicans wrested control of the board in a tightly fought election. Among other things, the Republican candidates promised to reduce property taxes by 20 percent across the board *and* freeze property assessments. The county government had accumulated a financial surplus during the previous administration, and the Republican candidates said it was time to get government off the backs of the people. Within a year the surplus was exhausted, and the county was in a deficit spending mode. The once enviable bond rating dropped precipitously as investors lost confidence in the county's leadership and its ability to meet its obligations. The grass grew long in county parks, and other services were reduced dramatically to balance the now strained budget. The strategy was political genius but fiscal folly.

To Shift Blame to a Scapegoat. Retrenchment strategies send a powerful message to key stakeholders. Often the implied if not explicit message is one of blame. The program or service that is cut is portrayed as expendable, ineffective, wasteful, or worse. The programs or services that are cut become the scapegoats for all the troubles of the organization, often unjustifiably. Thus retrenchment can be a means of deflecting attention away from top management's responsibilities or a smokescreen hiding the fact that management has no realistic, long-term strategy to address the issues or that its original strategy has turned out to be wrong.

To Play Budgetary Round Robin. When organizations encounter sustained periods of retrenchment, sometimes managers will take the easy way out by rotating cuts around the various programs in the organization's portfolio. These cuts are akin to across-the-board cuts except that they are implemented sequentially rather than all at once. Thus the retrenchment strategy amounts to little more than the implied statement, "It's your turn to carry the burden for the rest of us."

Concluson

After the lengthy discussion of organizational closure, it is difficult to close this chapter with an upbeat tone. But I return to the theme presented at the beginning of the chapter. Retrenchment *is* and *must be recognized as* an important option in public and nonprofit managers' strategic arsenals. Sometimes, retrenchment is necessary to turn around a struggling organization. Other times, more dramatic methods of retrenchment are called for, including divestment of parts of a portfolio or closure of the entire organization. Even closure, although normally repugnant to any self-respecting manager, must be acknowledged as a viable strategy under certain circumstances.

In the end, nothing will test your skill as a manager like a retrenchment strategy.

Getting Started

---

1. Are there any programs or services in your organization's portfolio that are candidates for retrenchment? What forces have created this situation? What are the options?

2. Have you been affiliated with a significant organizational retrenchment in the past? How was that strategy developed? What went well? What went poorly? What did you learn?

3. How should Clairsville cope with its financial crisis? Are there lessons from the turnaround of Duquesne University that can be applied to Clairsville? What divestment options are most attractive for Clairsville?

7

Stability Strategies

The literature on strategic planning has conditioned us to believe that a deliberative and reflective examination of our organizations will nearly always result in the formulation of a *new* strategy, or at least a significant change in the direction of the organization. Usually the focus of the planning process is on growth or retrenchment. Rarely, it seems, do planners and executives talk about strategic options that will help an organization simply continue along its current course, hold on to its current portfolio, or maintain its present size.

But organizational stability is a perfectly legitimate strategic objective (Wheelen and Hunger, 1992). Indeed, it may be the most frequently pursued objective among public and nonprofit organization, especially during turbulent times.

Banksville Human Services Center

Ned Callery was delighted when Maura Richey, the state's deputy secretary of public welfare, paid an unexpected but welcome visit to his agency, the Banksville Human Services Center (BHSC).* Richey's visit gave Callery the opportunity to showcase the work of his agency and also to do some impromptu lobbying for certain

* This example is adapted from Leslie, 1992.

items on the fall legislative agenda in the state capital. But Richey seemed to have other things on her mind, and after a brief tour of the agency, she asked if she could meet alone with Callery on a matter of some urgency.

Callery could hardly believe his ears as Richey wasted little time getting to her point. She wanted Callery to apply for funds controlled by the Governor's Office in order to establish an assessment and referral program for people suffering from physical, emotional and mental disorders that might prevent them from finding and keeping decent jobs under the state's new welfare system. Richey said that BHSC was the perfect agency to play a critical coordinating role in the emerging managed care network that the governor wanted to establish, on an experimental basis, as part of the state's welfare reform program: "I probably shouldn't say this, Ned, but I could almost guarantee that we would fund such a proposal from your agency. You could practically write your own ticket on this project. It's the perfect chance to expand your program of services beyond crisis intervention. If you get this contract, BHSC will be given the central coordinating role in this part of the state, involving a wide network of other social service and health care organizations." It seemed that Richey could hardly contain her enthusiasm for the idea. She admitted that she had followed the progress that BHSC had made over the past few years and was impressed by its potential: "I've gone out on a limb with the governor by giving all of my support to BHSC on this project," she said. "The governor has a lot riding on this demonstration project, and I just know that BHSC is the agency to pull it off."

Callery was flattered by the attention that BHSC had received from Richey and the Governor's Office. Until recently, BHSC had struggled in relative anonymity as a small nonprofit social service organization that provided a wide range of services to families in need—individual and family counseling, economic assistance, housing referrals, job training, and other services. BHSC had been conceived as a sort of one-stop shop for social services, an idea hatched among a group of professors in the Department of Social Work at the local university. In its early years, though, BHSC had barely survived and had once come perilously close to bankruptcy. Only an eleventh hour rescue by the United Way saved the day.

Callery had been hired as the executive director two years ago and immediately launched a strategy of aggressive growth. During his interview for the job, he impressed the board by asserting that BHSC had been far too timid in its strategy. He was convinced that BHSC was well positioned to respond to the many needs brought about by the national welfare reform effort. He provided an impromptu environmental scan and portfolio analysis during his interview, showing that BHSC had some comparative advantages that had not been exploited. He said that only an aggressive growth strategy would ensure the future of BHSC.

Callery soon lived up to his promise by securing several major grants, including a national demonstration grant, to integrate several types of family services that had previously been spread among different agencies with little coordination. He also added a sophisticated and highly effective advocacy division, which had played an important role in crafting the state's welfare reform bill. BHSC grew horizontally as well as vertically. It had opened three branch offices in the last six months, providing easier access to families in need. Moreover, new services had been added to the portfolio, including a drug and alcohol assessment and referral program. In the past two years, BHSC had nearly doubled its budget, with proportionate growth in the number of paid and volunteer staff.

As he listened to Richey conclude her pitch, Callery felt justifiably proud of what he and his staff had accomplished. In many respects, Richey's overtures were confirmation that BHSC was an agency on the move. This could be the right opportunity to launch BHSC on a trajectory of continued growth and greater statewide influence for many years to come.

"Your idea is very interesting, Maura," Callery said. "I am inclined to submit a proposal. But I need to give it some serious consideration and talk with my staff about it. Of course, in order to make a major commitment like this, I'll need the endorsement of my board of trustees. Coincidentally, they have a meeting at the end of next week. I'll put this at the top of their agenda and will give you an answer then."

Richey pressed on, "OK, Ned, but don't take too long. The window of opportunity may close very rapidly. The Governor's Office is very high on BHSC right now, but there are other agencies that have been lobbying for this assignment. The governor would like us to make a decision soon in order to avoid increasing pressure." As he walked her out of the building, Callery assured Richey that this opportunity would be his top priority.

When Callery returned to his office, his mind was racing. There was much to do before sharing the idea with his staff and the board of trustees. He decided to devote the weekend to preparing a preliminary assessment of the impact the program would have on his agency. How many people would be needed to staff the new program? What skills would they need? Would the program have a significant impact on facility space? How would it affect the mission of BHSC? The staff and trustees would have many questions, and he wanted to be as thorough as possible.

Even before beginning his analysis, however, Callery was bothered by a nagging feeling. He should have been euphoric about Richey's proposal. After all, she had practically told him that the program was his if he wanted it. But he was beginning to suspect that BHSC might be biting off more than it could chew. He was even more skeptical after completing his weekend analysis. He estimated that no fewer than fifteen new staff, twelve professionals and three clerical workers, would be needed to support the program. This would represent a 50 percent increase in staff size. The coordinating program would likely need its own offices and support infrastructure, including a very elaborate information system for tracking clients through the maze of social service and health care providers who would be part of the managed care network. Ned wondered whether the culture of the managed care program would be compatible with the culture of the traditional BHSC services. And he wondered whether BHSC would need to stretch the interpretation of its mission in order to accommodate the new program.

Ned also worried about his clients, the individuals and families who had come to rely on BHSC for a wide variety of services and advice. BHSC had become a kind of community center in a blighted neighborhood—a place where people gathered to gossip and share news, hold neighborhood meetings, and just pass the time with friends. How would the radical expansion of the portfolio affect this informal mission of BHSC? Would BHSC be able to remain in its current facility? It seemed likely that the organization would need to move to a larger building in order to accommodate everyone under one roof. Or perhaps the various parts of the organization could be housed in different locations around town.

Finally, there was the political uncertainty connected to the program. The governor was facing a tough opponent in next year's election, a candidate who was strongly opposed to the state's welfare reform program, including the managed care component. Most political experts gave the governor no more than a 50 percent chance of reelection. Some insiders said his chances were even worse.

Beyond all the facts and figures, however, Callery simply had a gut feeling that now was not the appropriate time to be taking on a significant new responsibility. He scheduled a Monday morning breakfast meeting with his board chair, Lorna DeFazio, to discuss the idea with her. "On the one hand, the past twenty-four months have brought dizzying growth to BHSC," he told Lorna. "The staff are stretched to the limit. We have not had time to develop the administrative infrastructure to keep pace with the growing portfolio of programs, not to mention our new branch offices. Most days we just fly by the seat of our pants, making up the rules as we go along. We need time to consolidate the gains we have made over the past two years. Also, this new program would fundamentally alter our relationship with nearly every other social service agency in the region and perhaps with our clients in this neighborhood. We would become the gatekeeper for clients and funds. We have good relations with these agencies now, but I am sure that this program would create some tensions for us that might affect the success of our other programs.

"On the other hand, there are huge risks in not taking on this program. I suspect we will lose favor in the Governor's Office. A chance like this may never come along again. This could be our one opportunity to really solidify our position. If only Maura had brought us this opportunity next year, or even last year before we undertook all these new responsibilities! Despite its appeal, I'm worried that now is not the right time for us to take on this major new responsibility."

Lorna was surprised by Ned's ambivalence toward the opportunity. Was this the same guy who had boldly pushed BHSC to the forefront of the human services market? Over the past two years Callery had taken some risks that had made even the most entrepreneurial board members a little nervous. "Can we afford not to take this opportunity?" she thought. "But maybe now is just not the right time."

Ned Callery faces a very difficult decision. His organization is desperately in need of some breathing room and a chance to consolidate its recent gains. A period of stability would help BHSC develop the operating procedures, policies, and administrative infrastructure needed to support and sustain its expanded role. But what will happen if Callery turns down the opportunity that Maura Richey has practically handed to him on a silver platter? Will BHSC lose credibility in the Governor's Office? Will it lose momentum? After all, growth opportunities don't always happen just when we are ready for them. What message will Callery send to the employees and the board if he decides to turn down this opportunity? Will they conclude that he has become complacent?

Stability strategies are designed to help your organization protect and preserve its current position in the environment. Stability may be the appropriate course of action when your organization, like Callery's, has not yet emerged from a period of intense growth (or retrenchment) or when your strategic environment is changing very rapidly. In many cases, stability strategies are designed to be *short term,* to cover periods of transition or extreme environmental turbulence when the wisest course is to move very slowly if at all. Under such circumstances, one might legitimately argue that stability strategies are not *strategies* at all but *tactics* that help your organization make the transition from one phase to another.

But sometimes organizations follow a stability strategy for years. This does not mean that these organizations are stagnant. Indeed, they may continually develop new products and services for their community, and they may continually adopt management innovations to enhance their efficiency and effectiveness. But their objective in these moves is not to grow or retrench. Their objective is to remain more or less constant in terms of size and scope of service.

There is much to be said for stability in public and nonprofit organizations. Let's now examine some of the strategies that organizations follow when they want to ensure their stability.

Types of Stability Strategies

There are several types of strategies your organization can follow if you wish simply to stabilize its position (Wheelen and Hunger, 1992). A *status quo* strategy maintains the current status and direction of your organization. A *captive* strategy tries to shelter your organization from an increasingly hostile environment. A *pause* strategy may be appropriate following significant growth or retrenchment or other substantial organizational change. Finally, an *incremental* strategy continually tests the waters, making marginal adjustments as needed.

Status Quo Strategy

When using a status quo strategy, your organization will try to hold onto its current position in the marketplace, neither seeking gains nor looking for opportunities to cut back. Henry Mintzberg reminds us that organizational strategies, contrary to popular belief, are relatively stable (Mintzberg and Waters, 1982; Mintzberg and McHugh,

1985). Most often, a change in strategic direction takes place gradually and in small steps. Oftentimes, organizational strategies are essentially status quo strategies.

Sometimes this stability of organizational strategies is a by-product of the natural forces of organizational inertia and internal politics, which combine to stymie proposals for radical change with a barrage of bargaining maneuvers and compromises. At other times, however, the status quo strategy may be consciously and strategically chosen as the best approach under certain environmental circumstances.

But a status quo strategy is not a passive or *do nothing* strategy. Here are some proactive steps to take if your organization has consciously decided to follow a status quo strategy.

Be extremely vigilant for sudden changes in your organization's strategic environment, especially external developments that might erode the attractiveness of that environment. Relatively stable industries are often at the mature stage of the industry life cycle. The next stage might be decline, in which case you must be poised to take aggressive steps to respond to this circumstance, perhaps by retrenching or diversifying into other products or services.

Refine and enhance your organization's ability to monitor competitive trends and to continually monitor its industry for threats and opportunities. A status quo strategy provides a good opportunity to refine (or develop) environmental scanning techniques, benchmarking methods, competitive intelligence systems, and performance monitoring systems and databases.

Make modest but steady investments in research and development (R&D). Now might be a good time to do research and development on new programs and services that your organization could offer if its current industry suddenly turns sour.

Make efforts to protect your organization's current position in its industry by focusing on efficiency, productivity, and effectiveness in the delivery of programs and services. It is important to avoid becoming complacent with your organization's current production processes or its current methods of distributing its programs and services. A status quo strategy presents a good opportunity to make a modest investment in TQM or other continuous improvement quality initiative. TQM assumes that the fundamental mission and products of your organization will remain relatively stable. Its aggressive cousin, reengineering, is more appropriate for volatile environments and conditions of rapid organizational change.

Invest in employees' professional development. This will help members of the organization avoid complacency when status quo strategies are implemented and will also let you take advantage of this relatively stable period to develop the next generation of leaders in your organization.

Make continuous improvements in methods of outcome assessment. A status quo strategy provides a good opportunity to refine the methods your organization uses to determine how successful (or unsuccessful) it is in meeting community needs. Because your clients and portfolio are relatively stable, you should be better able to monitor outcomes longitudinally.

Continue to advocate the need for community investments in your organization's mission. Status quo strategies can lull funders, volunteers, grantmakers, and donors into a false sense of security or complacency. A status quo strategy must not be falsely interpreted as a sign that the community needs your organization addresses have become less urgent.

In general a status quo strategy provides a good opportunity for your organization to take stock of itself and its environment. It also provides a good opportunity for your organization to invest in the strategic management systems that will give management the information it needs to change strategy when the environment changes.

Captive Strategy

A status quo strategy will not stabilize an organization if the environment starts turning hostile or if the organization's position vis-à-vis other providers starts becoming less viable. Under these increasingly threatening circumstances, an organization may eventually be forced to divest or liquidate (see Chapter Six). But let's assume that there is still some life in the organization. It has provided a valued service and can continue to provide that service *if* the managers can buffer it from the increasingly hostile environment. Management might try to seek shelter much as a small boat tries to race to harbor before a gathering storm.

In the business world, such an approach is called a captive strategy. Using this strategy, a small company or one that will soon lose its competitive edge tries to find a stronger company that will be a benefactor of sorts by purchasing a large portion of the weaker company's products, thus guaranteeing at least temporarily the continued existence of the weaker company. Typically the benefactor purchases at least 75 percent of the of the captive company's product (Wheelen and Hunger, 1992). The captive company is of course relieved of many of the normal burdens of trying to compete in the increasingly hostile environment. For example, because it relies heavily on a single customer, its marketing and distribution costs are dramatically reduced. But the stability of this cozy and secure arrangement comes at a price. The captive company often gives up some of its autonomy to the benefactor company, including perhaps its personnel policies, its R&D programs, and even its freedom to sell its product to other buyers. Moreover, if the relationship sours, the captive organization stands to lose the most. The captive company becomes a de facto division or branch of the dominant company, but without the formality of a merger or acquisition.

In the nonprofit sector, some social service agencies are virtually captives of government agencies on which they rely for, say, 75 to 80 percent of their revenues. An agency that specializes in juvenile counseling, for example, might be a de facto captive of a county's Department of Child and Youth Services. Sometimes these arrangements evolve gradually over many years. But in other instances a nonprofit organization actually searches for the secure shelter provided by a sole source contract with a secure benefactor. On the one hand such an arrangement is very attractive because the captive nonprofit organization is essentially relieved of the need to engage in fundraising, marketing, and new product development. On the other hand it is in danger of losing much of its autonomy, becoming a kind of shadow government agency. If the policies or priorities of the government benefactor should change, the nonprofit captive will be in serious trouble because it has such a high stake in the relationship.

If you are considering a captive strategy for your organization or if you are already in a captive relationship with another organization, you should consider following these precautions:

Select a stable benefactor. Naturally, if you are going to place your organization's future in the hands of another organization, you want that organization to be as stable and secure as possible. You do not want 75 percent or more of your revenues to come from an organization that is itself in a precarious position. For example, it would be risky to align your organization with a county agency or bureau of state government that is notorious for its internal political squabbling or that has historically been a political football for the legislature. Certainly, you cannot control the stability of your benefactor, and the sailor's advice "Any port in a storm" may apply to your organization's situation. Nonetheless, if your organization is going to become a captive to another organization, you will want to pick one that is as stable as possible.

Negotiate multiyear contracts, if possible. Even though government contractors may not be willing to give your organization a multiyear commitment to provide them with certain services, you should try to negotiate terms that provide at least a moderate amount of stability and predictability. For example, you should demand significant advance notice if the benefactor decides not to renew the contract. Also, you should have the protection of clearly defined performance criteria for both your organization and the contracting agency.

Provide your benefactor with multiple services, if possible. Try to avoid a situation in which your organization's benefactor depends on your organization for one and only one service. If possible, negotiate an arrangement to provide several services because this diversification may protect your organization from becoming a victim of shifting political priorities.

Find ways to make your organization indispensable to the benefactor. By pursuing a captive strategy, your organization has placed its fate in the hands of the benefactor organization. It is therefore in your organization's interest, and entirely ethical, to make that relationship as valuable as possible to the benefactor. Indeed, the objective of the captive organization is to create a situation of mutual dependence, wherein the benefactor organization needs the captive as much as the captive needs the benefactor. If the relationship is one way, the captive's stability is in peril.

Build and maintain your own constituency. Even in the most stable captive relationship, your organization should never completely sacrifice its autonomy. Its autonomy in this case extends well beyond its formal legal status as an independent corporate entity to include the maintenance of its own constituency, separate from that of the benefactor agency. Your organization's stability within the relationship will be enhanced if the benefactor agency perceives that it has its own support network and stakeholders who will advocate for its interests.

Be vigilant for change in the benefactor's priorities. In a captive relationship, your strategic planning must be extended to include the environment of your benefactor agency as well as your organization's own strategic environment. Your organization's fate now rests in the benefactor's hands, for better or worse. Your environmental scanning must now focus on the threats and opportunities for the benefactor so your organization can position itself to play a continuing role in the benefactor's strategic priorities.

Obviously a captive strategy has certain advantages. But the costs and potential pitfalls are significant as well. Captive strategies will likely become even more prevalent as government agencies increasingly turn to nonprofit organizations and for-profit firms in their ongoing process of *devolution*. But management should not be lulled into a false sense of security simply because it appears that the contract that supplies 75 percent or more of an organization's revenues seems secure. Government priorities may change, and the relationship that seems to serve a captive organization so well today may become the chains that sink it tomorrow.

Pause Strategy

Following a period of dramatic change, your organization might want to temporarily pause in order to consolidate and to adjust to its new state (Wheelen and Hunger, 1992). Assume, for example, that your organization has recently added several branch offices in neighborhoods not previously served by it. Your organization may need time to adjust to the new demands created by this strategy of horizontal growth. New employees must be hired and trained; new clients must be served; perhaps totally new services must be added to your portfolio. This is essentially the situation facing Ned Callery in the case at the beginning of this chapter. Similarly, if your organization has recently retrenched, you will need to reassign workloads and duties, adjust operating procedures, and work more closely with clients to ensure some continuity of service.

Under these conditions, your organization may want to temporarily follow a pause strategy. The pause strategy is similar to the status quo strategy except that it has an explicit purpose—to help an organization adjust to a recent change. Also, a pause strategy is by design a temporary strategy. In fact, some people might be inclined to call this a *tactic* not a strategy because it is short term and designed to respond to a very specific set of organizational circumstances.

If you select a pause strategy, consider supporting it with the following actions:

Identify specific goals and outcomes. A pause strategy is designed to help an organization recover from a recent change in its scope and size or a recent trauma. A pause strategy is not a *resting* strategy.

Therefore you should identify specific goals and outcomes to be accomplished by the pause strategy. Perhaps the goal is the restoration of community confidence or the consolidation of recent gains from a growth strategy. Whatever your organization's goals, you should try to be very clear about them and about how you will know the organization has been successful in achieving them. Explicit goals will send an important message to employees and other stakeholders that the pause strategy is not simply an institutional rest period. Rather it is designed to accomplish specific objectives, and it will be abandoned when those objectives are met.

Establish deadlines. A pause strategy is not a long-term venture. It is a short-term adaptive mechanism. As such, it should include deadlines for the accomplishment of goals and these deadlines should be communicated to employees and other stakeholders. This sends a clear message that the pause strategy will have a discrete beginning, middle, and end. It will also enhance the accountability of people who work with you.

Communicate expectations. As implied in the previous points, a pause strategy should be accompanied by a clear message from the leader about what he or she expects from the organization during this phase of its development.

Provide the support needed to accomplish the goals. Many employees will be under extreme stress during a pause strategy. For example, they might be expected to take on greater workloads (following a growth or retrenchment strategy) and at the same time design administrative systems to accommodate that larger load. The temptation is to manage the crisis first and worry about the infrastructure later. If you really want the pause strategy to be successful, you will need to provide employees with the resources to make the changes you envision.

A pause strategy can help an organization stabilize its environment. But it is not a long-term approach. Eventually, management will need to move on to the next phase of the growth or retrenchment strategy.

Incremental Strategy

When the environment is changing too rapidly to be predictable or you anticipate a change that will affect your organization in significant ways, you may want to base your strategy on small, incremental steps rather than bold moves or no moves at all. An incremental strategy may be an organization's best choice when the environment is in flux, but the organization cannot afford to simply wait out the storm because a status quo strategy will weaken its marketplace position.

For example, in 2000, the health care industry is clearly in a state of dramatic flux and profound uncertainty. Today, the leaders of hospitals and health systems seem to have a more cautious attitude toward acquisitions and diversification into marginally related health care products like long-term residential care. Many people believe there will be a major backlash against managed care, leading some hospitals to a back-to-basics approach. However, the industry continues to be buffeted by dramatic change. Private, for-profit hospitals continue to gain market share. Medical technology is racing ahead at a blinding pace. And the labor market, especially the market for skilled registered nurses, is in a state of dramatic flux. Indeed, the health care industry may have been more predictable at the dawn of the Clinton administration, when there was an intense national debate about the possibility of a national health care system.

Under these conditions, how should hospitals and other health care organizations develop their strategies for the future? On the one hand they cannot afford to sit back and wait for the future to become more clear because the rest of the industry will pass them by. On the other hand, bold strategic moves such as major acquisitions or diversification into ancillary health services might be very risky in the current environment. Thus some health care organizations are choosing to follow an incremental strategy, taking small steps and trying to retain as much flexibility as possible, given the different directions the industry might take.

Incrementalism can be a viable strategy, especially when the following considerations are kept in mind (Quinn, 1978, 1980a, 1980b, 1982):

Cultivate multiple sources of strategic intelligence. In a turbulent environment you may find that your organization's formal systems for environmental scanning are nearly useless, because they cannot track the rapid (almost daily) pace of change. In this case, you need to tap other intelligence sources—networks of policymakers, lobbyists, advocacy organizations, consumers, professionals, and other stakeholders—who might be able to offer unique and potentially valuable insights on the environment.

Pursue tactical solutions but do not lose sight of the bigger picture. Incrementalism is an effort to break big problems down into small components that may be solved more readily. But you should not lose sight of the bigger picture. The experience of the U.S. military in Vietnam is often used as a somber reminder that tactical victories can be seductive and can distract attention from the bigger picture and the absence of an overall strategy.

Try to design flexibility into your incremental strategy. An incremental strategy is most helpful when it is amenable to change and adaptation as the environment changes. Sunk costs can be a trap here. They can convince you that your organization must stay the course when in fact flexibility is called for.

Develop a capacity for experimentation. Incremental decision making is most effective when accompanied by continual monitoring and evaluation of the decisions that are made. This requires a commitment of resources to formulate and test hypotheses regarding the effects of your incremental strategies.

The incremental approach has many attractive features, especially when the environment is complex or changing so rapidly as to preclude holistic strategy development. It is especially appropriate when it is *consciously chosen* as a strategy. Problems develop, however, when organizations slip into a mode of *permanent* incrementalism, locking themselves in an endless cycle of small, incremental strategy adjustments even when the environment calls for more dramatic action. These organizations become calcified and rigid. They lose the ability to innovate. Quite often they lose any comparative advantage they may have one time enjoyed.

Defensive Strategy

Finally, I must at least briefly mention strategies designed to stabilize an organization by essentially buying time. Defensive maneuvers and delaying tactics can be effective short-term strategies. They are a recipe for disaster, however, in the longer term.

The objective of a defensive maneuver or delaying tactic is to help the organization survive in its current form through a period of temporary instability in its environment. Often the objective is to maintain public confidence in the organization during periods of temporary distress. For example, you might choose a defensive maneuver when it would allow you to avoid retrenching in response to an environmental challenge and thus to avoid sending distressing signals to important constituencies. Your hope would be that the challenge would pass and that therefore there is no need to threaten public confidence in your organization.

For example, private companies will sometimes prop up, or artificially sustain, their profit margins during temporary downturns in sales by delaying discretionary expenditures on such items as research and development on new products, maintenance, marketing, and employee training. The decision to temporarily cancel or delay these expenditures is not readily apparent to anyone except insiders and the most vigilant industry analysts. Thus stockholders and also more casual observers see that the company's profits remain robust, and therefore their confidence in the company remains high. Obviously such a strategy—often called a *profit strategy* (Wheelen and Hunger, 1992)—is not appropriate in certain industries and certainly not likely to be successful as a long-term strategy. The airline industry, for example, was accused of deferring maintenance expenses during the intense price competition of the 1980s. Although their reported profits remained high, they may have damaged their credibility in the eyes of the public (Wheelen and Hunger, 1992).

Public and nonprofit organizations have their own delaying tactics and defensive maneuvers, many of which may be prudent in the short term but foolhardy if followed for a longer term. Often the motive for adopting such tactics is political and designed to sustain or create public confidence when the organization is threatened by external forces. Several years ago, for example, the city of Pittsburgh sold its water treatment plant in order to resolve a budgetary crisis without raising taxes, which the mayor had promised not to do. This was an entirely legal maneuver, but it violated a fundamental norm of prudent public finance—never sell capital assets to cover short-term operating expenses. The city's bond rating dropped as soon as investors and bond analysts discovered the move. But taxpayers were relatively oblivious to it. All they knew was that the mayor had fulfilled his promise not to raise taxes and had somehow found a way to balance the budget.

McMurtry, Netting, and Kettner (1990, pp. 76–77) recommend several stabilizing approaches, such as increasing fees, increasing workloads, freezing salaries, and relying more on volunteers. These defensive maneuvers and delaying tactics may work well in the short term, but they are not likely to serve your organization well as a long-term strategy. They may buy time, but they come at a cost to your organization's credibility.

When Stability Is a Viable Strategic Option

There are several conditions under which your organization may want to consider a stability strategy.

To Respond to Uncertain Market Conditions

Wheelen and Hunger (1992) say that stability strategies are appropriate for a successful organization operating in a market that (1) is facing the prospect of little or no growth or (2) is in such great flux that opportunities and threats cannot be predicted with any degree of accuracy. In the first instance the organization may lack the skills needed to diversify into other industries but yet be reluctant to invest heavily in its current line of business if the prospects for a good return on the investment are poor. In the second instance the organization simply cannot afford to take a chance on any dramatic change in its direction because it has no ability to predict what the environment will offer.

Under these conditions a stability strategy will work better for a moderately strong organization than it will for a weak organization. The stronger organization can afford to wait out the storm in an uncertain environment. But the same environment might be extremely threatening to a weak organization, perhaps prompting more drastic actions such as liquidation or bankruptcy (see Chapter Six) or even a high-risk investment in a growth strategy (see Chapter Five).

To Consolidate Gains

An organization that has recently emerged from a period of sustained growth may need time to adjust to its new size and profile. Let's say your organization has recently added new services to its portfolio and expanded its market area to include neighborhoods and clients it has not previously served. The organization will need time to adjust to these new responsibilities. Employees will need to be hired, trained, and socialized to organizational norms and values. Information systems will need to be developed or modified to handle new clients and services. Policies and procedures will need to be revised to ensure accountability under the new circumstances. The problem of adjustment is compounded if your growth strategy includes diversification or vertical integration strategies (see Chapter Five). Under these circumstances the learning curve will be especially steep as your organization adjusts to entirely new industries and markets.

To Adjust to Retrenchment

Retrenchment, like growth, is sometimes followed by a period of stability so that people in the organization can adjust to the new downsized organizational structure. It is likely that a retrenching organization will need to expand employee job descriptions, reengineer the way it provides goods and services to the public, and perhaps even eliminate parts of the portfolio or the administrative infrastructure. After each major phase of retrenchment, your organization may find it necessary to pause, if only briefly, in order to adapt to the new organizational design. A short-term stability strategy may help your organization cope effectively during periods of retrenchment, when its resources are stretched to the limit.

To Protect a Leadership Position in a Stable Market

High-performing organizations do not rest on their laurels. In the private sector high-performing organizations usually leverage their comparative advantages with aggressive growth strategies in an effort to gain an even stronger hand over their competitors.

But in the public and nonprofit sectors there are times when there is little to be gained by aggressive growth strategies. Suppose, for example, that your organization is the dominant provider of programs and services for which the demand and community support seem steady but not growing. Your organization's position has been secured by its past performance and community reputation. There are no significant threats from new entrants, and there are no substitute products on the horizon. At the same time, there is no prospect for dramatic growth in the demand for the programs and services the organization produces. Therefore a growth strategy would not likely pay dividends.

One option would be to diversify into programs and services that have higher growth potential. But let's assume your organization is prevented from diversifying by the limitations of its legal mandate or that you are simply not interested in diversifying because other lines of programs and services look no more attractive than the line your organization currently occupies. In addition, in the public and nonprofit sectors diversification often is precluded by political and jurisdictional constraints.

In this mix of circumstances your organization's only viable option may be to hold its course in its current line of programs and services. Your focus should be to continue to build on your comparative advantages in serving the community with a particular portfolio of programs and services. Naturally, you should keep a watchful eye out for opportunities and challenges that may arise, never becoming complacent with your organization's dominant position in the industry. But at least for the foreseeable future, a stability strategy might be the most viable approach.

To Stabilize Revenue Streams

Many nonprofit organizations operate in a volatile fiscal environment. Their revenues are up one year and down the next, depending on the success of their fundraising efforts and the fickleness of the philanthropic community. Sometimes these organizations crave stability and may even have a legitimate claim to demand stability because of the central role they play in the community. There may be a cogent argument therefore for these organizations to seek out a single benefactor or sponsor who will support the bulk of their activities. Many nonprofit organizations that serve children and youths, for example, may receive 70 to 80 percent of their revenues from contracts with county and state government agencies. They are in effect captives of these government agencies. By virtue of their fiscal dependency, they have become a kind of quasi-governmental organization. Their autonomy suffers, but their financial stability is enhanced by the relationship.

To Meet Community Demands
for Continuity of Service and Direction

Public and nonprofit organizations respond to pressing public needs that often cannot be met in the private marketplace. These needs are usually enduring, not fleeting. The poor will always be with us, and like the rest of us, they will always need food, clothing, and shelter. Roads are not likely to become obsolete soon, and so they will need to be maintained in safe condition. Criminals are not on the endangered species list, so we will always need police to protect the public safety.

Although the public's taste for commercial products may be very changeable, its demand for public goods is relatively stable. Salipante and Golden-Biddle (1995) make a convincing argument that public and nonprofit organizations should position themselves to continually respond to these relatively stable public needs, not flit from one product or industry to the next as businesses sometimes do in order to survive in volatile markets.

Conclusion

There are many circumstances in which a stability strategy may be appropriate—environmental turbulence, organizational trauma, and financial insecurity. But beyond these strategic rationales, there are other reasons to carefully consider a stability strategy for your organization.

According to Salipante and Golden-Biddle, a strategic orientation toward stability rather than toward radical change can facilitate the survival of public and nonprofit organizations by (1) keeping each organization loyal to its historical roots, the practices and routines that have made it valued in its community and the time-tested practices that have helped it survive difficult challenges in the past; (2) maintaining the continuity of each organization's core expertise, so that workers can develop expertise that has a long payback period; and (3) customizing any change so that it fits with each organization's mission and past routines and builds public confidence in the organization.

Getting Started

1. During what periods in your organization's history has the dominant strategy been one of stability? What environmental

conditions prevailed during those periods? How long did the strategy stay in place? What prompted a change in the strategy?

2. What would you do if you were Ned Callery in the case presented at the beginning of this chapter? Is his situation different from that of Barbara Jenkins in the case presented in Chapter Three?

8

Collaborative Strategies

Public and nonprofit organizations are under intense pressure to do more with less, stretching their scarce resources further and further. Growth strategies, when successful, may enhance your organization's capacity to deliver more and more services, but growth strategies also consume more resources. Collaborations and cooperative arrangements between two or more organizations offer one promising way to accomplish more without necessarily adding more resources. In addition, there are powerful political forces that are driving public and nonprofit organizations toward collaborative (versus competitive) relations with their peer organizations. For example, the media and other critical observers have noted that nearly thirty thousand nonprofit organizations receive letters of certification each year from the Internal Revenue Service. They say that this level of growth inevitably leads to duplication of service and counterproductive competition among nonprofits for scarce community resources (Gaul and Borowski, 1993).

Whatever the motivation, many people are calling on public and nonprofit organizations to cooperation with each other rather than compete with each other (Huxham, 1996).

The American Heart Association, New York City Chapter

When the New York City chapter of the American Heart Association (NYCAHA) needed to cut costs, it looked at its options.* It could cut the scale of its educational and research programs designed to reduce individuals' risk of heart attack and stroke. It could eliminate some programs altogether. It could cut administrative expenditures. Or it could reduce its support staff and ancillary activities like lobbying and information management.

The NYCAHA opted to follow the last two strategies but in a novel way. Instead of taking a slash-and-burn approach, NYCAHA decided to team up with two of its "competitors," the National Multiple Sclerosis Society and the Arthritis Foundation. These organizations were suffering the same difficulty that NYCAHA faced—finding sufficient resources to carry out their many functions in a era of austerity in the health care industry. Beginning with a casual luncheon conversation, the CEOs of NYCAHA and the National Multiple Sclerosis Society talked about the prospect of sharing certain ancillary functions. First, they focused on lobbying. NYCAHA employed a full-time lobbyist who worked with legislators, volunteers, grassroots advocacy organizations, doctors, and the people NYCAHA served. Could the lobbyist possibly advocate on behalf of other comparable organizations? Certainly the players and the issues overlapped whether one was advocating more research on heart disease or more services for people afflicted with arthritis. Of course, the organizations did compete for scarce resources, but they also shared many core values, aspirations, and objectives. Later these two executives approached the Arthritis Foundation as a third partner.

It was decided that the lobbyist would work for all three organizations, each paying one-third of her salary. One day she might have a meeting with a legislator about antismoking legislation on

* This example is adapted from Wiesendanger, 1994. Copyright © 1994 by Faulkner & Gray, Inc. Reprinted with permission.

behalf of the NYCAHA. The next she might talk to the same legislator (or others) about access to health care on behalf of her other two employers. On certain issues, she might stress that all three organizations support the same core principles, but she could also explain each organization's nuances and priorities.

Other efforts to reduce expenditures in the NYCAHA focused inward. "Basically, we asked ourselves, 'What are our strengths? And what can be done at a lower cost by farming it out, making more dollars available for programs and the things we're really all about?'" said Michael Weamer, executive vice president of NYCAHA (Wiesendanger, 1994, p. 35). NYCAHA executives decided to protect the core mission and technology of the organization, concentrating on the funding and coordination of research. But again they found that ancillary functions might be reengineered. They decided for example to outsource the work of processing memorial gifts made to the NYCAHA to the AHA's state office in Syracuse.

And NYCAHA continues to look for collaborative ventures with the National Multiple Sclerosis Society and the Arthritis Foundation. The three organizations have discussed joint fundraising activities and a shared computer network among other options.

Types of Cooperative Effort

There are several types of cooperative venture, varying in complexity and in the level of commitment they require from the participating organizations.

Resource Sharing

The organizations in the case just described are involved in the most straightforward type of cooperative effort—*resource sharing*. They have decided to share the services of one lobbyist, and they are exploring other opportunities for resource sharing, perhaps involving information systems and databases.

Resource sharing is the most elementary type of collaborative effort but extremely effective. The parties agree simply to share the cost of certain portions of their administrative or service delivery infrastructure or to jointly purchase and share a resource they do not currently possess. The goal of such an arrangement is usually quite simple and straightforward—to save money by sharing a resource or to acquire a resource that none of the participating organizations could afford or justify on its own. Two suburban communities might agree to purchase an expensive sewer cleaning machine that neither could afford (or fully employ) on its own. Two small nonprofit organizations might agree to jointly purchase an integrated information system or even an office building that neither could afford on its own.

Resource sharing arrangements require a moderate level of administrative oversight, but they do not involve a significant or pervasive commitment from all members of the organization. In fact, depending on the nature of the resources being shared, the parties to the agreement may have very little direct interaction with each other after the initial agreement is struck. All participants retain complete organizational autonomy, and their interaction with each other is essentially limited to the use of the shared resource.

But this relatively simple form of cooperation can provide the essential foundation for more elaborate and ambitious collaborative efforts later on. Familiarity and trust can be built through resource sharing arrangements, and the participating parties may soon discover that they have in common larger strategic issues that may warrant a deeper commitment to each other. The two municipalities that share a sewer cleaning machine soon may discover that they also share many of the same problems in maintaining their total capital infrastructure. After a successful experience with sharing the sewer equipment, they may conclude that additional cooperative ventures will be even more beneficial. They may decide that a larger commitment, perhaps involving other neighboring communities, is needed to address the problem. Ultimately they may decide that they need to create a new regional organization, a joint venture (as discussed later), such as a council of governments (COG) or a regional sewer authority that is capable of issuing bonds and doing regional planning. In other words, every journey begins with a single step, and a resource sharing agreement can be the first step toward a more ambitious collaborative venture (Kearns, 1989).

Joint Ventures

A *joint venture* is a more complex and ambitious type of cooperative arrangement, involving commitments from two or more organizations to undertake a major project or to jointly address a strategic issue or community need. For example, several nonprofit organizations may decide that a major community need or problem, such as gang violence, is not being adequately addressed by any existing organization working alone. They may then decide to work together to address the issue. Or two federal agencies may come to the conclusion that their individual efforts are not enough to combat white-collar crime. They may then decide to form a joint task force to address the issue.

A joint venture can take many forms. In its most elementary form, a joint venture has as its objective a single project with a discrete beginning, middle, and end. This type of joint venture does not necessarily require a sophisticated infrastructure to hold it together. Instead the participating organizations simply agree to distribute responsibility among themselves for the various obligations and responsibilities associated with the project. They map out the project steps and stages and then simply parcel out various parts to each participating organization. They may meet periodically to review progress and to redefine the needs, and there may be an interorganizational team of employees assigned to carry out the project. But there is relatively little formal infrastructure holding the joint venture together. This type of informal joint venture is sometimes used to undertake a well-defined project such as a fundraising event, for example, or a venture that essentially sustains itself over time.

A more complex type of joint venture involves larger projects with more open-ended agendas and for which goals and their attainment may be more subjectively determined. Such projects may involve the creation of an interorganizational task force or other coordinating body that is formally charged with undertaking the project on behalf of the participating organizations. This task force may have all the attributes short of formal incorporation of an autonomous organization, and it may last for months or even years.

This type of joint venture may involve relatively complex and sensitive negotiations among the participating organizations on such issues as the mandate for the task force, who will lead the joint venture, how it will be governed, and when it will come to a close.

The distinguishing feature of a joint venture, whether simple or complex, is that it is intended to undertake a particular project or to address a particular need. Although the level of commitment is high in comparison with simple resource sharing, the venture still has definite boundaries and any change or extension of these boundaries will require renegotiation among the participating organizations.

Strategic Alliances

Strategic alliances are the most ambitious type of cooperative arrangement and also the most open ended. A strategic alliance is a commitment by two or more organizations to join forces to address a wide range of strategic issues that affect attainment of their respective missions. Strategic alliances go far beyond normal interorganizational dealings but fall short of a formal merger or consolidation. Often a strategic alliance will involve the creation of a new organization, charged with undertaking a variety of activities on behalf of the participating organizations.

For example, if several neighboring communities decide to create a council of governments, then they must make a commitment to the formation of a new corporate entity that will undertake various projects on behalf of the participating members. The COG will likely have a charter describing its purpose, a set of bylaws describing how it will be governed, and policies and procedures for its daily management. This type of strategic alliance is usually reserved for highly open-ended agendas and goals. In other words, the participants envision that the alliance will evolve over time to address a variety of opportunities and challenges, from the simple to the complex. The COG, for example, might facilitate the member communities' joint purchase of expensive equipment such as a fleet of new police cars. The objective here is simply to achieve some cost savings for the individual communities via a bulk purchase. But the COG may also engage in far more ambitious (and ambiguous) tasks such as recruiting new industries to the area, developing a comprehensive land use plan, overhauling the zoning ordinances, or negotiating tax sharing arrangements among the member municipalities. Nonprofit organizations sometimes form regional or statewide alliances to engage in lobbying, public education and advocacy, joint purchasing, and resource sharing.

Strategic alliances require a higher level of commitment than resource sharing arrangements, but the payoffs are potentially much greater as well. Table 8.1 summarizes the key features of the three types of cooperative ventures just described.

Motivations for Interorganizational Cooperation

There are many reasons why public and nonprofit organizations should consider cooperative ventures as part of their portfolios. An organization may be under intense pressure from powerful constituencies to collaborate with peer organizations. Grantmaking federations like the United Way are encouraging collaborative efforts among nonprofit human service organizations, and some foundations have made collaboration a condition for receiving funds. Or an organization might make a deep commitment to a collaborative strategy because management believes collaboration is in the best interests of the organization and the communities it serves.

Some Good Reasons to Cooperate

Here are some good reasons to cooperate with other organizations.

TABLE 8.1 Types of Interorganizational Cooperation.

	Resource Sharing	Joint Venture	Strategic Alliance
Description	An agreement between two or more organizations to share selected resources such as people, equipment, or information used to accomplish their respective missions.	A commitment by two or more organizations to jointly undertake a project or initiative to address a strategic issue facing the organizations or to address an unmet need in the community.	A formal commitment by two or more organizations to formally join forces to undertake a variety of long-term strategic initiatives, often open ended.
Objective	To increase efficiency and effectiveness in the use of scarce resources, or to allow the cooperating organizations to acquire resources they would not be able to afford or justify on their own.	To leverage the resources and expertise of the participating organizations, thereby allowing them to accomplish together what none of them could accomplish acting alone.	To undertake open-ended initiatives involving some resource sharing, some joint venturing, and some long-term commitments for as yet unspecified strategic initiatives that are in the best interests of the participating organizations.
Infrastructure	Often not needed. The participating organizations may establish an advisory committee	Often takes the form of a co-ordinating body such as a temporary task force, an advisory	Typically involves the creation of a formal organizational mechanism like a coalition,

	or assign an employee to oversee and manage the arrangement.	committee, a special commission, or a network.	confederation, consortium, league, or partnership.
Risk	Relatively low, depending on the financial commitment made by each organization. Virtually no impact on your mission, goals, or autonomy.	Slightly higher, depending on the strength of the commitment to work collaboratively toward a common goal. Substantial commitments of time and other valuable resources may be required and organizational mission and goals may be affected.	Relatively high, due to commitment to form an alliance with another organization just short of a merger or consolidation. Controversy may arise over governance, shared power, and distribution of costs and benefits.
Formality	Minimal infrastructure. May be entirely informal, based on a handshake between two executive directors. Or may be more formal, based on a contract that specifies all parties' rights and obligations.	Depends on the nature of the objective. When it is modest, such as coordinating an event, the agreement may be relatively informal. When it is to address a long-standing community problem or other controversial task, the participants will likely make a far more formal commitment.	Typically high, involving contractual commitment to the alliance, mandatory obligations to its support and maintenance, and specified rights and obligations.

Source: Adapted from Winer and Ray, 1994, p. 22.

To Advance the Mission of Your Organization. As with every
other strategy discussed in this book, the prime reason to pursue a
collaborative strategy is to advance your organization's mission and
your organization's contributions to the communities it serves. If
the cooperative venture does not meet this critical test, it is not
worth the effort. The cooperative arrangement should help your
organization accomplish something (or acquire the resources to
accomplish something) that it could not accomplish or acquire on
its own.

This criterion should be met by all organizations participating
in a collaboration, not just one or two. Therefore it becomes more
difficult to meet as more organizations join the cooperative venture.
It is probably unrealistic to expect a cooperative arrangement to be
equally beneficial to all participants. Some will inevitably benefit
more than others. But, in the end, each participant must be able to
say unequivocally that the cooperative venture contributes mean-
ingfully to the accomplishment of its own mission.

***To Grow or to Otherwise Expand Your Impact in the Commu-
nity.*** Cooperative arrangements can be a powerful mechanism for
external growth (see Chapter Five). For example, acting alone your
organization might not be able to afford to open a branch office or
might not have sufficient leverage to vertically integrate by acquiring greater control of supply and distribution channels. A cooperative venture with another organization might help it accomplish
these objectives with a lower level of risk and financial commitment than would be required if it pursued the growth strategy on
its own.

Thus a cooperative venture might help your organization
strengthen its position in its strategic environment by expanding its
service area or by controlling production and distribution costs
more effectively than other providers do. A cooperative venture is
a viable way to enhance your organization's comparative advantage
relative to other organizations without encountering some of the
risks inherent in internal growth strategies.

To Retrench Without Diminishing Your Quantity or Quality of Services. The attractive paradox of cooperative strategies is that you can use them either to grow or to downsize your organization. When used as part of an overall retrenchment strategy, a cooperative venture may help your organization hold services at their current level while using fewer resources. Resource sharing arrangements, for example, might accomplish this objective. The organizations in the opening case study in this chapter were facing the prospect of retrenchment that might have cut into some of their core services. Then they discovered ways to save money (and those core services) by sharing their government relations activities.

A cooperative venture may be especially helpful to a small and young organization that is retrenching and perhaps threatened with extinction. The dilemma, of course, is that vulnerable organizations typically have a difficult time finding partners because they may bring little or nothing of real value to the cooperative arrangement.

To Reduce Unproductive Duplication of Services. Another worthy motive for cooperation takes a community-wide perspective. This motive is to reduce redundancy among a group of peer organizations, all of whom provide similar or complementary services to the community. What is redundancy? The answer to that question is not as simple as managers might first assume. Essentially, redundancy is defined by the market. Go to the dairy case at your local supermarket, and count the number of brands of orange juice for sale. There is significant redundancy in that market because there is sufficient consumer demand for marginal (but seemingly infinite) variations in the attributes and prices of orange juice products. But consumers and especially funders of public and nonprofit programs and services have a lower tolerance for redundancy because they perceive it to be a waste of scarce community resources. They do not detect an overall improvement in quality as a result of competition. Rather they see only duplication of services.

So at one level redundancy is a subjective construct. At another level it is defined fairly clearly and perhaps ruthlessly by the marketplace. Whatever one's definition, a cooperative venture can reduce or eliminate some types of duplication.

To Create Synergies, Making the Whole More Than the Sum of Its Parts.   Another noble objective of a cooperative venture is to leverage the resources of two or more organizations into something even more powerful and beneficial to the community. A joint venture or strategic alliance might be used, for example, to attract more resources to the community in the form of grants or intergovernmental transfers. Or a successful joint venture might inspire other organizations to follow that venture's lead and could become a template for them to emulate, thereby spreading the benefits of cooperation beyond the boundaries of the original agreement.

To Enhance Visibility and to Build Community Support for a Worthy Cause.   Collaborative strategies often have higher levels of community visibility than even the most ambitious individual efforts of organizations acting alone. The media, for example, often respond favorably to announcements of cooperative ventures because they capture the imagination and tap into cooperative values and ideals that many Americans hold to be part of the bedrock of the nation. Thus a collaborative venture may give your organization a platform from which to advocate certain policy issues or causes, and this advocacy may have greater credibility because it is supported not only by your organization but by your organization's partners as well.

There is power in numbers, and a collaborative effort will also attract the attention of political officials and other community leaders. For example, a state legislature may look first to its state's League of Municipalities to test the reaction to a proposed piece of legislation affecting local governments in the state. The legislators know that the league will be able to mobilize support or opposition when the bill comes up for a vote. Better to have the league involved early on in the deliberations and to solicit its members' opinion and involvement in the drafting process than to have the league emerge later in opposition to the bill. This strategic alliance greatly enhances the power of the members, some of whom are too small to have a meaningful input into the bigger political agenda. Together, however, their power is increased geometrically.

Some Questionable Reasons to Cooperate

There are a few dubious reasons to seek out cooperative arrangements with other organizations. Fortunately, most of these will surface before the agreement is consummated.

To Use Collaboration as a Crisis Management or Avoidance Tactic. When the wolf is at the door, an endangered organization might seek a cooperative arrangement in order to survive a while longer. This last ditch effort, even if temporarily successful, will likely only delay the inevitable. The organization might want to drastically reduce its administrative overhead, and perhaps it harbors hope that the cooperative venture will allow it to eliminate certain support positions like clerical support or MIS personnel. In the long run, however, these savings will probably be trivial in comparison with the organization's financial troubles. A cooperative venture will rarely save a dying organization. Moreover, a dying organization will have trouble finding partners for a collaborative venture unless its management lies or hides the truth about its difficulties.

To Use Collaboration as a Public Relations Tactic. As I mentioned earlier, a collaborative effort oftentimes attracts favorable media attention. This public relations bonanza is short lived, however, and by itself it is a poor motivation for a cooperative venture. Even though it may be rare for media coverage to be a primary motive for cooperative ventures, it is easy for participants in a cooperative venture to inflate the venture's significance in order to attract as much favorable media attention as possible. The chances are that you, like me, have attended more than a few press conferences or cocktail receptions where a new "community-wide collaboration," "public-private partnership," or "strategic initiative" has been announced with great fanfare. Food and drinks are served. Posters and brochures are on display. Then, one-by-one, community leaders, politicians, and advocates take their turn at the podium to announce and endorse the new venture and to seize a few moments of favorable publicity for themselves. But the event is soon forgotten and the collaborative venture fades into the programmatic landscape or is abandoned or is incorporated into yet another new program to be announced at yet another press conference.

To Satisfy Funders or Other Important Stakeholders. The motivation for entering a collaborative arrangement with another organization is sometimes external pressure. Grant guidelines, for example, may specify collaborative strategies as a condition for funding. State legislatures may demand that municipalities and counties engage in intergovernmental cooperation before they can qualify for certain contracts or fund transfers. Certainly such demands are powerful motivators and catalysts, and they are not inappropriate as long as they do not cause organizations to simply go through the motions of a collaboration in order to satisfy the most narrow interpretation of the mandate or guidelines. Unfortunately, mandates often produce just that kind of behavior—minimal compliance in order to qualify for the reward.

It probably goes without saying that cooperative ventures are most successful when all partners enter the arrangement of their own accord and with full commitment to the spirit as well as the literal interpretation of the mandate.

Barriers to Collaboration

Even successful collaborative ventures encounter problems and barriers that threaten their viability. Anticipating these problems can help you prepare appropriate responses.

Turf Mentality. Government organizations at all levels—national, state, and local—tend to think in terms of jurisdictions and boundaries. Sometimes these are geopolitical boundaries, such as those separating two county governments, and sometimes they are operational jurisdictions, such as those separating a local police force and the FBI. Whatever their origins, these boundaries can become political *turf* that (in the minds of parochial stakeholders) must be defended. Private nonprofit organizations can also succumb to this turf mentality, especially in a competitive environment where many nonprofits are fighting to retain their existing markets or to expand into new ventures.

Conflicting Cultures. Every organization has a culture—a collection of values, beliefs, norms, and assumptions—that provides the invisible but very powerful framework within which people work. Cultures form gradually over time, and they are very difficult to change. Some organizational cultures, for example, are highly normative. They dictate how people dress for work, how they interact with clients and with each other, how newcomers are "oriented" to the social system, and how unacceptable behavior is "punished." Other cultures are more relaxed but equally pervasive in their effect on organizational behavior. The cultures of public and nonprofit organizations can be especially powerful because these organizations are driven so strongly by their missions and core values. Private for-profit firms are dedicated to maximizing value for shareholders. Public and nonprofit organizations, in contrast, exist to fill a need or address a societal concern. They attract people who are deeply committed to the organizational missions and those who have the professional skills needed to attain these missions. Thus these organizations tend to build up powerful and compelling cultures around those missions and around the professional disciplines that support the mission.

If the culture of your organization has become calcified and inflexible, it can be a significant barrier to cooperative ventures with other organizations. Members of your organization might perceive a prospective partner as "different from us." For example, a collaborative venture between two social service organizations broke down because one of the organizations had a consensual culture, in which important decisions were traditionally made by the group, whereas the other organization had an action-oriented culture, in which all important decisions were made by the founding executive director. The employees in the consensual organization could not tolerate the "paternalism" of employees in the action-oriented organization, whereas the employees in the action-oriented organization lost patience with the "indecisiveness" and "dysfunctional democracy" of the consensual organization.

Mixed Loyalties and Role Conflict. A collaborative strategy calls upon employees and other stakeholders to divide their loyalties. On the one hand they are asked to look out for the interests of their parent organization, and on the other hand they are asked to be attentive to the goals of the collaborative venture. Sometimes these two objectives will conflict with each other, and employees will feel that their loyalties are divided. If forced to choose, they may fall back to familiar terrain by defending their turf and their culture.

Similarly, collaborative strategies may impose role conflict on employees. As members of an interorganizational team or task force, they may ask themselves, When should I represent my team and when should I represent my organization, and what if neither the team nor my organization is adequately representing my clients? In other words, a collaborative venture may place even greater stress on employees who are already feeling role conflict between loyalty to their clients and loyalty to their organization.

Lack of Sustained Commitment and Leadership. Collaboration is an idea in good currency right now. Many public and nonprofit leaders are jumping on the bandwagon by making public pronouncements in favor of collaborative ventures and perhaps even committing their organizations to specific collaborative efforts. A windfall of goodwill and even grants and contracts may come from such public posturing. But if the leader is not committed to the collaborative venture for the long term, it will surely fail.

Some leaders launch collaborative ventures with the best of intentions, not merely to gain short-term benefits, but then they lose their nerve when the venture encounters its first serious challenge. Employees quickly detect the leader's loss of confidence in the effort, and in turn, they too begin to distance themselves from it.

Lack of a Track Record of Successful Collaborations. There is good reason for the old saying that "nothing breeds success like success." The theory of organizational ecology suggests that organizations learn to be successful by overcoming threats and becoming progressively stronger and smarter if they are fortunate enough to make it through their vulnerable youth and adolescence.

But the concept of interorganizational collaboration is still quite new in the public and nonprofit sectors, and therefore many organizations simply do not have much experience to draw upon. Even mature organizations may be neophytes in the game of joint ventures. Their lack of experience makes their fledgling efforts at cooperation especially vulnerable. The cycle of failure continues if an initial effort sours the attitude of leaders and employees toward subsequent opportunities that may arise.

Logistical Barriers and Fundamental Incompatibility. Finally, some collaborative ventures fail or never really get off the ground because the partners have fundamental incompatibilities. These may be operational. Perhaps the two organizations operate on different fiscal years, use fundamentally different accounting systems, or have other policies and procedures that are fundamentally at odds with each other. Quite often such logistical barriers can be overcome, especially in the more modest types of cooperative venture such as simple resource sharing or simple types of joint ventures. Logistical barriers may be significant, however, for strategic alliances.

Initiating and Sustaining Cooperative Arrangements

Collaboration among public and nonprofit organizations is a topic that has attracted a lot of attention lately (Mattessich and Monsey, 1992; Winer and Ray, 1994; Butterfoss, Goodman, and Wandersman,

1996). From this growing body of research, it is possible to summarize the characteristics that seem to contribute to successful collaborative ventures as well as the barriers that often impede or destroy such ventures.

Cooperative ventures seem to be most successful under the following conditions:

- When the participating organizations have complementary missions
- When each organization contributes something of genuine value
- When the participating organizations have a high level of mutual trust and respect
- When there are agreed-upon mechanisms to resolve conflict and adapt the arrangement to changing circumstances
- When there is strong leadership that continually endorses the collaboration and provides resources to support it
- When the organization can draw upon a history of collaboration

Complementary Missions, Visions, and Goals

Participants in a cooperative arrangement should have complementary, though not necessarily identical, missions and aspirations. Say, for example, that Organization X, a nonprofit health advocacy organization operating in several states on the West Coast, is thinking about franchising its services through Organization Y, a Chicago-based social service agency. The two organizations have vastly different missions and aspirations. X envisions itself as a national health advocacy and research organization. Y simply wants to enhance the range and quality of services it offers in the Chicago area. The franchise arrangement will help X extend its market area and perhaps even lay the foundation on which X could become an affiliate-based organization with national visibility. The cooperative arrangement may also help Organization Y enhance its portfolio of services to better serve its local community.

Clearly, the missions, aspirations, and goals of Organizations X and Y are different. But they are complementary and fully compatible. Through the arrangement, X might take a major step toward establishing national visibility, and Y might expand the portfolio of services it can offer to people in the Chicago area.

Sometimes the compatibility (or incompatibility) of missions and aspirations is so readily apparent that it does not need to be explicated and dissected. At other times, however, what may appear to be compatibility may be an illusion. It is worth the time and effort to fully discuss your organization's mission and your potential partner's mission, as well as each organization's self-interests, before making a significant commitment to the arrangement. Here are some approaches that may be helpful:

Compatibility of missions. Take the time to read and discuss your organizations' respective mission and vision statements. If you or your prospective partners do not have formal mission and vision statements, you should be especially diligent in discussing your respective purposes and aspirations.

Compatibility of values. Look closely at your organizations' respective values, beliefs, and operating philosophies. Again, these do not necessarily need to be identical, but they must be complementary. Is your organization in fundamental agreement with the values and operating philosophies of the partner organization? In what ways, if any, might those values and operating philosophies be at odds with your organization's mission? Will they consistently produce priorities for your partner that are different from your own? Will they lead to a clash in the way the two of you do business?

Synergies. Try to be as clear as possible about what *complementary* means to you and to your prospective partner. How do your respective missions work in concert? What are the prerequisites for success in your respective missions? Where and how significantly do your respective missions diverge?

Try to be as clear as possible about how pervasive the compatibility of values must be to sustain a long-term relationship. For example, the American Civil Liberties Union and the Ku Klux Klan may have compatible interests and visions in one very narrow respect (the belief that Klan members have a right to free speech), leading perhaps to a short-term partnership with respect to specific litigation or controversies. But the incompatibility of these two organizations on other more pervasive aspects of their respective mission precludes a long-term relationship.

The Value Brought to the Relationship: Symbiosis, Mutual Dependence, and Self-Interest

Each participant in a cooperative arrangement must bring something to the table that is needed or at least valued by the others. One organization might bring specific skills while another brings political clout and credibility. One organization might bring high capacity for production and quality control while another brings a sophisticated distribution network. The skills or attributes they bring should be complementary and able to work together in synergy to accomplish the organizations' respective missions and aspirations.

Organizations of vastly different sizes and resources can still bring complementary resources to the cooperative arrangement. In the example just discussed, Organization X brings a host of resources to the franchise arrangement, including a sophisticated research and development staff, close ties to health policy experts and national political leaders, and a strategic plan for certain types of health advocacy programs and services. Organization Y, though much smaller than X, brings a network of distribution centers in the Chicago area and the ability to communicate to a different audience about certain health issues. Organization Y may also have a grassroots presence that can reach audiences heretofore inaccessible to Organization X.

Most relationships, whether interorganizational or interpersonal, are devoted at least in part to preserving mutual self-interests. We form friendships and more intimate relationships out of love, and, true, we do try our best to unselfishly meet our partner's needs even when ours are not met. But we also meet our own needs in these relationships. We marry for security, for companionship, and perhaps even for social acceptance in a society that values marriage. We seek out friends in order to avoid loneliness and perhaps even to reinforce the notion that we are attractive and interesting to others.

Similarly, organizations do not seek partners out of a sense of altruism. They seek partners and collaborative ventures because they have come to the conclusion that these ventures will serve their own interests, as well as society's interests, better than they can serve these interests on their own. One-sided relationships rarely last, and even when they do, they rarely produce desirable results.

Although it is always difficult and risky to be perfectly explicit about your own self-interests, it is worthwhile to discuss the following questions with your prospective partner.

- What is your own organization trying to achieve via the cooperative relationship and how might your prospective partner help you achieve that? What is your prospective partner trying to achieve and how might your organization help?

- How do your organization's strengths and weaknesses specifically match up with those of your prospective partner?

You should be candid about the resources you think your organization can bring to the arrangement and ask your prospective partner to be equally candid. Certainly you should do your *due diligence* prior to entering the arrangement by examining the financial and performance records of your prospective partner. You should also find out as much as you can by talking to people who are familiar with the organization. Ultimately, however, you must have the face-to-face discussion with the representative of the other organization in which each of you talks about what your organizations can and cannot bring to the relationship.

Mutual Trust and Credibility

It is perhaps trite to say that interorganizational relationships are most successful when based on mutual trust. But what is trust, and how is it established in a relationship? Trust is an intangible, relative, and subjective construct. Trust is built on performance; trust is created when all participants in a collaborative strategy carry through on their end of the bargain.

Perhaps trust is truly built up only over time, but here are some indicators of trust that should be tested prior to entering a cooperative arrangement:

- Does your prospective partner have a history of exemplary performance, delivering services in a timely and effective manner with positive outcomes for the community? Is its history characterized by stability and continuity, or has it followed an erratic and chaotic path? Has its organizational strategy been coherent and reasonably consistent?

- Has your prospective partner followed through on what it has publicly promised to do? For example, has it followed through on what it pledged to do in its formal strategic plans? If not, does it have good reasons for changing directions?

- In your discussions with your prospective partner, have its representatives consistently and faithfully delivered information or products to you as promised?

- Does your prospective partner walk its talk? That is, has it ever intentionally or unintentionally promised more than it could deliver?

Management of Conflicts, Differences, and Changing Circumstances

Regardless of how carefully you select your partners, no cooperative arrangement can be expected to be totally free of conflict. Indeed, any relationship that is totally free of conflict is likely to be pretty boring, if not stagnant and nonproductive. Conflict, in moderation, is a sign of a healthy and vital relationship.

Therefore you should neither search fruitlessly for a conflict-free relationship nor suppress conflict when (not if) it arises. Rather, the key is to work with your partners to develop ways to confront and resolve conflicts when they occur. Part of this process is attitudinal, and part of it is procedural. The attitudinal part involves recognizing and valuing differences between your organization and your partner organizations. Each comes to the relationship with different strengths and weaknesses. Although these sometimes produce conflicts in terms of frames of reference and priorities, they also are complementary and help organizations accomplish things together that they could not accomplish alone. Seeing the positive side of these differences, especially when one is in the middle of a conflict, is easier said than done. Still, it is essential to work continually to develop respect and appreciation for the differences that each organization brings to the cooperative enterprise.

The procedural part of the process involves establishing routines through which your organization and its partner can periodically review their respective priorities and negotiate differences when they occur. Experts on conflict resolution tell us that we should focus first on our respective values and objectives, leaving the mechanics for achieving those objectives till later (Fisher and Ury, 1981).

Another important feature of successful cooperative ventures is the ability of the organizations to modify the arrangement as circumstances change. In today's dynamic environment the conditions that provide the original catalyst for the cooperative venture will quickly change. The organizations then need to decide whether the cooperative venture still makes sense, and if so, how it must be modified to respond to the new circumstances. There is a delicate balance in any cooperative arrangement between *structure* (which ensures that expectations, responsibilities, and outcomes are clearly understood) and *flexibility* (which is essential to adapt to changing conditions and needs).

Strong Leadership

Cooperative ventures require strong leadership from start to finish. The leaders of an organization must be uniquely positioned to provide the catalyst for cooperative arrangements. First, they must be the architects of an organizational philosophy that makes collaboration with other organizations a realistic prospect. This might involve writing a statement about collaboration and making it one of the values and operating philosophies that accompany the mission statement. Even before doing this, however, organizational leaders may need to gradually build awareness of the benefits of collaborative arrangements and encourage openness to such arrangements among employees, elected officials, and trustees who either have never thought about the prospect of collaborating with other organizations or who are opposed to the notion. This is an educational process that may take months or even longer. But it is the responsibility of the leaders (the primary boundary spanners) of the organization to translate their observations of the external environment (including the growing pressure for collaboration from foundations and other grantmaking organizations) into terms that the internal stakeholders can understand and appreciate.

Providing leadership for a culture that accepts the possibility of interorganizational collaboration is easier said than done. Sometimes even the most obvious benefits of joint ventures escape the notice of leaders who are locked into a parochial view of the world around them. Consider the following example. A recent gathering of criminal justice experts focused on innovative methods of crime fighting and prevention. One of the speakers, a police chief from a small financially distressed municipality, spoke with passion and vision about the need for leaders like himself to be in direct contact with "the streets" by riding in patrol cars, making arrests, mentoring junior officers and so on. Then, almost off-handedly, he mentioned that he was not able to do as much of this as he would like because he was working two jobs to support his family and he had only recently returned from the temporary lay-off he had to take when his municipality could not meet the police payroll near the end of the fiscal year. A member of the audience asked the chief if his town had considered a joint venture with its neighboring communities to provide full-time, twenty-four-hour police protection. The chief responded blandly, "We don't want to give up our autonomy and the 'personal touch' that our residents have with the police department." Apparently autonomy is more important than public safety in this community. This same type of *pathological parochialism* ("Pathological Parochialism," 1999) has kept many communities from participating in regional 911 programs, preferring instead to have emergency dispatch operations handled by their local police stations.

Second, leaders must have the vision to see specific needs and strategic opportunities that might be candidates for collaborative ventures with other organizations. They need to put flesh and bones on the organization's vision by identifying concrete projects where collaborative ventures will allow the organization to accomplish something with a partner that it cannot accomplish alone. This part of the educational process will help key stakeholders envision tangible outcomes and prospects for collaboration and may help convince them that an organization is serious about making collaboration part of its strategic portfolio.

Third, leaders must be at the forefront of efforts to keep collaborative efforts on track when (not if) they hit snags and suffer setbacks. Collaborative ventures, like any interpersonal relationship, suffer through bad times as well as enjoy good times. During disputes among partners and during times when the desired outcomes of the cooperative venture are not materializing, the skeptics will be quick to condemn the arrangement and argue for a hasty retreat. When leaders are convinced of the partnership's value, they must continually advocate for the arrangement.

Finally, leaders must provide tangible support to the cooperative venture in the form of resources, time, energy, and political capital. Nothing will demonstrate their commitment to a collaborative strategy more forcefully than devoting resources to it. For example, the organization may need to offer additional training to employees, provide release time to them, supply office space, or make other tangible commitments to the collaborative venture. Research on organizational innovations like TQM, quality circles, and reengineering demonstrates over and over again that leaders must make a sustained commitment of resources in order for these efforts to succeed.

Conclusion

Collaborative ventures represent an important and attractive set of strategic alternatives for public and nonprofit organizations. Many funders and political leaders have grown impatient with what they perceive to be redundancies and needless competition among public and nonprofit organizations. They believe, with some justification, that public and nonprofit organizations ought to put the public interest ahead of organizational interests. If the public's needs can better be served by two organizations working in concert, then those organizations have a moral obligation to do so. Even when organizations operate in their self-interests, collaboration sometimes makes far more sense than competition. It offer a mechanism to enhance an organization's comparative advantages, not diminish them. Collaborations might actually enhance and help preserve an organization's autonomy in the long run, even though it sacrifices some autonomy in the short term.

But despite the high moral and operational arguments in favor of collaboration, there are many barriers to overcome. The private for-profit sector may have a slightly less emotional approach to collaborative ventures when it is clear that the venture will improve long-term profitability for shareholders. But even the private sector abounds with examples of failed joint ventures and a pervasive culture of protectionism and suspicion about collaborative efforts.

Getting Started

1. Does your organization have an explicit philosophy on collaboration with other organizations? Does your organization have a track record of collaboration? What forces have shaped your own attitudes toward collaborative strategies?

2. In what specific ways could your mission be advanced by a collaborative strategy? What are the major barriers to employing successful collaborative strategies in your organization?

PART THREE

Strategy in Practice

9

Implementing Strategic Decisions

Strategy implementation is a vast topic and the subject of book-length studies (for example, Galbraith and Kazanjian, 1986; Ripley and Franklin, 1986; Pressman and Wildavsky, 1984). Thus a full treatment of implementation issues is beyond the scope of this chapter. Instead, I address some of the most important issues by focusing on four of the following five sets of factors that your organization should consider as it moves from strategy formulation to strategy implementation. The fifth set of factors is discussed in the final chapter.

Organizational structure and design. What type of organizational design will help your organization advance the strategy it has chosen, whether that strategy is growth, retrenchment, or stability? How will the structure of your organization be affected by its strategy? These questions accept the notion that form follows function and therefore that the structural design of your organization should be tailored to the strategy you have selected (Chandler, 1962; Miles and Snow, 1978; Miller, 1986). Naturally, your organization cannot make wholesale changes in its structure every time it marginally adjusts its strategy, but certain design principles discussed below will be helpful if your organization makes significant changes in strategy.

Staffing and human resource management. What staffing and personnel management approaches will advance your strategy? Will a strategy of growth, retrenchment, or stability have an impact on your organization's current approach to human resource management? Management's flawless logic and brilliant insights might be the genesis of your organization's strategy, but the execution of that strategy has to be handled by employees. The strategy will place demands on them and will require their full involvement and support.

Information and strategic control. What types of information systems and management controls will help you to monitor and adjust your organization's strategy as needed? How will you keep tabs on whether the strategy is being implemented as planned? What kind of information should you gather along the way? Will it be possible to make midcourse corrections if things go wrong? How will you keep your organization's strategy on track? Strategies are not locked in stone. Implementation of a strategy may actually change the environment by, for example, prompting counterstrategies from other organizations. Maintaining a watchful eye on your organization and on the external environment is a crucial task during the implementation phase.

Measures of success. What type of outcomes should be specified in advance? How will you know whether your organization's strategy has been successful? It is hard to know whether a strategy is successful unless you specify in advance what general objectives you are trying to achieve. "Implementation cannot succeed or fail without a goal against which to judge it" (Pressman and Wildavsky, 1984, p. xxii).

Political feasibility. What stakeholders will support the strategy you have chosen, and how might they help with implementation? Conversely, what stakeholders will likely oppose your strategy? (Political considerations are discussed in the Conclusion of this book.)

It should be said at the outset that strategy *formulation* and *implementation* should not be thought of as two separate parts of the strategic management process. Rather, they are fully integrated. As managers develop strategies they should think ahead to issues they might encounter when the organization tries to implement the strategy. A brilliantly conceived strategy that is politically infeasible is of no use to anyone. Thus, in earlier chapters, I highlighted some of the most important implementation issues associated with each of the strategies presented. This chapter takes a more systematic approach to implementation. However, there are no universally accepted recipes or rules for ensuring successful implementation of a strategy. For example, there is no simple way to match the ideal organizational design to a selected growth strategy. The approach your organization selects will be influenced by many factors including its mission and mandate, its history and culture, the skills of its workforce, and the extent to which it must be accountable for specific processes and outcomes. For example, if you work in government, you may have little or no ability to significantly alter the structure of your organization, which may be dictated by its legal mandate. Nonetheless, as you ponder how best to implement a chosen strategy, you will likely need to consider questions of structure, staffing, information, and measures of success and use whatever degrees of freedom you have to make these components work *for* your strategy, not *against* it.

The Edgewood Housing Authority

Dave Adams, executive director of the Edgewood Housing Authority (EHA), took a deep breath as he emerged from the meeting of the board of directors. The board had just approved a strategic plan that would significantly affect the mission of EHA and its portfolio of housing programs and services. Adams is very pleased with EHA's new strategic plan, but he knows that implementing it will pose many challenges.

Here are some of the important components of EHA's new strategy.

Mission. The mission of EHA will be to facilitate access to quality housing and essential social services for the residents of Edgewood. This new mission both expands and constrains the scope of

EHA's activities. Previously, EHA served almost exclusively the desperately poor who live in public housing developments that are highly concentrated and segregated from the hubs of social and economic opportunity. Now, under new federal guidelines for public housing, EHA will promote mixed-income housing developments and scattered site housing, much of which will be privately operated. EHA will also be responsible for enhancing access to social services and economic opportunities for residents in a holistic approach designed to break the cycle of dependence on public housing.

Financing structure and constraints. Historically, EHA has accomplished its mission by using a mixture of publicly owned and privately owned housing units and complexes. New federal financing procedures will increase the pressure on EHA to improve the quality and competitiveness of its publicly owned housing relative to private suppliers' housing. EHA is now one of many suppliers of housing in a competitive marketplace.

Characteristics of EHA housing stock. As in most cities, the housing stock owned by EHA is dominated by aging, high-density apartment complexes located in very poor neighborhoods, far from economic opportunities and with limited access to social services. The new plan calls for EHA to demolish many of these housing units and to develop scattered-site housing units and smaller apartment units located closer to jobs, transportation, and other amenities.

Tenants. EHA will serve a greater variety of tenants through mixed-income housing developments that include both public housing and market-rate units. EHA will also provide access to a variety of social services for these tenants, including job training, child care, and other support services.

Management philosophy. EHA's management philosophy will be defined by the competitive housing market. Many of EHA's potential customers will now have choices via portable housing certificates and subsidies, and EHA will have to compete for its market share against private and nonprofit housing suppliers. Its portfolio of assets must be managed just like a business portfolio, with attention to cost effectiveness, competitiveness, customer preferences, and financial performance.

The new direction and priorities for EHA are a mixture of many strategies addressed in previous chapters. For example, part of the new strategy is based on *horizontal growth* and *concentric diversification*, because the EHA has made a commitment to serve new market segments with a wider array of services. There is also a significant element of *retrenchment* in the new strategy, especially *divestment*, as the EHA demolishes much of its aging housing stock and gets into the business of real estate brokerage in place of the business of being the sole provider of subsidized housing. In addition, the EHA strategy is one of *collaboration*, because it calls for a new working relationship with private housing suppliers, nonprofit social service agencies, and other public and private organizations.

Dave Adams will face many challenges as he tries to implement this complex new strategy. He will need to consider the impact of the strategy on the structure of EHA, its human resources, and its information and control mechanisms. The strategy will likely encounter political resistance from various stakeholders as well. Some residents and businesses have already expressed opposition to the strategy, saying that they don't want subsidized housing units in their neighborhood.

Throughout this book, I have focused on growth, retrenchment, and stability as an organization's overall strategic options. This discussion of implementation will follow the same template.

Implementing Growth Strategies

If you decide that a growth strategy is appropriate for your organization, your next task is to design an implementation approach to put the strategy into effect. Much will depend on whether the strategy is based on horizontal growth, vertical integration, or diversification.

Implementing Horizontal Growth Strategies

Horizontal growth strategies generally involve the addition of new service areas, expanded markets, and types of consumers not previously served by the organization. Although horizontal growth usually does not involve significant new additions to a portfolio of programs and services, it can strain the existing organizational structure and require changes in staff, information systems, and measures of organizational performance. Here are some approaches to consider as your organization implements its horizontal growth strategy.

Organizational Structure and Horizontal Growth.   Most organizations begin their lives with a simple *functional* design. As they grow, this simple structure evolves into a larger and more complex bureaucracy. But bureaucracies are fundamentally functional designs too, just enlarged to handle a greater variety of tasks. The building blocks of such a design, or structure, are the functions performed by the organization as it delivers its programs and services to the community.

A functional structure usually includes cells such as service delivery, finance and accounting, procurement, facility management, administration, human resource management, public relations, and so on. All of these functional cells support the organization's portfolio of programs and services. Most government bureaucracies are organized along functional principles, which are designed to maximize control and accountability for outputs. Functional structures can also be extremely efficient for organizations that have well-practiced routines for producing a very limited range of programs and services in a stable environment. But the high level of centralization in a functionally based organization can create problems when the organization tries to grow horizontally (Boyne, 1996).

When implementing a horizontal growth strategy, your organization may want to consider changing over to a *geographical* approach to organizational design. In a geographical structure, the key elements are regional or perhaps simply neighborhood units—the northern office, the southern office, the downtown office, and so on. In a geographical structure, support functions such as accounting and procurement are either centrally located in the home office or duplicated in each geographical unit.

When your organization expands its market area, you will likely want to decentralize some decision making to make it easier to tailor programs and services to meet the needs of different market areas. A geographical structure will support this objective in several ways. First, this structure allows your organization to be more responsive to local needs in each sector of its expanding market. Branch offices are more in touch with local needs and can quickly mobilize resources to respond to those needs. Second, a geographical structure will facilitate tracking organizational performance by region. This allows you to monitor the outcomes of the growth strategy, tracing which regions or markets have been most successful. Third, a geographical structure will develop executive talent and leadership among managers in each of the geographical units because these managers must behave much like mini CEOs. This can be extremely important as the organization develops a plan for leadership succession.

However, a geographical structure will also complicate management in the following ways.

Balancing control and delegation.   Your organization must decide how much central control it ought to retain in the home office and balance this against the autonomy desired by the branch offices.

Adding layers.   Your organization will have to contend with another layer of management manifested in the branch managers, each of whom will develop his or her own agenda and priorities.

Maintaining consistency of purpose.   The consistency of the organization-wide strategy will be challenged by geographical units that want to develop their own strategies rather than adapt to the larger strategy.

Duplicating functions. Your organization may experience duplication of support services and other administration functions as each geographical unit begins to grow in sophistication and depth.

Goal displacement. Managers will need to work hard to maintain the supremacy of and allegiance to the organization-wide priorities and strategies, as the decentralized branches will be tempted to put their own goals ahead of the organization's.

If your organization currently has a simple functional structure, it may be able to accommodate a measure of horizontal growth without changing that structure. It could simply add more personnel to handle the expanded production and distribution challenges, remembering to add supervisory personnel also to ensure that spans of control do not become overwhelming. Eventually, however, the centralized functional structure will begin to falter under the added responsibility of serving diverse and possibly far-flung populations.

Dave Adams, for example, might be able to handle EHA's expanded scope of service with the organization's existing structure, but he should seriously consider adding branch offices that could provide closer contact with neighborhoods where EHA has never before had a presence. The branch offices would be better able to assess neighborhood conditions, needs, and opportunities for subsidized housing. They would also be able to assess political issues far more accurately and sensitively than the central bureaucratic structure could. Establishing direct lines of communication with various neighborhood groups as well as with coproducers such as Realtors would be helpful as EHA moves from the model of concentrated high-density housing to dispersed and low-density housing.

Staffing and Horizontal Growth. One of the key challenges you will face when implementing your organization's horizontal growth strategy is developing an approach to human resource management that balances the competing pressures for autonomy and coordination among the geographical units. As EHA begins to serve a wider geographical area, and perhaps adopts a new organizational structure to match, there are likely to be frequent and increasingly intense conflicts between line and staff personnel and especially between central headquarters and the branch offices. The branch offices will naturally push for autonomy and may even compete against one another for scarce resources. The regional managers will constantly implore Adams to recognize their needs first or to bend a rule here and a procedure there to accommodate their unique circumstances and needs.

As your organization grows horizontally, be prepared to spend more time and energy communicating with regional offices and coordinating their tasks and priorities. You will need to focus on maintaining lateral as well as vertical communication throughout the organization. Consider these tactics.

Make greater use of teams. Functional teams that transcend geographical regions can promote communication, resource sharing, and consistency of practice throughout the organization (Gummer, 1995).

Rotate staff. Rotation of regional managers and other key staff can sensitize them to issues facing each part of the organization.

Use meetings. Bring staff together regularly to share progress, to do strategic planning, and to communicate with each other (Shera and Page, 1995).

Provide incentives. Hold regional managers accountable for lateral coordination, and provide performance incentives accordingly.

Get out of your office and encourage other staff to do the same. Staff in the central office must have a firsthand understanding of what is happening in the geographical units. The prospects for staff-line conflicts are much higher when managers remain cloistered in the central office.

Horizontal growth will pose many challenges to your organization's human resource management system. From a human resource perspective, a horizontal growth strategy can be the most difficult growth strategy to implement because it is a hybrid of a simple functional structure and the more complex structures described later.

Information, Control, and Horizontal Growth. As suggested by the previous discussion, a horizontal growth strategy requires vigilant oversight to ensure that it does not work against the goals and objectives your organization is trying to pursue. For example, horizontal growth can quickly result in *diseconomies of scale* unless certain staff and support functions remain centralized in the home office. If each geographical unit has its own fully staffed support infrastructure, then there will be duplication of these resources and eventually loss of coherence throughout your organization's growing system of service delivery as each region develops policies and procedures to suit its own purposes. Also, retaining central control of support functions and infrastructure can help combat the phenomenon described in Chapter Five of adding capacity in lumps, which Michael Porter (1980) observes is a typical problem with growth strategies.

However, it is also possible that the workings of your organization might be quite compatible with allowing each geographical unit to have its own support infrastructure and to function essentially like an autonomous organization. Remember, there are no universal rules for developing one best organizational structure.

When implementing a horizontal growth strategy, your organization must take precautions against the natural phenomenon of *goal displacement*. This occurs when units, divisions, or regional offices begin to see their own goals and objectives as more important than those of the total organization. Unit managers are critically important in combating this phenomenon. But central leaders and staff can also fall victim to goal displacement, especially if they begin to envision their organization as nothing more than a collection of regional delivery systems. Thus management must keep a system-wide perspective on the organization's mission, goals, and strategy.

As your organization sets performance targets for each geographical unit, it should not focus exclusively on outputs or outcomes related only to that unit's coverage area. Some of the objectives should be tied to organization-wide priorities that transcend the unit's unique needs and circumstances. Hold geographical units accountable to these organization-wide priorities, and reiterate the priorities over and over again in meetings.

In the case of EHA, Dave Adams will likely need to overhaul his organization's information systems, budgeting systems, and financial control systems as the horizontal growth strategy proceeds. Networked information systems will allow the neighborhood offices to access the information they need on, say, housing opportunities in other parts of the city, access to jobs, and availability of social services like public transportation and day care for children. This information will be critical as the neighborhood offices of EHA provide housing assistance services. The neighborhood offices should also have the capability to input information needed by the EHA central office to monitor neighborhood office performance. Budgeting and accounting systems will need to track important financial indicators for each of the geographical units as well as for the entire system. These adjustments will be expensive and must be taken into account as Adams plans his implementation expenditures.

Goal Attainment and Horizontal Growth.   Lastly, as you contemplate an implementation approach for your organization's horizontal growth strategy, you must have in mind a measure of success or failure. How will you know if the horizontal growth strategy is successful? What exactly is your organization trying to accomplish with the strategy? Here are some frequently used objectives for horizontal growth strategies.

Market penetration and market share.   These performance measures are often at the heart of a horizontal growth strategy. They should be measured carefully whenever your organization is competing with another provider of programs and services.

Return on investment.   Each new component of a horizontal growth strategy, such as a new regional office, represents an investment of scarce resources. When financial performance is an important consideration, construct a break-even model, and carefully monitor the return on investment for each geographical unit.

Geographical coverage. When your organization is not in a competitive position, its primary objective with a horizontal growth strategy might simply be to expand its geographical coverage. Thus coverage itself might be measure of success for a horizontal growth strategy.

Economies of scale. In production organizations, a primary objective of horizontal growth is to achieve the economies and efficiencies that accompany larger-scale production and distribution systems. Your organization needs to be able to measure unit production costs, both fixed and variable, for this measure to be useful.

Responsiveness to local needs. The goal of an organization's horizontal growth strategy may have little to do with economies of scale, market shares, or unit costs. If you are interested primarily in tailoring your organization's programs and services to meet the unique needs of various constituencies, then you should develop measures of responsiveness and consumer satisfaction.

Dave Adams must be especially careful to fully explain the new goals and objectives of EHA to his many constituencies. His staff are accustomed to very limited activity and output measures for EHA. Now they will be held accountable for far more diverse and rigorous outcomes. Also, the citizens of Edgewood will have questions and perhaps concerns about EHA's new goals for its role in their community.

Implementing Vertical Growth Strategies

Vertical growth is primarily a process-oriented strategy, the objective of which is to gain greater control of supply and distribution systems. Thus many of the implementation questions focus on process issues.

Organizational Structure and Vertical Growth. A vertically integrated organization needs a structure that coordinates the processes of supply, production, and distribution. There must be a smooth and

uninterrupted flow among these three components of a fully integrated organization. If these parts of the process are not closely
coordinated, the organization will immediately lose many of the
advantages of vertical integration and will be negatively affected by
such downsides of vertical integration as higher fixed costs.

When your organization has adopted a strategy of vertical
growth, a *process* model of organizational design may help it coordinate the integrated components of supply, production, and distribution. The building blocks of a process model, or design, are the
key flows of the activities of the organization as it acquires resources,
transforms those resources into programs and services, and then dis-
tributes those programs and services to the public. Thus, for example, a vertically integrated hospital system might be organized into
three divisions: one for the HMO it owns (which affects the flow of
patients into the system), another for the hospital itself (where
much of the treatment and research takes place), and a third for the
physician practices (which are crucial components of the distribution system).

Vertically integrated organizations need high levels of lateral
coordination among the various parts of the organizational process.
Thus, as you prepare to implement a vertical growth strategy, you
may want to consider the use of process teams and task forces to
promote effective coordination at each stage of all of the organization's production processes.

Staffing and Vertical Growth. Perhaps the greatest staffing challenge your organization will face when implementing a vertical
growth strategy is finding senior executives with the extraordinary
skills needed to manage a fully integrated organization. Senior staff
will no longer enjoy the full benefit of outside suppliers and distributors who offered expertise and advice as well as materials and
services. They will need to master these functions and processes
themselves. Among the many types of skills needed by senior executives in vertically integrated systems are the following:

- A wide lens perspective on the total organization, understanding in extraordinary detail the flows and linkages within the organizational system

- A narrow lens perspective on the details of each major aspect of the integrated organization—supply, production, and distribution

- Extraordinary expertise in cost control methods

- An external perspective that replaces the information formerly supplied by vendors and distributors

Only exceptional managerial talent can effectively run and control a vertically integrated organization.

A related challenge is to staff your organization's human resource division with highly skilled professionals and provide them with the resources they will need to supply exceptionally skilled people at all levels of the organization. Your human resource staff will be significantly challenged by a vertical growth strategy. Suddenly they will be responsible for recruiting, training, and evaluating a vastly expanded range of professionals. Your organization may need to hire human resource professionals who have significant experience in vertically integrated organizations.

Information, Control, and Vertical Growth. Cost control will be a significant challenge as your organization grows vertically. As described earlier, many variable costs associated with supply and distribution networks will become *fixed costs* in a vertically integrated system. Fixed costs, of course, have a significant impact on an organization's fiscal performance. Thus, your organization's implementation plan should include intensified efforts to control fixed costs.

Another concern in a vertically integrated organization is how to remain in touch with technological developments and innovations. The self-sufficiency of a fully integrated organization can come at the cost of isolation or at least insulation from the outside world. If your strategy is to succeed, your organization's in-house supply and distribution systems must be as sophisticated and competitive as those formerly supplied by vendors.

A vertically integrated organization needs people with special training to help with so-called make or buy decisions: Should we make this component ourselves or buy it from an outside vendor? Optimization models, cost-benefit analysis, and other quantitative techniques of management science will become a more important component of your organization's skills portfolio. Naturally, the sophistication of your organization's management information system will also need to be addressed to ensure that the system is capable of helping managers make these decisions quickly and accurately.

Goal Attainment and Vertical Growth. There are several important outcomes of a vertical integration strategy that should be monitored closely. One desired outcome is to reduce the organization's reliance on outside vendors and distributors and thereby to stabilize its supply and distribution systems. This stability might be measured in many different ways, such as price, availability, and quality. These are very important measures of the success of a vertical growth strategy.

Another related objective of vertical integration is to develop the in-house capability of tailoring programs and services to meet the needs of diverse consumers. In other words, vertical integration should give your organization a greater ability to *differentiate* its programs and services and get out of the one-size-fits-all approach. Thus you should carefully monitor your organization's success in meeting the unique needs of special constituencies.

Finally, vertical integration provides a foundation for other types of growth, including horizontal growth and diversification. Vertical integration typically raises the stakes for competitors by increasing their potential entry and exit costs. Thus one measure of success might be the extent to which your organization's vertical growth strategy has given it a larger and more secure market share.

Implementation of Diversification Strategies

Like the other growth strategies, diversification will usually require substantial changes in an organization's structure, staffing, and information and control systems.

Organizational Structure and Diversification. Diversification requires an organizational design that can accommodate an expanding portfolio of programs and services. When your organization chooses a diversification strategy, it is likely that you will want to give each of your organization's programs and services more autonomy than, say, a geographical unit in a horizontal growth scenario. This is especially true when each component of the portfolio serves a different purpose, operates in a distinct business environment, generates its own streams of revenue, and requires its own strategy to survive and prosper. This is the situation Barbara Jenkins envisions for the Lakeview Women's Center and Shelter in the Chapter Five case study. Each of the three components of her diversified organization will have a separate and unique purpose. This is not to say that the consulting, advocacy, and service delivery components of LWCS will not be related. But they will serve fundamentally distinct purposes, interact with their own sets of stakeholders, and be subject to unique environmental forces. They will be analogous to semiautonomous business units under the roof of one holding company.

Dave Adams is also trying to decide how to implement the diversification strategy of EHA. EHA now has at least three distinct program and service components in its portfolio: housing units built and managed by EHA; housing units supplied by the private sector; and social services to enhance prospects for residents of subsidized housing. Although these components interact as a system, they have individual identities, purposes, funding streams, and outcomes.

In the private sector many diversified companies use a *decentralized business unit* design, much like that envisioned for LWCS by Barbara Jenkins. In such a structure the building blocks are the diversified business units or product lines. Typically each semiautonomous unit will have its own structure, based on the unique functions or processes that are essential to the fulfillment of its purpose (see the previous description of functional and process designs). Certain support functions common to all the units, such as personnel, finance, and research and development, are typically kept in the central office to enhance coordination across the units. Such a structure has many advantages for the diversified organization, including the following:

- It delegates authority to business unit managers, who are assumed to know their business better than anyone else.

- It allows business units to take responsibility for their own strategic plans.

- It allows business units to adopt the functional or process structures that make sense for them.

- It creates a clear accountability system that places responsibility for performance squarely on the shoulders of the business unit managers.

- It gives the CEO the freedom to plan the corporate strategy.

But a decentralized structure also has many potential disadvantages. For example, it leads to duplication of many support functions in each of the business units and can create dysfunctional rivalries among business units.

The most difficult problem is achieving the appropriate level of coordination and integration in the decentralized system. *Interdivisional teams*, however, can provide advice on how to coordinate key functions and processes. For example, if some diversified business units have customers in common or rely on the same vendors for materials or distribution logistics, the teams can help develop policies and procedures to ensure that dealings with these stakeholders are consistent across the business units and to protect against inefficient duplication of effort.

Diversified organizations sometime use *venture teams* to provide advice to top leadership on new business opportunities and investments. These teams are composed of people who are trained to carefully evaluate opportunities for diversification. They may, for example, be skilled at identifying organizations for possible acquisition or merger. They likely will be adept at identifying emerging markets and needs for new services. They should have an organization-wide perspective so they can assess the impact of any new venture on the existing mission, structure, and culture of the organization. Sometimes they will have the legal or technical skills to conduct due diligence assessments prior to the acquisition of another organization or to explore a new market. Venture teams may be temporary, formed in response to a specific opportunity, or a permanent part of the organizational structure.

If your organization's diversification strategy progresses to extreme levels, you might adopt an organizational design based on *strategic business units* (SBUs). This design is often used by conglomerates in the business world. Its basic elements are groups of strategically related business units, clustered together and reporting to a group vice president who in turn reports to the CEO. A broadly diversified organization might organize its structure around three or four SBUs each of which might contain several strategically related subsidiaries or product lines. The SBU design has many advantages, such as these:

- It provides a mechanism to coordinate the activities of closely related business units.
- It supports strategic planning at the logical level of the organization.
- It provides a way to track performance according to strategic environments, not just isolated business units.

But, as with any organizational design, there are disadvantages to the SBU model as well. Sometimes the grouping of strategically related businesses can be arbitrary and counterproductive. Also, the group vice presidents must be given broad discretionary authority to plan and execute SBU strategy. Otherwise they will become little more than an added layer of management between unit managers and the CEO. The SBU model also poses extreme challenges of coordination. Again, boundary spanning teams can help you develop and enforce an organization-wide perspective in each of the SBUs. But it will be a constant challenge to maintain this perspective in a system that is inherently fragmented.

Staffing and Diversification.   Diversification strategies pose special problems for the human resource function. Unless your organization's diversification strategy is based on acquisitions, you will need to staff diversified business units with existing staff and new staff hired explicitly to fulfill the strategy. Thus, from the outset, your organization's diversification strategy should be based on the concept of *transferable skills*. For example, if your organization has acquired vast experience in advocacy in one domain of public policy, those skills might be transferable to other domains. Or perhaps your organization has acquired significant expertise in logistics planning and implementation. This skill might be transferable to another line of programs and services that also rely heavily on logistical competence. Identification of these transferable skills among existing staff is one of the most important human resource functions in a diversified or diversifying organization.

The hiring function is also very important in a diversified organization. Your organization might delegate authority for hiring to the decentralized product lines or SBUs. This is the appropriate strategy when each unit requires highly specialized expertise. However, under some circumstances, you may want to retain the hiring function in the central office. This may be appropriate when each product line is closely interrelated, and you want to ensure coordination and central control over personnel decisions. If the hiring function is centralized, your organization should recruit people with transferable skills, who can contribute to several diverse parts of the organization.

Sometimes, however, transferable skills must be developed. Dave Adams will likely need to develop a training program that is in sync with EHA's diversification strategy in order to develop skills in his employees that will advance that strategy. Most EHA employees are skilled in housing management—infrastructure, lease administration, maintenance, conflict resolution, and so on. Now they will need skills in brokerage, referral, social needs assessment, and outcome measurement.

Some diversified organizations rely on *job rotation* to build transferable skills and to reinforce a shared culture that transcends each business unit. Building a shared culture in a diversified organization is even more difficult than it is in horizontally or vertically integrated organizations. Each diversified business unit is likely to have its own customers, a unique line of programs and services, a distinct professional career path, and an individualized set of performance standards. All these unit features will work against developing and sustaining the notion of *one organization—one mission*. Managers' leadership skills will be severely tested by a diversification strategy.

Leadership succession also presents special challenges in a diversified organization. Managers, and especially the CEO, must be knowledgeable (at least at the strategic level) about each of the organization's diverse business units. They must know each unit's programs and services, the competitive environment in which it works, the technologies it uses, the customers it serves, and the emerging forces that will affect its future. They must be able to converse intelligently and sometimes forcefully with unit or group vice presidents, who will usually clamor for priority attention or more resources. The CEO, indeed, may be the only one in the organization who truly understands the interrelationships of its various business units and how each of them separately and all of them together contribute to the organization's mission. Thus, most of all, the CEO must be the spokesperson and advocate for that organizational mission, continually teaching and prodding others in the organization's growing empire to keep that mission at the forefront of all they do.

Although Dave Adams is unlikely to get to handpick his successor, the new strategy for EHA certainly should affect his approach to developing the skills of the EHA executives just below him so that they are primed to take his place when he leaves or retires, if one of them is selected to do so.

Information, Control, and Diversification. Keeping track of the performance of a diversified organization is a difficult task. Reports from diversified business units must be carefully designed to ensure that management gets all the information it needs to monitor unit performance, but not more information than managers can handle.

Budgeting plays a critical role in successfully implementing a diversification strategy. The corporate budget cycle must be carefully planned and implemented to ensure that unit vice presidents have sufficient time and information to do their own budgeting. Moreover, an organization may need to make adjustments to its overall budgeting policies and procedures to allow greater flexibility in the allocation of resources. A diversified organization often needs to move money from one activity to another to capitalize on emerging opportunities or to resolve crises in discrete parts of the organization. *Capital budgeting* will likely be an essential tool as your organization diversifies. Capital budgeting allows you to keep track of the many capital requirements your units have for equipment, facilities, land, and other fixed assets. Capital budgeting can also help you establish protocols for these financial outlays in terms of their return on investment.

Michael Porter (1985) comments on the need to create and maintain *synergy* and *interrelationships* in diversified organizations. Control of diversified organizations is simplified when the various units share information on common markets, shared technology, and overlapping production processes. When implementing a diversification strategy, an organization must focus its strategic planning systems on the horizontal relationships among the diverse units as well as the vertical relationships between the central office and these units.

Above all, control and information in diversified organizations begins with a clear and universally understood *mission* for the organization as a whole and for each of the business units. First, it is absolutely essential that each business unit fully understands and embraces the organization-wide mission. Second, each unit must understand and accept its respective role in advancing that mission. Some units may exist primarily to generate earned revenue to subsidize the charitable or public service activities of other units. If so, these *profit centers* must understand and embrace this role. Others may exist primarily to enhance the public image of the organization, producing little in terms of tangible goods and services. If so, they must embrace that role and its functions. When the respective missions and synergies of all parts of the organization are fully understood in relation to the overall mission, then the choice of appropriate performance indicators follows naturally.

Goal Attainment and Diversification. In the private sector, diversification is often used by organizations whose core business is threatened. Diversification allows a threatened organization to transfer its skills and competencies to other, more promising lines of business. Thus the measure of success in a diversified business organization is often survival and metamorphosis.

In the public and nonprofit sectors, diversification may achieve these outcomes:

- Diversify and increase your organization's revenue streams.
- Stabilize your organization's revenues by reducing its reliance on volatile or insufficient revenue sources.
- Enhance your organization's self-sufficiency.
- Increase your organization's flexibility.
- Improve your organization's responsiveness to community needs.

All of these imply valid performance measures with which to assess the success or failure of a diversification strategy. Ultimately, however, you cannot judge a diversification strategy simply in terms of revenues or outputs. The prime objective of diversification, or any growth strategy discussed in this chapter, is to contribute to the fulfillment of your organization's mission. Will diversification contribute to your organization's mission? Will it be a better organization with a diversified structure than with its current mix of programs and services? Will diversification add to your organization's "public value" (Moore, 1995)?

Diversification strategies can be especially seductive and even mesmerizing, and so the tail can quickly begin to wag the dog. It is tempting and easy for managers to become consumed with monitoring the financial performance of subsidiary organizations or even their nonfinancial performance. The key performance indicator, however, is whether each of them alone and all of them together add value and contribute to fulfillment of the organization's mission.

Table 9.1 summarizes the suggestions presented in the first part of this chapter. It is also useful to summarize some of the growth issues facing Dave Adams. This is what he must do.

Design an organizational structure for EHA that can accommodate the new types of housing and support services EHA offers and the new neighborhoods and clients it serves. A geographically based organizational structure will be more responsive to neighborhood needs and issues than a centralized bureaucracy. And a product-based structure will allow Adams to track the performance of his expanded portfolio. Perhaps a hybrid structure based both on geography and services will be most appropriate for EHA as it implements its new strategy.

Assist the EHA staff in performing their new duties. Training and coordination will be key features of his implementation plan. Adams will need to consider how to balance the need for autonomy among the regional offices and the professional specialties with the need to coordinate their activities to achieve a truly integrated system of housing and social services.

Develop new monitoring and control systems. The new strategy will likely require a complete overhaul of EHA's information and

TABLE 9.1 Implementing Growth Strategies.

Growth Strategy	Organizational Design to Support the Strategy	Implications for Staffing and Human Resource Management	Implications for Monitoring and Controlling the Strategy	Measures of Success
Horizontal Growth	Functional design or geographical design.	Understand greater potential for line and staff conflict and field or home conflicts. Consider rotation of staff to build system-wide perspective. Use interregional task forces to ensure functional coordination.	Understand that diseconomies of scale can result without central control of shared functions. Be aware that span of supervisory control may become a problem in a functional structure. Be prepared and budget for at least some duplication of functions in a geographical design. Guard against goal displacement on the part of functional units or geographical locations.	Improvements in market share, economies of scale, geographical coverage, responsiveness to local needs, and efficiency and effectiveness.

Vertical Integration				
Process model of organizational structure. Process task forces and teams help ensure smooth transition from input to throughput to output.	Establish performance targets by region, but relate them to organization-wide mission and goals.	Install extraordinary management competence at senior levels. Focus training and development on process objectives as well as substantive knowledge and skills.	Focus coordination and control mechanisms on ensuring smooth interface of processes. Control operating costs (this is essential). Be aware of loss of innovation due to insulation from the outside.	Reduced transaction costs and improvements in efficiencies, economies of scale, stability of supply and distribution channels, and ability to tailor products to different needs (product differentiation).

TABLE 9.1 Implementing Growth Strategies, *continued.*

Growth Strategy	Organizational Design to Support the Strategy	Implications for Staffing and Human Resource Management	Implications for Monitoring and Controlling the Strategy	Measures of Success
Diversification	Product line or divisional structure (group).	Focus on developing transferable skills in employees.	Track performance by line with product-line budgets and financial statements.	Improvements in revenue diversification and stability, buffering against cyclical markets or unstable revenue sources, self-sufficiency, and responsiveness to community needs.
	Interdivisional teams help ensure coordination.	Use job rotation, forums, and continual training to build transferable skills.	Monitor expenditures on fixed assets with capital budgeting.	
	Venture team helps plan and design foray into new line of business.	Maintain organization-wide role in hiring and training.	Establish synergy between product lines (common markets, technology, production).	
	Partial centralization of key support functions like procurement and logistics, but decentralization of functions like program development and marketing.		Control for mission drift.	
			Build in performance incentives to encourage units to interrelate.	
			Conduct horizontal as well as vertical strategic planning.	

control systems. A dispersed and diverse system of delivering housing services combined with new types of relationships with other providers will strain the existing system beyond its capability. Most important, Adams will need to think about how to measure outcomes as well as outputs.

Carefully communicate the goals of the new EHA. Adams will need to polish his communication and conflict resolution skills to keep the new system on track. Previously the mission of EHA was limited but very clear—to supply housing to people in need. Now the mission is more diffused and likely more controversial. Stakeholders will interpret this mission in many different ways to suit their own preferences and agendas. Adams must balance their need for specificity with the political strategy of flexibility.

Implementing Retrenchment Strategies

Like growth, retrenchment will have effects on an organization's structure, staff, and information and control systems and on the measures it uses to assess success or failure. But these effects will likely vary depending on the type of retrenchment strategy—turnaround, divestment, or liquidation—managers have selected.

Implementing Turnaround Strategies

Recall from Chapter Five that turnaround strategies generally involve a back-to-basics approach, which requires a renewed focus on fulfilling the organization's core mission, building staff competencies to deliver programs and services, and reducing the costs of production. If your organization is engaged in a turnaround strategy, that strategy will have implications for organizational structure, staffing, and control systems.

Organizational Structure and Turnarounds. Depending on the mission and tasks of your organization, operating efficiency might be enhanced if you implement your turnaround strategy with a functional structure in which the division of labor between staff and line functions is clear and support activities are centralized. This approach may support one of the key objectives of a turnaround strategy—the reduction of operating costs.

A functional bureaucracy may be quite appropriate if your organization engages in relatively routine production processes in a stable environment. A functional structure, with its centralized control, offers the added advantage of allowing the leader of the organization to closely monitor and adjust the turnaround strategy as necessary.

The problem of course is that a functional structure can inhibit innovation and creativity, which may be critically important to the success of a turnaround strategy. If your organization engages in non-routine production processes, in which programs and services must be tailored to the needs of clients, then a functional bureaucracy will stymie the kind of quality improvement and product differentiation that are hallmarks of successful turnaround strategies. Under these circumstances, you will likely be better off implementing your organization's turnaround strategy with a pared down product-based or geographically based organizational design, even though these designs have some inherent inefficiencies and might keep operating costs higher than you would like.

The key design principle when implementing a turnaround strategy is to consolidate and build the organization around *core competencies* as much as possible in order to reduce operating costs and to refocus attention on the core mission, although not to the extent of squelching innovation or losing contact with key constituencies.

For example, my academic department enjoyed many years of growing budgets and diversification of programs and services. The twenty or so faculty had gradually evolved a wide array of academic specialties and niche programs that catered to narrow markets and individual teaching and research interests. We had the luxury of hiring faculty to fill very specialized niches, almost to the extent of losing sight of our core purpose and educational portfolio. Then, over the past five years, the department's growth curve leveled and eventually reversed. We found that we were spread far too thin over too many areas of teaching and research. We could no longer afford this diversified strategy. Our turnaround strategy has been based in part on a structural reconfiguration in which faculty and the courses they teach have been consolidated into three areas that represent the essence—back to basics—of our educational mission. The consolidation has re-created a critical mass of competency in each of these three academic areas, which has actually fueled rather than diminished innovation and creativity. Faculty are once again talking to each other, designing integrated curricula, and drawing on the natural synergies between them. Prospective students now know that we are not trying to be all things to all people, but that we are differentiating our products on the basis of a few key attributes.

Staffing and Turnarounds.   I pointed out in Chapter Six that turnaround strategies require employees who know and have experience with the organization's line of programs and services. Successful turnarounds often begin with intensive efforts to rebuild and re-emphasize basic skills and competencies in the delivery of core programs and services. This will likely require an investment in employee development with an emphasis on basic techniques.

If possible, minimize managerial instability during a turnaround. An organization's turnaround strategy can be severely jeopardized by the defection or loss of key managerial talent. Strive to create an environment in which the best managerial talent will have strong incentives to stay and help bring the organization back from the brink. Some managers may be intrigued by the challenge and exhilaration of being part of a successful turnaround. Many will want the invaluable managerial experience and authority that they may acquire. Others, however, may demand different types of rewards for staying with the ship. Your organization may not be able to afford these demands, but try to retain the best talent if possible. If you must make managerial changes, try to make them quickly and at the beginning of the turnaround so that the new managers will be on board for nearly its full duration.

Turnarounds provide an excellent opportunity for leadership development and executive succession. Observe your subordinates carefully. Give them as much authority and autonomy as they can handle. Crises and organizational adversity bring out the very best (and also the worst) in managers. A turnaround may bring the cream to the top.

Information, Control, and Turnarounds. When you are implementing a turnaround strategy, your organization's information and control mechanisms must focus on several indicators.

Significant and sustained reductions in operating costs. Many public and nonprofit organizations are not accustomed to carefully monitoring operating costs relative to revenues. Careful monitoring of fixed and variable costs is required for break-even analysis. Analysis of selected financial ratios can also be an important monitoring and control tool, especially for turnaround strategies (see Anthony and Young, 1994). Reengineering is a management tool that has produced dramatic reductions in operating costs for some organizations (Hammer and Champy, 1993). Yet this approach, which requires a total redesign of production processes and procedures, is very demanding and can be risky for organizations engaged in turnaround strategies.

Program quality. During turnaround strategies you should intensify your interaction with clients and other important stakeholders in order to continually monitor their perceptions of the quality of your organization's programs and services. Cost cutting alone will not carry a turnaround strategy. Your organization must sustain or, better yet, improve the quality of its programs and services in order to rekindle public faith and trust. Total Quality Management and methods of statistical process control can be important tools for sustaining and improving program quality.

Boundary spanning information systems. Turnaround strategies require close contact with key constituencies. Your organization must listen to their needs, respond to their concerns, and even solicit their assistance in reversing the decline. You cannot afford to become isolated in your efforts to reduce costs and improve quality. Perhaps more than any other strategy discussed in this book, turnaround strategies demand mechanisms for continually monitoring the strategic environment and listening to key constituencies.

Your organization's mission statement is a control instrument that should not be overlooked when implementing a turnaround strategy. If indeed that turnaround strategy is based on a back-to-basics philosophy, then the place to begin conveying this message to employees and other constituencies is with the organization's mission statement. A revitalized mission statement can help everyone in your organization stay focused on core programs and services during the turnaround strategy.

Goal Attainment and Turnarounds. The objective of a turnaround strategy is to reverse the fortunes of an organization that is threatened with demise or stagnation unless something is done. Reversal of fortune might take several forms:

- Restoring the organization to a solid fiscal condition
- Restoring public confidence in the organization
- Bolstering the perceived legitimacy of the organization in the eyes of political overseers, regulators, accrediting agencies, and the like
- Enhancing the quality and effectiveness of services
- Stemming or reversing the tide of employee attrition
- Improving employee morale
- Increasing public investment in the organization, such as philanthropic contributions, volunteer support, and improved bond ratings that open up access to capital markets

There are other outcomes as well, but this list illustrates the kinds of outcomes that need to be monitored and reported to key constituencies. Progress may come in small increments during a turnaround, and you may find that your organization takes a step backward for every two steps forward along the way. It's easy to lose sight of what you are trying to accomplish unless you keep the prize clearly in view.

Implementing Divestment and Liquidation Strategies

The downsizing, elimination, or transfer of selected parts of an organization's portfolio has important implications for the organization's structure, human resource system, and information and control mechanisms. Here are some suggested approaches.

Organizational Structure and Divestment. When your organization has decided on a divestment strategy that involves the closure or transfer of programs, you will almost certainly need to consolidate administrative overhead functions to achieve the efficiencies and cost savings sought by this strategy. Centralization of control and use of a functional support infrastructure is the usual approach to consolidation. As with turnaround strategies, however, try to accomplish this in a way that will not cripple your organization's innovative capabilities.

The structural paradox is that divestment can become a spiral of decline if it significantly reduces an organization's ability to stay in touch with the communities it serves, to offer programs and services of high quality, and to respond effectively to emerging needs. Therefore, if possible, consolidate functions and programs in a way that sustains *synergy* among people and functions in the new streamlined structure. For example, if the divestment strategy involves the closure of a division or a branch office, and the plan is to absorb at least some of those employees into other parts of the organization, try to do so in a way that creates skill synergies rather than just transplanting those workers from one unit to another. Of course this is easier said than done, which is why divestment is usually so traumatic for organizations.

The board of EHA, for example, has decided to demolish many of EHA's old housing units now that EHA is adopting a new model of service that integrates housing and social services. In effect, EHA is divesting a major part of its historical role as a direct provider of housing. Its new role focuses more on ensuring that quality housing is provided in Edgewood by a mixture of public and private sources. Consequently, Dave Adams must decide what to do with the people and infrastructure formerly devoted to maintaining EHA's vast capital plant. Attrition and layoffs may solve part of the problem. But EHA still needs personnel who understand how to maintain quality infrastructure, whether that infrastructure is provided by EHA or private landlords. Keeping these people centralized in the EHA home office might enhance efficiency, but it is not likely to promote the new mission of EHA.

The first to be selected for divestment are often programs or support functions deemed *nonessential*. Unfortunately, they may be programs like employee training, communications, research and development, and community relations, which keep the organization in touch with the outside world. The elimination of these functions and programs may only hasten the decline of the organization or make the prospects for a successful turnaround even more remote.

The use of various teams will be helpful, especially when your organization's divestment strategy involves a new or intensified relationship with another organization. This will be the case when the strategy involves contracting out functions to another organization, ceding responsibility to another organization, or collaborative service delivery. Transition teams and task forces can be an effective implementation tool for anticipating and solving problems that are bound to occur in the transfer or sharing of program and service responsibility.

Staffing and Divestment. Most divestment strategies involve at least the prospect of laying off some employees. This requires attention to a host of issues such as employment contracts, severance policies, and outplacement counseling. The employees who remain will likely need additional training so they can absorb the functions of those who have been laid off. Just as important, the layoffs will create new group dynamics among the employees who remain. New patterns of relations will be required as the organization adjusts to new work flows.

As you anticipate staffing needs, do not neglect the need to fully inform and assist clients and other stakeholders who will be directly affected by the divestment strategy. You will likely need to assign staff to community liaison activities to minimize the disruptive effects and, if necessary, to assist with moving clients from your organization to another agency. These staff members should be especially skilled in communication, coordination, conflict resolution, and logistics. They should also be effective in interpersonal relations and able to deal empathically with others.

If the divestment strategy is to liquidate the organization, the typical trickle of attrition will become a raging torrent as the organization's best employees will immediately begin to find jobs elsewhere. If the liquidation will be implemented over several months or more, managers will find it challenging to cover essential operations as they gradually phase out the organization. Delegation of authority will be needed to cover the essential operations as the organization winds down, but it will also weaken leaders' control of the organization during the delicate procedure of closer.

Information, Control, and Divestment. Divestment strategies need to be monitored carefully to ensure that they are producing the desired objectives. The prospects for negative unanticipated consequences are high because the elimination of programs or functions usually has ripple effects throughout the organization and the communities it serves. Here are some information and control issues to keep in mind:

Exit costs. What costs, tangible and intangible, will your organization incur as it eliminates programs and services? Can these exit costs be minimized?

Deferred savings. When will your organization start to realize savings from its divestment strategy? Quite often the savings will not accrue till later.

Accountability. If you plan to transfer services to another organization yet retain ultimate accountability for those services, what information will be necessary to monitor program quality and effectiveness?

Protection of the operational core. Information and control mechanisms should focus on the operational core of the organization—the administrative systems and processes necessary to fulfill its core purpose and mission. When the operational core is threatened by divestment strategies, the essence of the organization may be in jeopardy.

Unanticipated consequences. Carelessly designed and implemented divestment can produce a cycle of decline in an organization. Develop mechanisms that allow bad news to flow upward so you will know when the strategy is not serving its desired purpose.

Members of the management team need to work very closely together during a divestment strategy to monitor information, control the strategy, and make adjustments as necessary. The organizational leader must keep lines of communication open and be accessible to the rest of the management team and to employees. Divestment strategies require a commitment to two-way communication.

Rumors will run rampant during divestment as employees and other stakeholders speculate about future cuts. There will be lots of second-guessing as people question the cuts already made and offer opinions on future cuts. To make matters worse, some of the organization's best employees will abandon ship during divestment because they will have better opportunities elsewhere.

All of this combines to place enormous burdens on an organization's information and control systems during implementation of a divestment strategy.

Goal Attainment and Divestment. Some of the desired outcomes of a divestment strategy are cost savings, renewed focus of organizational energy on the core mission, and reallocation of resources to programs and functions in which the organization has real comparative advantages.

Ultimately the objective of a divestment strategy is to create a foundation on which the organization can grow and prosper again in the future. If the divestment strategy cuts deeply into the operational core, the long-term sustainability of the organization may be threatened.

Table 9.2 summarizes some suggested approaches to the implementation of retrenchment strategies. And it is also helpful to consider a summary of the divestment issues facing Dave Adams and EHA.

Develop structures to facilitate the new mission. As EHA transfers more and more responsibility for housing to the private sector, Adams would be wise to make extensive use of transition teams to troubleshoot and to ensure that essential programs and services do not fall through the cracks.

Decide how to downsize some of EHA's former functions to achieve greater economies without damaging EHA's capacity to innovate and serve its clients. The employees who previously managed EHA's vast capital infrastructure have skills that are readily transferable to the new mission. They know about issues of safe construction and security; they know about preventive maintenance; they know about land management. These skills have natural synergies with the new EHA mission. For example, the housing maintenance staff could work with landlords and with residents to run training programs and technical assistance services to ensure that the new stock of housing is high quality and remains so.

Make use of information and control systems that allow tracking of the retrenchment strategy. As EHA gets out of its original lines of business and into others, Adams must develop monitoring and control systems to make sure that the transition takes place smoothly. There are high exit costs associated with EHA's strategy, and Adams must keep the EHA board fully informed of these costs. Also, he

TABLE 9.2 Implementing Retrenchment Strategies.

Retrenchment Strategy	Organizational Design to Support the Strategy	Implications for Staffing and Human Resource Management	Implications for Monitoring and Controlling the Strategy	Measures of Success
Turnaround	Consolidate structure to focus on core programs and services. Maintain boundary spanning mechanisms to support innovation and client contact.	Invest in core competencies; return to basics in skills development. Invest in leadership development; try to minimize managerial instability.	Monitor reductions in operating costs with financial and operational ratio analysis. Monitor improved program quality with methods like TQM.	A refocusing on the core mission, reductions in operating costs, renewed public confidence and legitimacy for the organization, and greater public investment in the organization.
Divestment	Consolidate overhead functions. Use transition teams to troubleshoot.	Consolidate resources in a way that creates or sustains synergies among functions and	Monitor issues like exit costs, deferred savings, protecting the operational core, and	Cost savings, renewed public confidence in the organization, and positioning for later

TABLE 9.2 Implementing Retrenchment Strategies, *continued.*

Retrenchment Strategy	Organizational Design to Support the Strategy	Implications for Staffing and Human Resource Management	Implications for Monitoring and Controlling the Strategy	Measures of Success
		the employees who perform them. Invest in retraining. Prepare to lose some of your best employees.	sustaining the organization's accountability mechanisms to key constituencies. Monitor community reactions to divestment in order to avert a crisis of confidence and other unintended consequences of divestment.	stability and possibly growth.
Liquidation	Disband the organization in an orderly way. Use teams to assist clients and employees.	Recognize that the best employees will be first to leave. Plan to sustain critical operations during phased liquidation. Delegate authority.	Control rumors and develop ad hoc mechanisms to monitor and sustain critical tasks.	Enhanced public well-being from freeing up resources to be distributed to other organizations or other needs.

will be ultimately accountable for the performance of housing providers that he does not directly control. Thus he will need to work closely with landlords and Realtors and with other nonprofit organizations to ensure that he has the information he needs to monitor the quality and effectiveness of the housing services.

Be clear about the desired outcomes of the divestment strategy. EHA is divesting some of its portfolio in order to reallocate resources to other needs. In addition, there is no doubt that EHA will be a smaller organization than it has been in the past.

Implementing Stability and Collaborative Strategies

Stability and collaborative strategies are not likely to involve radical changes in organizational structure, staffing, or information and control systems. Nevertheless these implementation issues should not be taken lightly. Much can go wrong with these strategies if their implementation is not handled carefully.

Implementing Stability Strategies

It is tempting to think of stability as a passive strategy that requires no forethought regarding implementation. But stability, like growth and retrenchment, should be a consciously chosen strategy designed to respond to specific types of environmental threats and opportunities. Implementation of a stability strategy involves making specific choices about organizational structure, staffing, information and control systems, and measures of success.

Organizational Structure and Stability. Stability strategies give you the opportunity to strengthen organizational structure rather than radically change it. You can take advantage of a stability strategy to refine operating procedures and flows of information and to strengthen systems of authority and accountability. Note that this does not necessarily mean making these structural components more rigid, centralized, or calcified. Indeed, if your preferred organizational structure is a decentralized product design, then a stability strategy will give you the opportunity to design more effective delegation methods and institutionalize the autonomy you are trying to create within each of the product lines.

Staffing and Stability. Stability strategies provide the perfect opportunity to invest in human resources. Managers should take advantage of a stability strategy to review the organization's approach to employee recruitment, training, professional development, benefit systems, and other parts of the human resource management system. Are these systems well matched with the organizational strategy and with the environment?

It is especially important to think about employee development, keeping an eye on the future and preparing for likely changes in strategy. Do you foresee another period of sustained growth on the horizon after the stability strategy has accomplished its goal? Or is retrenchment a likely scenario? Regardless, the key question to ask is whether your organization's human resource management system is well positioned for what might lie ahead. A stability strategy provides a window of opportunity—perhaps a very narrow window— during which an organization can make some important investments that will produce substantial dividends later.

Information, Control, and Stability. Recall from the discussion in Chapter Seven that stability strategies are sometimes used when the environment is changing so rapidly or future events are so uncertain that a wait and see approach is the most prudent. Under such conditions, vigilance is the order of the day, and an investment in the organization's information and control systems is appropriate. Stability strategies provide a perfect opportunity to fine-tune the organization's skills in benchmarking, outcome measurement, competitive intelligence, research and development of new programs and services, financial and operational controls, break-even analysis, ratio analysis, and general environmental scanning.

During times of environmental turbulence, it is useful to culti-vate multiple information sources as a check and balance on your organization's traditional intelligence systems, which may not be reliable. Intensify contacts with clients, regulators, lobbyists, acad-emics, competitors, and anyone else who can provide insights into what the future might hold. Be prepared to adjust or abandon the stability strategy when you are confident that the environment has become more predictable.

Goal Attainment and Stability.   Do not allow your organization's stability strategy to have a numbing effect. This strategy was se-lected to accomplish specific objectives such as refinement of the organizational design, improvement of the human resource systems, and preparation for the next wave of environmental opportunities and challenges. But you must also remain flexible about the objec-tives you want to accomplish with this strategy. For example, if the environment suddenly provides excellent opportunities for growth or if conditions unexpectedly demand immediate retrenchment, then you must be prepared to abandon the stability strategy even though it has not yet achieved all the objectives you originally had in mind.

Implementing Collaborative Strategies

Collaborative strategies sometimes fail when the partners in the collaboration do not anticipate and prepare for the effects that the strategy will have on the structure and administrative processes of the organization. Collaborative strategies can have far-reaching impacts on the organization.

Organizational Structure and Collaboration.   A key decision in collaborative arrangements is whether or not to establish a new orga-nizational structure to manage the strategy. Simple resource sharing arrangements do not need much oversight, but a joint venture or strategic alliance might require a temporary or permanent administrative infrastructure. The decision depends on a variety of factors including the complexity of the collaborative venture, the risks involved, and the symbolic value of establishing a visible administrative mechanism. In general, it is wise to err on the side of simplicity. In other words, keep the administrative infrastructure as small as possible without jeopardizing the success of the venture. It can be increased later if need be, but it is difficult to dismantle this infrastructure once it has been established.

Ad hoc administrative mechanisms can be very useful when pursuing a collaborative strategy. In the business world, corporations sometimes establish temporary committees or teams to look for acquisition or merger opportunities. These teams, which often include representatives of the board of directors, work quietly so as not to attract the attention of outsiders. Typically these teams will dissolve when their work is accomplished or no longer needed. In the public and nonprofit sectors, venture teams can accomplish the same purpose. As mentioned earlier, these ad hoc, interdisciplinary teams are charged with scanning the environment for opportunities for particular kinds of ventures, including collaborative arrangements. Once a collaborating partner has been found, design and implementation teams representing both organizations work to ensure smooth implementation of the strategy.

Staffing and Collaboration. Collaborative strategies can place new demands on your organization's human resource management system. As with other strategies discussed here, training will likely be an issue as the organization must find employees who are skilled at undertaking the particular type of collaborative strategy you have in mind. Just as important, however, are the intangible factors that can jeopardize a collaborative strategy, such as a clash of organizational cultures.

Your organization's human resource professionals should participate in the design and implementation of collaborative strategies.

Information, Control, and Collaboration. Organizational leaders must play an active role in monitoring and controlling collaborative strategies. Even though many of the technical details of collaboration can be delegated, it may be difficult to delegate oversight. The complications that arise often involve conflicts over issues that only organizational leaders can resolve, such as organizational priorities and philosophies. At the same time, collaborative strategies by definition afford organizational leaders less control than they had before and are likely to restrict access to information to a greater extent than any other strategy discussed here. This is because at least some of the information leaders need to monitor the success of the strategy is likely to be controlled by the partner organization. Leaders are usually able to negotiate access to this information, but it will never be quite as accessible or easily analyzed as the information that their own organizations produce and control.

Thus, when negotiating the objectives of a collaborative arrangement—whether a simple resource sharing agreement or a complex strategic alliance—try to reach agreement early on with your partners on precisely what information will be gathered to monitor and adjust the arrangement.

Goal Attainment and Collaboration. The objectives of a collaborative strategy are almost limitless. As noted in Chapter Eight, collaboration can be used as an instrument of growth, retrenchment, or stability. Moreover, some positive (and negative) outcomes will not be foreseen. Whenever you bring two organizations together, synergies will take place that have not been predicted.

Thus, as with the other strategies discussed here, there is utility in remaining flexible about desired goals and objectives. Naturally, you will have some goals that are explicit and that must be reinforced again and again with employees and other stakeholders in order to build support for and commitment to the collaborative strategy. But other objectives may simply emerge or evolve as the collaborative venture matures.

Table 9.3 summarizes the process of implementing stability and collaborative strategies. And once again it is helpful to visit EHA and the issues Dave Adams should consider as he implements the new strategy that calls for collaboration.

Using teams. Coordinating and transition teams may be helpful as EHA works more closely with social service agencies, private Realtors, neighborhood groups, and other stakeholders. EHA is in effect now playing a brokerage and coordinating role in the system. Consequently, Adams and his staff will need to play a lead role in facilitating communication among all parties.

Changing a culture and overcoming culture clash. EHA will be challenged to be more competitive in terms of the quality, price, and location of the housing units it owns and operates. The culture at EHA may be somewhat complacent after many years of near monopoly in the business of subsidized housing. Adams will need to work to build a new competitive culture at EHA. In addition, the EHA staff will be working more closely with other organizations, such as social service agencies, that have cultures that might clash with EHA's.

Negotiating information access. As the central player in the new integrated housing and human services system, Adams will need access to information from all the agencies involved with the system.

Retaining flexibility on goals. Although there are some specific goals for the new system, Adams should remain open to beneficial outcomes that cannot be foreseen.

Conclusion

The implementation factors presented in this chapter provide a useful template for anticipating some of the most prevalent roadblocks to successful implementation. I have never encountered a situation in which implementers of a strategy or policy did not eventually confront choices regarding organizational structure, staffing, information and control, and assessment of outcomes.

TABLE 9.3 Implementing Stability and Collaborative Strategies.

	Organizational Design to Support the Strategy	Implications for Staffing and Human Resource Management	Implications for Monitoring and Controlling the Strategy	Measures of Success
Stability strategy	Refine standard operating procedures, authority structure, and other structural features to advance the strategy.	Invest in professional development.	Develop more diverse and sophisticated sources of information about external trends. Invest in internal information systems to monitor performance and quality.	Specify goals for this strategy to avoid complacency or inertia.
Collaborative strategy	Make use of inter-organizational teams, task forces, and committees.	Watch for clash of cultures, role conflict, and mixed loyalties. Provide additional training in teamwork, conflict resolution, and collaboration.	Negotiate access to information with your partner organizations.	Specify goals but also remain flexible to accommodate emerging goals.

Still, these four factors represent only the generic issues you are likely to encounter during the implementation process. Other idiosyncratic issues will undoubtedly arise to either facilitate or thwart your implementation efforts. Some of these issues are political, and they are discussed in the Conclusion to this book.

Getting Started

1. Think of an implementation project in which you were involved that went very well. What happened to make the implementation so smooth?

2. Think of an implementation project that went very badly. What happened to make it so troubled?

Conclusion

Balancing Politics and Strategy

By placing a discussion on politics at the very end of this book, I may risk criticism from readers who will say that I included it only as an afterthought. But many political considerations have been discussed and illustrated throughout this book even though they may not have been labeled as such. For example, political trends and events have a huge impact on the strategic environment of public and nonprofit organizations, as presented in Chapter One. Political considerations may affect the model of strategy development selected by an organization, as discussed in Chapter Two. In Chapters Three and Four I said that business models of environmental scanning and portfolio analysis must be adapted to the political and social missions of the public or nonprofit organization. And in the chapters dealing with growth, retrenchment, stability, and collaboration, I repeatedly focused on the centrality of mission and mandate.

Still, there are a few points worth repeating and several additional issues to explore in order to give the political environment the attention it deserves.

Strategy as Policy

First, there is no escaping the fact that in formulating or helping to formulate a strategy for your organization, you are in effect making and advocating policy, and thus you become a player in the ancient political game of deciding who gets what, when, why, and how. The notion that public administrators are merely detached professional implementers of policies handed down from the formal political process has long ago been discredited, both in theory and in practice. Still, there is no shortage of current journal articles debating the limits on administrative discretion in public and nonprofit organizations (Behn, 1998; Bellone and Goerl, 1992; Terry, 1993; Kaboolian, 1998).

Organizational strategy is much more than making routine administrative decisions about how best to accomplish a specific task or function. It commits the organization's resources to a direction and a set of priorities. The strategy is a tangible manifestation of executive vision for the organization, and that vision will have implications for the long term.

There are risks in exercising leadership and vision. But it is not much safer to stand on the sidelines and wait for the strategy to be handed to your organization on a silver platter by elected officials or nonprofit trustees. First, you will grow old waiting for the formal political or policymaking process supply an explicit strategy, because that is not what those processes are designed to do. Second, the general public and your organization's clients will likely hold *your organization* (not its political overseers) accountable for any inaction. So, from professional and political perspectives, it is better to enter the game as a full-fledged player than to await instructions on the sidelines.

Naturally, you can't play the game recklessly. There are, after all, still assigned roles in the political and policymaking process. Elected officials and nonprofit trustees have their roles and public and nonprofit administrators have theirs. Officials and trustees will vigorously defend their roles, and administrators must work within theirs. You can play safely by following a few commonsense political rules of thumb:

Develop strategy from your mandate and your organization's mission. If you cannot easily defend your strategy as a way to advance your organization's legal mandate or authorized mission, you are setting yourself up for criticism as someone who is willing to circumvent the political or policymaking process in order to advance a personal vision.

By the same token, use all of your mandate, formal and implied, when necessary. Elected officials are given their mandates by the ballot box. Nonprofit trustees get their mandates from charters and bylaws. You too have a mandate, perhaps specified legally or negotiated in the form of employment contracts or annual performance standards. When William Ruckelshaus returned to rescue the Environmental Protection Agency from scandal and mismanagement, he demanded and received a broad mandate from President Reagan to manage the EPA as he saw fit.

Balance entrepreneurship with due process. Entrepreneurs often have the luxury of answering only to themselves. They can make decisions and take actions with little consultation. Public and nonprofit leaders must work within an authorizing environment in which their decisions are legitimized by a formal process. Know your authorizing process and work within it.

Link your strategy to perceived public needs. Ultimately, your job is to make the best possible use of the assets that have been entrusted to your stewardship. In a political sense, "best possible use" generally refers to meeting needs or taking opportunities that are compelling to a significant number of people in the population even if they do not directly benefit from the action. Compelling arguments for a strategy might be made on the basis that it promotes social justice, limits government involvement in solving a problem, encourages free markets, or fosters other popular political values.

Engage key stakeholders in the strategy formulation process. It is political folly to spring a strategy on key stakeholders at the last minute and beg their support. They must be involved or consulted at some point earlier on in the process if the organization wants to ask for their support later.

This is not a complete list of recommendations of course, nor will heeding it guarantee that you will be a successful player in the political process. Political skills are acquired through practice and experience.

Strategy as Advocacy

Having crafted a strategy within a political environment, you must *sell* the strategy to someone. Organizational leaders cannot simply *present* a strategy to overseers with a detached professional assessment of the pros and cons. They must *advocate* the strategy. They show their *passion* for the strategy. They *teach* overseers to see the environment and the strategic options from the leaders' perspective. And they also remember that they will be held accountable for what they have advocated. Here are some advocacy skills drawn from Mark Moore (1995, pp. 106–171) and from experience.

Identify stakeholders, their values, and their power. The first step is to determine who must be *sold* on the strategy in order for it to be successful. Who has a stake in the outcome of the strategy? Who will have a role in the success or failure of the policy? What type of support do you need from these stakeholders—tacit, explicit, or operational? What kind of power do they have? Are they organized in coalitions, or are they isolated from each other? Which stakeholders can be influenced by your actions, and which ones are beyond your control?

Define problems, opportunities, and choices. Advocacy does not begin with selling your preferred strategy. It begins with selling your preferred definition of the issues and choices related to an agenda. Your first task is to determine whether or not you can influence the agenda by influencing the way decisions and choices are defined and discussed. If you can lead significant stakeholders to adopt your view of the opportunities and challenges in the environment, then they will be far more likely to embrace your strategy as well.

Use others to advocate for your position. Others can help you advocate for your strategy, especially when they are viewed as credible sources. Cultivating allies in the media and among special interest groups, legislative staff, and beneficiaries can be a powerful advocacy technique.

Use data judiciously and ethically. Sometimes so-called hard data, such as results of program evaluations, can help you justify your strategy. At other times a simple story or real-life testimonial from an important stakeholder can be far more effective than data. A sense of timing and context is important. In either case, never stretch the truth.

Balance principle with flexibility. Advocacy of strategic options may lose credibility when it is perceived as strident preaching. It is wise to be firm on the strategic objectives you want the organization to achieve (growth, retrenchment, or stability) but flexible on the means to achieve those outcomes.

As an advocate in the political process you will find that you stand in opposition to others who are advocating different strategies or promoting an entirely different cause in the zero-sum scramble for finite resources. Although it is useful to try to understand and anticipate the moves of these competitors, your best bet is to tend your own garden first—make the best possible case for your strategy rather than denigrating others' strategies.

Strategy as Negotiation

We all learned in our first political science course that policymaking is an endless process of negotiation, bargaining, and compromise. Although this book has explored many *rational* management methods and concepts, the nonrational process of negotiation also plays a significant role in strategy development and implementation. Fisher and Ury (1981) outline a process of "principled negotiation" that is useful for understanding how to reach agreement through nonadversarial negotiations. But in the world of politics, negotiations are sometimes adversarial and attempts to introduce principles may even be used against you. Here are some basic ground rules for negotiating in a political environment, drawn from Zartman and Berman (1984) and from personal experience:

Select those with whom you are willing to negotiate. You do not need to negotiate with everyone who has a stake in your strategy and who has expressed a viewpoint. Not every voice is heard or acknowledged in the political process. You may decide to negotiate only with people who are viewed as legitimate representatives of broad interests or of large groups of stakeholders.

Decide when to negotiate. The timing of negotiations may give you or your adversary the upper hand. If you have a choice, wait until conditions favor your preferred strategy.

Understand precedents. Negotiations, whether in a courtroom or in a management suite, often are driven by precedents that are invoked by one or both parties to bolster their respective cases. What precedents will affect perceptions of the strategy you are advocating? It will be useful to know, for example, if your preferred strategy has failed miserably or succeeded spectacularly in another organization. Also, you might be able to invoke sunk costs to bolster your position if your organization has already made investments that need time to produce dividends.

Know your tolerance for suboptimization. Compromise is almost always suboptimal from the perspective of the negotiators because none of them gets all of what he or she wants. Before launching negotiations, therefore, it will be useful to think about where you are willing to compromise and where you will stand firm. It probably is best, however, to keep this calculus to yourself so that you do not give up more than you need to.

Negotiation of strategic direction must be monitored carefully to ensure that the essence of your strategy survives intact.

Strategy as Planned Organizational Change and Innovation

Strategy often involves a change or modification in direction, goals, and objectives. Therefore certain stakeholders will sometimes resist change. They may resist because the strategy will affect their power or career path within the organization. They may resist because they do not understand the forces driving the strategy or because they view the strategy as arbitrary or impulsive or because they lack the skills to implement the strategy and are stonewalling as long as possible to avoid exposing their vulnerabilities. Finally, the resistance may be bureaucratic rather than personal. In other words, organizational inertia can stymie even the most vigorous and well-intentioned efforts.

Whatever the reason for organizational resistance, a few simple practices can help reduce it.

Develop empathy. As you develop a strategy, think about its impact on employees, clients, and other organizations, and try to empathize with their perspectives. If you have a lot of yourself invested in the strategy, it may be difficult to step back and view it objectively. You may need the assistance of trusted confidants or outside consultants to help you see the strategy from a perspective other than your own.

Share ownership of the strategy. Although I am not a zealous advocate of bottom-up planning, it can be valuable to share ownership of a strategy with key stakeholders. Involve them in the environmental scanning process, for example, so that they can see for themselves the threats and opportunities in the organization's strategic environment.

Overcome resistance. In my experience, it is usually best to overcome resistance by strengthening the case for your preferred strategy rather than spending time and energy combating the resistance head on. Eventually, however, you need to know when it is time to exercise your leadership by expressing the vision for the organization and inviting others to participate or not, at their choosing.

Create a learning organization. Resistance may be lessened by portraying the strategy as part of a continual process of organizational learning rather than as a long-term dictate that is locked in stone. Obviously this approach cannot succeed if it is mere rhetoric. Employees and others will judge your words in the context of your past actions. If you have not promoted organizational learning in the past, it is unlikely to be accepted as a rationale for your strategy now.

Strategy as Accountability

Finally, the development of an organizational strategy puts the leadership of the organization squarely on the firing line. As a player in a political process, you must understand the rules by which you and others are held accountable. When Alice Rivlin was appointed first director of the Congressional Budget Office (CBO), she had a vision (and a strategy) to craft the CBO as a congressional "think tank." She knew, however, that many powerful members of Congress desired a far less expansive vision for the CBO and had ensured that some very specific outputs were incorporated into the authorizing legislation. Rivlin knew that she was first and foremost accountable to those mandated activities and that she could not pursue her larger vision until those must-do activities were accomplished very well.

Returning to the theme of Chapter One, this closing chapter reminds us that public and nonprofit organizations cannot be run just like businesses. Yet, on reflection, it is clear that quite a few of this chapter's suggestions for astute political management would not be out of place in a corporate boardroom. Even in the private sector, executives must develop strategies consistent with the corporate charter and mission. They must advocate for their strategies, selling them to key stakeholders including boards of directors and powerful investors. They must sometimes negotiate strategic actions, and they must overcome resistance to change. Finally, perhaps even more so than administrators in the public sector, private executives are held accountable for the outcomes they do or do not produce.

In these pages I have tried to provide a balanced perspective on the concepts and tools of strategic management. Some of them have direct applicability in public and nonprofit organizations, and others must be significantly modified. But they are *tools*, not recipes. They should be applied with discretion and augmented with the knowledge gained from your experience as a leader and manager.

Above all (and I wish again to make this point strongly) the cold logic of strategic management should never supplant the commitment and passion you feel for public service. Sometimes, therefore, the strategy you select for your organization will be driven simply by what you believe is right for the communities you serve. Your sense of community needs, the value of public intervention to meet those needs, and your commitment to make a contribution in this world may be all the justification you need to design and implement your strategy.

References

Allison, G. "Public and Private Management: Are They Fundamentally Alike in All Unimportant Respects?" Office of Personnel Management." Proceedings of the Public Management Research Conference, OPM Document no. 127-53-1. In J. M. Shafritz and A. C. Hyde (eds.), *Classics of Public Administration*. (3rd ed.) Pacific Grove, Calif.: Brooks/Cole, 1991. (Originally published 1980.)

Andrews, K. R. *The Concept of Corporate Strategy*. (Rev. ed.) Burr Ridge, Ill.: Irwin, 1980.

Angelica, E., and Hyman, V. *Coping with Cutbacks: The Nonprofit Guide to Success When Times Are Tight*. St. Paul: Amherst H. Wilder Foundation, 1997.

Anthony, R. N., and Young, D. W. "Accounting and Financial Management." In R. D. Herman and Associates, *The Jossey-Bass Handbook of Nonprofit Leadership and Management*. San Francisco: Jossey-Bass, 1994.

Behn, R. "What Right Do Public Managers Have to Lead?" *Public Administration Quarterly Review*, 1998, 58(2), 209–224.

Bellone, C., and Goerl, G. F. "Reconciling Public Entrepreneurship and Democracy." *Public Administration Review*, 1992, 52(2), 130–134.

Bielefeld, W. "What Affects Nonprofit Survival?" *Nonprofit Management and Leadership*, Fall 1994, 5(1), 19–36.

Bolman, L. G., and Deal, T. E. *Reframing Organizations: Artistry, Choice, and Leadership*. San Francisco: Jossey-Bass, 1996.

Boyne, G. A. "Local Government: From Monopoly to Competition? In

N. Ashford and G. Jordan (eds.), *Public Policy and the Impact of the New Right.* London: Pinter, 1993.

Boyne, G. A. "Scale, Performance and the New Public Management: An Empirical Analysis of Local Authority Services." *Journal of Management Studies,* 1996, *33*(6), 809–825.

Brinkerhoff, P. C. *Mission-Based Management: Leading Your Not-for-Profit into the Twenty-First Century.* Dillon, Colo.: Alpin Guild, 1994.

Bryson, J. M. *Strategic Planning for Public and Nonprofit Organizations: A Guide for Strengthening and Sustaining Organizational Achievement.* San Francisco: Jossey-Bass, 1988.

Bryson, J. M. *Strategic Planning for Public and Nonprofit Organizations: A Guide for Strengthening and Sustaining Organizational Achievement.* (Rev. ed.) San Francisco: Jossey-Bass, 1995.

Butterfoss, F. D., Goodman, R. M., and Wandersman, A. "Community Coalitions for Prevention and Health Promotion: Factors Predicting Satisfaction, Participation, and Planning." *Health Education Quarterly,* 1996, *23,* 65–79.

Chaffee, E. E. "Three Models of Strategy." *Academy of Management Review,* 1985, *10*(1), 89–98.

Chandler, A. D. *Strategy and Structure.* Cambridge, Mass.: MIT Press, 1962.

Claxton, G., Feder, J., Shactman, D., and Altman, S. "Public Policy Issues in Nonprofit Conversions: An Overview." *Health Affairs,* 1997, *16*(2), 9–28.

Corbin, J. "A Study of Factors Influencing the Growth of Nonprofits in Social Services." *Nonprofit and Voluntary Sector Quarterly,* 1999, *28*(3), 296–314.

Crimmins, J. C., and Kiel, M. "Enterprise in the Nonprofit Sector." In D. L. Gies, S. J. Ott, and J. M. Shafritz. *The Nonprofit Sector: Essential Readings,* Belmont, Calif.: Wadsworth, 1990. (Originally published 1983.)

Cronkite, W. *America's Cup: The Walter Cronkite Report.* Fairwind Productions, 1988. Videotape.

Day, G. S. "Diagnosing the Product Portfolio." *Journal of Marketing,* 1977, *41*(2), 29–38.

DeParle, J. "Slamming the Door." *New York Times Magazine,* Oct. 20, 1996, pp. 52–57, 68, 94.

DiIulio, J. J., and Kettl, D. F. *Fine Print: The Contract with America: Devolution, and the Administrative Realities of American Federalism*. Washington, D.C.: Brookings Institution, 1995.

Drucker, P. F. *Managing the Nonprofit Organization: Practices and Principles*. New York: HarperCollins, 1990.

Espy, S. *Marketing Strategies for Nonprofit Organizations*. Chicago: Lyceum, 1993.

Firstenberg, P. B. *The Twenty-First Century Nonprofit: Remaking the Organization in the Post-Government Era*. New York: Foundation Center, 1996.

Fisher, R., and Ury, W. *Getting to Yes: Negotiating Agreement Without Giving In*. New York: Penguin, 1981.

Galaskiewicz, J., and Bielefeld, W. "Growth, Decline, and Organizational Strategies: A Panel Study of Nonprofit Organizations 1980–1988." In Independent Sector, *The Nonprofit Sector (NGOs) in the United States and Abroad: Cross-Cultural Perspectives*. Washington, D.C.: Independent Sector, 1990.

Galbraith, J. R., and Kazanjian, R. K. *Strategy Implementation: Structure, Systems, and Process*. St. Paul: West, 1986.

Gaul, G., and Borowski, N. *Free Ride: The Tax-Exempt Economy*. Kansas City, Mo.: Andrews and McMeel, 1993.

Geneen, H., with Moscow, A. *Managing*. New York: Avon, 1984.

General Accounting Office, *Government Contractors: Are Service Contractors Performing Inherently Governmental Functions?* GGD-92-11. Washington, D.C.: Government Printing Office, 1991.

Goodsell, C. *The Case for Bureaucracy*. Chatham, N.J.: Chatham House, 1994.

Gruber, R. E., and Mohr, M. "Strategic Management for Multipurpose Nonprofit Organizations." *California Management Review*, 1982, 24(3), 15–22.

Gummer, B. "Go Team Go! The Growing Importance of Teamwork in Organizational Life." *Administration in Social Work*, 1995, 19(4), 85–100.

Hager, M. A. "Neither Adaptation nor Selection: 'Mission Completion' as a Rationale for Organizational Dissolution." Paper presented at the annual meeting of the Association for Research on Nonprofit Organizations and Voluntary Action, Indianapolis, Dec. 1997.

Hager, M., Galaskiewicz, J., Bielefeld, W., and Pins, J. "Tales from the Grave: Organizations' Accounts of Their Own Demise." *American Behavioral Scientist,* 1996, *39*(8), 975–994.

Hall, H. "Courting Tomorrow's Elderly." *Chronicle of Philanthropy,* Nov. 27, 1997, *10*(4), 24, 26–28.

Hambrick, D. C. "Some Tests of the Effectiveness and Functional Attributes of Miles and Snow's Strategic Types." *Academy of Management Journal,* 1983, *26*(1), 5–26.

Hamel, G., and Prahalad, C. K. "Strategic Intent." *Harvard Business Review,* May–June 1989, pp. 63–76.

Hammer, M., and Champy, J. *Reengineering the Corporation: A Manifesto for Business Revolution.* New York: HarperCollins, 1993.

Hasenfeld, Y. "The Administration of Human Services: What Lies Ahead?" In P. R. Raffoul and C. A. McNeece (eds.), *Future Issues for Social Work Practice.* Needham Heights, Mass.: Allyn & Bacon, 1996.

Hasenfeld, Y., and Schmid, H. "The Life Cycle of Human Service Organizations: An Administrative Perspective." *Administrative Leadership in the Social Services,* 1989, *13,* 243–269.

Hedley, B. "Strategy and the Business Portfolio." *Long Range Planning,* 1977, *10*(1), 9–15.

Hesselbein, F. "The 'How To Be' Leader." In F. Hesselbein, M. Goldsmith, and R. Beckard (eds.), *The Leader of the Future: New Visions, Strategies, and Practices for the Next Era.* San Francisco: Jossey-Bass, 1996.

Hofer, C. W. "Toward a Contingency Theory of Business Strategy." *Academy of Management Journal,* 1975, *18*(4), 785–810.

Huxham, C. *Creating Collaborative Advantage.* Thousand Oaks, Calif.: Sage, 1996.

Isenberg, D. "How Senior Managers Think." *Harvard Business Review,* Nov.–Dec. 1984, pp. 81–90.

Kaboolian, L. "The New Public Management: Challenging the Boundaries of the Management vs. Administration Debate." *Public Administration Review,* 1998, *58*(3), 189–193.

Kearns, K. P. "Communication Networks Among Municipal Administrators." *Knowledge: Creation, Diffusion, Utilization,* 1989, *10*(4), 260–279.

Kearns, K. P. "From Comparative Advantage to Damage Control: Clarifying Strategic Issues Using SWOT Analysis." *Nonprofit Management and Leadership,* 1992a, *3*(1), 3–25.

Kearns, K. P. "Innovations in Local Government: A Sociocognitive Network Approach." *Knowledge and Policy*, 1992b, 5(2), 45–67.

Kearns, K. P. "Accountability and Entrepreneurial Public Management: The Case of the Orange County Investment Fund." *Public Budgeting and Finance*, 1995, 15(3), 3–21.

Kearns, K. P. *Managing for Accountability: Preserving the Public Trust in Public and Nonprofit Organizations*. San Francisco: Jossey-Bass, 1996.

Kearns, K. P. "Mission Statements." In J. M. Shafritz (ed.), *International Encyclopedia of Public Policy and Administration*. Vol. 3. Boulder, Colo.: Westview Press, 1998b.

Knauft, E. B., Berger, R. A., and Gray, S. T. *Profiles of Excellence: Achieving Success in the Nonprofit Sector*. San Francisco: Jossey-Bass, 1991.

LaPiana, D. *Beyond Collaboration: Strategic Restructuring of Nonprofit Organizations*. Washington, D.C.: National Center for Nonprofit Boards, 1998.

Leslie, D. "To Grow or Not to Grow," in K. Koziol (ed.), *Nonprofit Management Case Collection*. Institute for Nonprofit Organization Management, College of Professional Studies, University of San Francisco, 1992.

Letts, C., Ryan, W., and Grossman, A. "Virtuous Capital: What Foundations Can Learn from Venture Capitalists." *Harvard Business Review*, Mar.–Apr. 1997, pp. 36–44.

Levine, C. H, Rubin, I. S., and Wolohojian, G. G. *The Politics of Retrenchment*. Thousand Oaks, Calif.: Sage, 1981.

Lindblom, C. E. "The Science of Muddling Through." *Public Administration Review*, 1959, 10(2), 79–89.

Lipsky, M., and Smith, S. *Nonprofits for Hire: The Welfare State in the Age of Contracting*. Cambridge, Mass.: Harvard University Press, 1993.

MacMillan, I. C. "Competitive Strategies for Not-for-Profit Organizations." *Advances in Strategic Management*. Vol. 1. Greenwich, Conn.: JAI Press, 1983.

Maranville, S. J. "Requisite Variety of Strategic Management Modes: A Cultural Study of Strategic Actions in a Deterministic Environment." *Nonprofit Management and Leadership*, 1999, 9(3), 277–291.

Massarsky, C. W. "Business Planning for Nonprofit Enterprise." In E. Skloot (ed.), *The Nonprofit Entrepreneur: Creating Ventures to Earn Income*. New York: Foundation Center, 1988.

Mattessich, P. W., and Monsey, B. R. *Collaboration: What Makes It Work:*

A Review of Research Literature on Factors Influencing Successful Collaboration. St. Paul, Minn.: Amherst H. Wilder Foundation, 1992.

McMurty, S. L., Netting, F. E., and Kettner, P. M. "Critical Inputs and Strategic Choice in Non-Profit Human Service Organizations." *Administration in Social Work*, 1990, *14*(3), 67–82.

Menefee, D. "Strategic Administration of Nonprofit Human Service Organizations: A Model for Executive Success in Turbulent Times." *Administration in Social Work*, 1997, *7*(21), 1–19.

Meyer, M. W., and Zucker, G. *Permanently Failing Organizations*. Thousand Oaks, Calif.: Sage, 1989.

Miles, R. E., and Snow, C. C. *Organizational Strategy, Structure and Process*. New York: McGraw-Hill, 1978.

Miller, D. "Configurations of Strategy and Structure." *Strategic Management Journal*, 1986, *7*, 233–249.

Mintzberg, H. "Patterns in Strategy Formation." *Management Science*, 1978, *24*(9), 934–948.

Mintzberg, H. "Crafting Strategy." *Harvard Business Review*, July–Aug. 1987, pp. 66–75.

Mintzberg, H. *The Rise and Fall of Strategic Planning*. New York: Free Press, 1994.

Mintzberg, H., Ahlstrand, B., and Lampel, J. *Strategy Safari: A Guided Tour Through the Wilds of Strategic Management*. New York: Free Press, 1998.

Mintzberg, H., and McHugh, A. "Strategy Formation in an Ad Hocracy." *Administrative Science Quarterly*, 1985, *31*, 160–197.

Mintzberg, H., and Waters, J. A. "Tracking Strategy in an Entrepreneurial Firm." *Academy of Management Journal*, 1982, *25*(3), 465–499.

Moe, R. "The 'Reinventing Government' Exercise: Misinterpreting the Problem, Misjudging the Consequences." *Public Administration Review*, 1994, *54*(2), 111–122.

Moore, J. "Peggy Charren's Closing ACT." *Chronicle of Philanthropy*, July 28, 1992, pp. 1, 25–26.

Moore, J., Rocque, A., and Williams, G. "A Debacle for Charities' Credibility." *Chronicle of Philanthropy*, June 1, 1995, *7*(16), 1, 24, 29.

Moore, M. *Creating Public Value: Strategic Management in Government*, Cambridge, Mass.: Harvard University Press, 1995.

Nutt, P. C., and Backoff, R. W. "Organizational Publicness and Its Implications for Strategic Management." *Journal of Public Administration Research and Theory*, 1993, *3*(2), 209–231.

Osborne, D., and Gaebler, T. *Reinventing Government*. Reading, Mass.: Addison-Wesley, 1992.

Oster, S. *Strategic Management for Nonprofit Organizations*. New York: Oxford University Press, 1995.

Peters, T. J., and Waterman, R. H., Jr. *In Search of Excellence*. New York: HarperCollins, 1982.

"Pathological Parochialism: 57 Communities Opt Out of 'Countywide' 911." *Pittsburgh Post-Gazette*, Mar. 25, 1999, p. A- 26.

Porter, M. E. *Competitive Strategy*. New York: Free Press, 1980.

Porter, M. E. *Competitive Advantage: Creating and Sustaining Superior Performance*. New York: Free Press, 1985.

Pressman, J. L., and Wildavsky, A. *Implementation: How Great Expectations in Washington Are Dashed in Oakland*. (3rd ed.) Berkeley: University of California Press, 1984.

Quercia, R., and Galster, G. "The Challenges Facing Public Housing in a Brave New World." *Housing Policy Debate*, 1997, 8(3), 535–569.

Quinn, J. B. "Strategic Change: 'Logical Incrementalism.'" *Sloan Management Review*, Fall 1978, 7–21.

Quinn, J. B. "Managing for Strategic Change." *Sloan Management Review*, Summer 1980a, pp. 3–20.

Quinn, J. B. *Strategies for Change: Logical Incrementalism*. Burr Ridge, Ill.: Irwin, 1980b.

Quinn, J. B. "Managing Strategies Incrementally." *Omega*, 1982, 10(6), 613–627.

Ring, P. S., and Perry, J. L. "Strategic Management in Public and Private Organizations: Implications of Distinctive Contexts and Constraints." *Academy of Management Review*, 1985, 10(2), 276–286.

Ripley, R., and Franklin, G. *Policy Implementation and Bureaucracy*. Florence, Ky.: Dorsey Press, 1986.

Roller, R. H., "Strategy Formulation in Nonprofit Social Services Organizations: A Proposed Framework." *Nonprofit Management and Leadership*, 1996, 7(2), 137–153.

Rose, R., and Peters, B. G. *Can Government Go Bankrupt?* New York: Basic Books, 1978.

Rosenman, M. *Nonprofit Sector Issues*. Washington, D.C.: Union Institute, 1998.

Ryan, W. P. "The New Landscape for Nonprofits." *Harvard Business Review*, Jan.–Feb. 1999, pp. 127–136.

Salipante, P. F., and Golden-Biddle, K. "Managing Traditionality and Strategic Change in Nonprofit Organizations." *Nonprofit Management and Leadership*, 1995, 6(1), 3–20.

Schmid, H. "Strategic and Structural Change in Human Service Organizations: The Role of the Environment." *Administration in Social Work*, 1992, pp. 167–186.

Schmidt, R. J. *The Divestiture Option: A Guide for Financial and Corporate Planning Executives*. New York: Quorum Books, 1990.

Senge, P. M. *The Fifth Discipline: The Art and Practice of the Learning Organization*. New York: Doubleday, 1990.

Sheehan, R. M. "Achieving Growth and High Quality by Strategic Intent." *Nonprofit Management and Leadership*, 1999, 9(4), 413–428.

Shelly, P. "AHERF to Meet Payroll," *Pittsburgh Post-Gazette*, July 24, 1998, pp. A1, A14.

Shera, W., and Page, J. "Creating More Effective Human Service Organizations Through Strategies of Empowerment." *Administration in Social Work*, 1995, 19(4) 1–15.

Simon, H. *Administrative Behavior: A Study of Decision-Making Processes in Administrative Organizations*. New York: MacMillan, 1947.

Skloot, E. "The Venture Planning Process." In E. Skloot (ed.), *The Nonprofit Entrepreneur: Creating Ventures to Earn Income*. New York: Foundation Center, 1988.

Steckel, R., and Lehman, J. *In Search of America's Best Nonprofits*. San Francisco: Jossey-Bass, 1997.

Stone, M. M., and Crittenden, W. "A Guide to Strategic Management Literature on Nonprofit Organizations." *Nonprofit Management and Leadership*, 1994, 4(2), 193–213.

Sutton, R. I. "Managing Organizational Death." *Human Resource Management*, 1983, 22(4), 391–412.

Sutton, R. I. "The Process of Organizational Death: Disbanding and Reconnecting." *Administrative Science Quarterly*, Dec. 1987, 32, 542–569.

Terry, L. "Why We Should Abandon the Misconceived Quest to Reconcile Public Entrepreneurship with Democracy." *Public Administration Review*, 1993, 53(4), 393–395.

Thompson, A. A., and Strickland, A. J. *Strategic Management: Concepts and Cases*. (6th ed.) Burr Ridge, Ill.: Irwin, 1992.

Thompson, J. D. *Organizations in Action*. New York: McGraw-Hill, 1967.

Tschirhart, M. *Artful Leadership*. Bloomington: Indiana University Press, 1996.

Ward, J. "Cancerous Growth: The Cancer Fund of America May Be Booming for All the Wrong Reasons." *Financial World*, Sept. 1, 1994, pp. 54, 56.

Weisbrod, B. A. (ed.). *To Profit or Not to Profit: The Commercial Transformation of the Nonprofit Sector*. New York: Cambridge University Press, 1998.

Wensley, R. "Strategic Marketing: Beta, Boxes, or Basic?" *Journal of Marketing*, 1981, *45*(3), 173–182.

Wheelen, T. L., and Hunger, J. D. *Strategic Management and Business Policy*. (4th ed.) Reading, Mass.: Addison-Wesley, 1992.

Wiesendanger, B. "Profitable Pointers from Nonprofits." *Journal of Business Strategy*, 1994, *15*(4), 32–39.

Winer, M., and Ray, K. *Collaboration Handbook: Creating, Sustaining, and Enjoying the Journey*. St. Paul, Minn.: Amherst H. Wilder Foundation, 1994.

Yankey, J. A. "Mergers, Acquisitions, and Consolidations in the Nonprofit Sector: Trends, Prospects, and Lessons." Paper presented at the conference "Nonprofit Organizations in a Market Economy" at the Mandel Center for Nonprofit Organizations, Case Western Reserve University, Cleveland, Nov. 1991.

Young, D. R. "Profitmaking by Nonprofits: Issues for Management." Paper presented at the conference "Commercial Activities of Nonprofits" at New York University, Nov. 15–16, 1988.

Young, P. "Management Accounting." In R. D. Herman and Associates, *The Jossey-Bass Handbook of Nonprofit Leadership and Management*. San Francisco: Jossey-Bass, 1994.

Zartman, I. W., and Berman, M. *The Practical Negotiator*. New Haven, Conn.: Yale University Press, 1982.

Zimmerman, F. M. "Managing a Successful Turnaround." *Long Range Planning*, 1989, *22*(3), 105–124.

Zimmerman, F. M. *The Turnaround Experience: Real World Lessons in Revitalizing Corporations*. New York: McGraw-Hill, 1991.

Index

184–186; organizational priorities at
each stage of, 185
Life cycle, program, 55–57, 66, 68–69
Lindblom, C. E., 33, 45
Lipsky, M., 3
Liquidation: and benefits of organizational
closure, 207–208; and factors contributing to failure of organization,
201–203; forces promoting and resisting, 199–201; and management of
organizational demise, 204–207; management skills for, 205–207
Living Masters jazz series, 35
Lloyd Weber, A., 110
Logical incrementalism, theory of, 45
LWCS. *See* Lakeview Women's Center
and Shelter case study

M

MacMillan, I. C., 119, 120, 121, 122, 123,
124, 125, 126, 127, 189
MacMillan's portfolio analysis, 119–128;
dimensions of, 121–122; matrix for,
123
Manchester Craftsmen's Guild, 33–37,
39–40, 43, 44, 47
Mandate, managing from, 7–11, 28
Maranville, S. J., 48
March of Dimes, 56
Market, strategic environment *versus*, 58
Markov, B., 51–107. *See also* Shadyside
Rehabilitation Clinic (SRC) case
study
Massarsky, C. W., 156
Mattessich, P. W., 257–258
McHugh, A., 224–225
McMurty, S. L., 235
Medicare, 73
Menefee, D., 13
Mergers, 158–159
Meyer, M. W., 200, 209
Midwest Arts Council, 110
Miles, R. E., 271
Miller, D., 271
Miller, E., 4 (fictional)
Millersburg Public Library (hypothetical
case), 3–22; in competitive environ-
ment, 5–6; mandate and mission of,
4–5; measurement of outcomes for, 7;
mission statement of, 11; new sources

or revenue for, 6; values and operating
principles of, 11–23
Minneapolis–St. Paul, Minnesota, 201
Mintzberg, H., 32, 41, 45, 224–225
Mission: compatibility of, 258–260; as
constraining force, 12–13; as empow-
ering force, 9–10; and interorganiza-
tional cooperation, 250; managing
from, 8–9; from mandates to, 7–11;
statement of, 10–11; tension between,
and costs, 181
Mission creep, 155
Mission statement, 10–12
Moe, R., 19, 29
Mohr, M., 117, 118, 119, 127
Monsey, B. R., 257–258
Moore, J., 213
Moore, M., 8, 29, 293, 320
Murray, J. E., Jr., 169, 170, 171, 174, 175,
176
Mutual dependence, 260–261

N

National Institutes of Health, 169
National Kidney Foundation, 56
National Multiple Sclerosis Society, 242
Negotiation, strategy as, 321–322
Netting, F. E., 235
New York City, 241
Nutt, P. C., 27–28
NYCAHA. *See* American Heart Associa-
tion, New York City Chapter

O

Obligations, moral and legal, in divestment, 196–197
Orange County, California, 16, 178, 206
Organizational strategy: interaction
between, and program strategies, 112
Organizational structure: and collaboration, 311–312; and diversification,
286–289; and divestment, 302–303;
geographical approach to, 276–278;
and horizontal growth, 276–278; and
stability, 309–310; and strategy implementation, 271; and turnarounds,
297–299; and vertical growth,
282–283
Osborne, D., 17, 184, 187

Ruckelshaus, W., 319
Ryan, W., 3

S

Salipante, P. F., 197, 239
Scale, diseconomies of, 280
Schactman, D., 159
Schmid, H., 37, 61
Schmidt, R. J., 184
Self-interest, 260–261
Senge, P. M., 45
Shadyside Rehabilitation Clinic (SRC)
    case study, 51–107
Sheehan, R. M., 43
Shelly, P., 106
Shera, W., 279
Similar programs and services, 54–55
Simon, H., 45
Single-purpose organizations, 202
Size and growth characteristics, assessing,
    62–65
Skloot, E., 154, 156
Smith, S., 3
Smith Foundation, 110, 125
Snow, C. C., 271
Stability strategies: to adjust retrench-
    ment, 236–237; Banksville Human
    Services Center (BHCS) case study
    for, 218–224; and captive strategy,
    226–230; and community demand,
    238–239; to consolidate gains, 236;
    and defensive strategy, 234–235; and
    incremental strategy, 232–234; and
    pause strategy, 230–231; to protect
    leadership in stable market, 237–238;
    as response to uncertain market condi-
    tions, 235–236; and revenue streams,
    238; and status quo strategy, 224–226;
    types of, 224–235; viability of, in cer-
    tain conditions, 235–239
Staffing. See Human resource management
Status quo strategy, 224–226. See also Sta-
    bility strategies
Steckle, R., 8
Strategic alliances, 246–247, 248–249
Strategic business units (SBUs), 288–289
Strategic environment: defining bound-
    aries of, 52–58; guidelines for defining,
    57–58; key driving forces of, 88–92;
    key economic characteristics in,
    59–74; level of competition in, 74–88;

versus market, 58; related programs
    and services in, 53–54; similar pro-
    grams and services in, 54–55; substi-
    tutable programs and services in,
    55–57; threats, opportunities,
    prospects in, 93
Strategic issue analysis, 130
Strategy: as accountability, 324; as advo-
    cacy, 320–321; as negotiation,
    321–322; as planned organizational
    change, 322–323; as policy, 317–320;
    and politics, 317–325
Strategy formulation: analytical approach
    to, 37–40; incremental approach to,
    44–48; visioning approach to, 40–44
Strategy implementation: and collabora-
    tion, 311–315; and diversification,
    286–297; and divestment and liquida-
    tion, 302–309; factors in move from
    strategy formulation to, 271–273; and
    growth strategies, 294–296; and hori-
    zontal growth, 276–282; and retrench-
    ment, 307–308; and stability
    strategies, 309–311, 315; and turn-
    around strategies, 297–302; and verti-
    cal growth, 282–285
Strickland, A. J., 59, 81, 182
Strickland, W., 33–37, 39–40, 43, 44, 47
Structure, organizational. See Organiza-
    tional structure
Substitutable programs and services, 55–57
Substitute products, 53, 86–87, 188
Success, measures of: and diversification,
    292–293, 292–297; and divestment,
    305–309; and horizontal growth, 281–
    282; and stability, 311; and strategy
    implementation, 272; and turnarounds,
    301–302; and vertical growth, 285
Sullivan, A. S., 110
Sutton, R. I., 204, 205–206, 207
Symbiosis, 260–261
Symbolic sacrifices, 214
Synergy: and compatibility of missions,
    258–260; and interorganizational
    cooperation, 252; need for, in diversi-
    fied organizations, 291

T

Tactics, strategies versus, 224
Technology, 91–92, 187
Terry, L., 318